They Think I Killed My Husband!

~Memoirs of the Wild Widow~

written by Marty Penate

They Think I Killed My Husband
~ Memoirs of the Wild Widow~ ® Copyright 2005
TXu001267535
All rights reserved; Except as permitted under the U.S. Copyright Act, no part of this publication may be reproduced, distributed, or transmitted in any form or by any means, or stored in a data base or retrieval system, without prior written permission of the publisher or author. May be cited for publicity purposes with proper credits given.

This book is a work of fiction. Any resemblance to real persons or actual events is coincidental.

ISBN#: 978-0-9842497-2-5
the United States of America Copyright Number:
TXu001267535
written by Marty Penate
edited by Martha Nelson
photographer, Michael Murphy
cover design by Martha Nelson

Printed in the United States of America

They think I Killed My Husband!

This book is totally fictional. Any incidences or names in this book are not real. So, if anyone thinks I am writing about him or her, I am not! If you think these may be inspired from a crazy talk show, they are not. But, I will say that this book was inspired from real life occurrences. The names have been changed to protect the guilty.

Dedicated to the loving memory of my husband and our two wonderful kids that had to grow up without him.

Never be afraid of telling the truth, no matter how bad it is. As long as you are alive, you can try to fix the problem especially with the help of the people that truly love you. (Because once you are dead, it doesn't really matter anymore. The problem will still be there even though you aren't.)

We must seize every opportunity for desire and enjoyment that comes our way, as long as we don't hurt anyone else in the process. Within seconds into the future, life can be lost. So should we live for instant gratification? We are taught to set and achieve our goals so we have a sense of accomplishment. I agree, but not by paying the price of misery and obsession with our goals that we forget about love and compassion from the people close to us while we are enjoying our time in mortality. Our loved ones could be whisked away in a split second. If we didn't share our accomplishments or the journey of achieving the accomplishments with the people we love, would we feel as much enjoyment from it? I doubt that. It is good to accomplish and to have careers, but please make time to enjoy life. You only have one. Your body is your temple, take care of it. Live life well and be happy.

Marty Penate

Chapter One

It has been almost two years since I lost the love of my life. Ralph wasn't the most handsome man, or the fittest, but he was mine and I was his. Ralph had jet-black hair and big, gorgeous big brown eyes with lashes any woman would die for that was framed with a thick, oblong face. His mocha olive skin was typical for his Latin background. He was only about 5'10" tall and a bit overweight, but he was still extremely strong. He resembled a Cuban Godfather type in looks and in his attitude. I was a few years younger than Ralph. I am a tall slender long-haired brunette with big brown eyes almost as pretty as Ralph's eyes. My life has been such a ride, not just since widowed, but long before that. I loved my husband very much. We were truly best friends and lovers. Sure, we argued, but who doesn't? We were with each other constantly. We ran our business together, lived together, raised our kids together, and went out together. I miss him very much. I can say without a doubt, I believe he loved and adored me.

One night, the weather was humid and cool in South Florida, but inside the nightclub it was and dark and an essence of smoke and cologne diffused into every crack and crevice. The club had a glow of black lights everywhere. All colors were distorted and jumping into your face. The carpet appeared to be covered with confetti and the bar counter tops were lit up with pale soft white neon lights. The decorations in the club were of wild jungle animals everywhere, with bamboo railings and a

They think I Killed My Husband!

tropical theme. I was on the dance floor, shaking my booty and having a good time. The atmosphere was like a dream with the fog and the black lights dimly lighting the bar. The lights in the disco area were spinning and so was my head from the drinks I had. My husband, Ralph just enjoyed being on the sidelines watching me dance. Then a slender girl with milky white skin and long flaming red hair piled on top of her head started to dance with me. She was dancing extremely close to me rubbing her breasts against my body. Our legs were intertwined with each other and our pelvis's were grinding in circling motions. She looked so delicious. I pressed my thirsty lips onto her soft, sweet rosy lips. That is what Ralph came to see. He loves to watch me kiss and make out with another girl. Then, the girl's boyfriend started to dance with us. I glanced over at Ralph. He was not at his usual spot. The girl turned around pressing her ass into my pussy when her boyfriend, a younger African-American man came and started to dance behind me. He was dancing behind me, grinding himself into my butt. He was pressing his big hard cock against my ass and rubbing it up and down my butt cleavage and with her in front of me, wiggling her ass across my pussy. I searched with my eyes around the club for Ralph, he finally returned to his seat. He did not look happy. His face was turning bright red and his eyes were bulging right out of his eye sockets! I was just made into a Pam sandwich, in which Ralph did not like. As the girl's boyfriend kept grinding himself into my ass, I felt another situation behind me that developed and grew hard! Ralph was fuming from jealousy and anger.

    He screamed at the guy, "Stay away from my wife!" The guy just swung his head back and laughed and ignored him. But, we were all still dancing. The tall, spindly red head turned around and I was kissing and dancing with the girl, unaware of the friction that developed between Ralph and her boyfriend. The next thing I realized, Ralph threw a drinking glass at this man! There was broken glass and ice all over the floor. The girl's boyfriend's head was bleeding. He ran off into the bathroom with his girlfriend bent over with her arms around his shoulders.. I looked at Ralph in total amazement.

"Why did you do such a thing?" I asked.

"He called you a whore." he replied.

"But that doesn't constitute you reacting the way you did!" I told him.

"Just get out of my way! I have to go find him to kick his ass!" Ralph blurted out.

"This isn't happening," I thought to myself.

During this chaos, Manny, a big body builder, came to me and asked where Ralph was. Manny was also the bouncer for the club. Manny was a broad shouldered Cuban man that took his body -building seriously. Manny had the prettiest baby blue eyes with black, thinning hair and milky white skin. I told Manny that Ralph went toward the front of the club to find that guy and kick his ass. Manny informed me that the guy had some friends here and one was out front waiting for Ralph. The police were also called to arrest Ralph. Manny was trying to find Ralph to help me get him out the back door.

I ran towards the front of the nightclub to find Ralph. I made it out the front door and found him in the middle of another fight with the guy's friend. This man was in his late twenties and was slim and more agile than Ralph. It all just seemed like a crazy dream. In the 10 years we have been together, had he lost his mind so terribly? All I could think to do was to get the hell out of there, now!

But nooooo, my hot-blooded Latin lover was quite adamant about pursuing his enemy of that moment. Manny raced outside to grab him from the arena that was made in the parking lot by the circle of spectators standing around watching the fight. Manny grabbed Ralph's arm. Ralph flung Manny from his grip like a small rag doll.

"Get the fuck away from me," Ralph steamed.

Manny was a body builder and was Ralph's equal weight. I couldn't believe Ralph had so much strength to manhandle Manny the way he did. I am watching this fiasco outside and wondering if this was really happening. I was helpless. I watched Ralph just fling Manny away from him. I was scared to get close to Ralph. I just sat down on the bench outside and watched in disbelief. I was numb all over. I felt like I was in a crazy nightmare.

The security guard was standing next to me. He was a tall slender man that has worked there for years. I asked him if he could get some help or try to stop it.

He answered me with a response I really didn't want to hear, "the police are on their way and I am not going to get hurt."

The two men that were fighting were bouncing around with their elbows bent and fists protecting their faces and abs. It looked as though I was watching professional boxers jumping back and forth in a boxing arena ready to go at the fight. Within a minute of the fight, I saw Ralph get sucker-punched in the face! Ralph fell backwards and did a backward roll and jumped right back on his feet! Then Ralph thrust himself towards his opponent and hit him across his jaw and knocked him out! That's when I had enough and went to him and told him the cops were on their way.

He just said, "I don't give a shit! I want to kick the other guy's ass!"

I looked for Manny with great desperation. Manny had retrieved another strong friend that delivers furniture for a living. His friend was a short, stout Puerto Rican with long curly black hair. Manny told me to get the car. It was in the parking lot, back a few rows. I ran and got the Mercedes and pulled up closer to the fight to pick up Ralph.

At that moment the red-head's boyfriend wanted to take over where his friend left off. That's when Manny grabbed Ralph and with the help of Manny's friend, they both were able to gain control of Ralph and put him into the passenger seat of our new Mercedes 500 SEL. I sped off as fast as I could go. Getting home after that bit of tribulation wasn't going to be an easy trick either. Ralph was very upset. He wanted me to turn around so he could go back and kick the other guy's ass too! I couldn't believe what I was hearing. Was he truly insane? The cops would get there any minute to arrest him and he wants to go back and fight. What would I tell the kids? Daddy is in jail for being stupid?

"I can't believe he sucker punched me!" Ralph said. He was so furious he grabbed the steering wheel of the Benz and jerked it around to force me to turn the car around. Avoiding a collision, I jerked the wheel back and told him to chill out! I reminded him that he was the one that started everything.

"No, I didn't. That girl's boyfriend did!" Exclaimed Ralph. It took another 15 minutes to calm him down. I had to make an irrational man understand and be above people that say things to piss you off, to provoke you into doing something that you wouldn't normally do. You must try to be smarter than they are, always. If you succumb to their manipulations, you are just showing your stupidity. He was sweating so much. His color looked pale too.

"Are you okay?" I asked. "You don't look so good."

"I'm okay," he replied, while looking at me with those big, gorgeous brown eyes of his. "Just a little over exerted. I must have pulled a muscle in my chest throwing that punch."

"Why? Are you hurt," I inquired alarmingly?

As he did a slow motion version of throwing that last punch, Ralph stated, "I'm fine. It just hurts here from throwing that punch."

The "here" area Ralph was referring to was his upper left chest area. The last thing on our minds was a heart attack. While driving I looked at Ralph a little closer. He was short of breath and in a cold sweat. He complained of heartburn and begged me to hurry home so he could take a shower.

"Do you want me to take you to the hospital?" I asked. "I will."

"No. I'm fine," Ralph said, wearily. " I just need a shower to feel better."

We arrived home finally. It was so good to see my dream home. We had just moved in to my big, beautiful, dream home right on the lake just months ago. It was a huge 5-bedroom/6 bath, old styled, yet brand new Victorian manor. I called it 'Vicky.' The color was pale yellow with green trim.

They think I Killed My Husband!

I pushed the button of the opener for the front gate to drive up to the house. I had to help Ralph into the house by letting him lean on me. He was so weak. It was hard to support most of his weight on mine. I pleaded with him to let me take him to the hospital. He said to just help him into the shower. He would be fine. I helped him into the walk-in shower and hoped he would be all right. I was very nervous. I peeked in the shower. I hadn't heard any movement for some time. Ralph was propped up against the glass block wall, the water just hitting him on the chest. He wasn't moving at all. He looked like a tired and beaten man.

When he finally came out of the shower, he did look better. I knew something was terribly wrong when Ralph broke out in a cold sweat instantly. Even after wiping it off, I could literally see the sweat pouring out of his skin.

That's when I asked him, "Do you think I should call 9-1-1?"

"Don't be silly," he said. "Just open the window. I am so hot."

"No!" I blurted. "It is cold outside. My uncle died after watching a game and sweating in a hot basketball gymnasium then going outside in below freezing temperature. He had a heart attack within minutes!"

Ralph muttered, "Don't be ridiculous. I am not having a heart attack. I am just hot. Would you please open the window? Now! God damn it!" He demanded loudly as he sat down on the bed.

"Okay, okay!" I blurted. I opened the window. I sat back down on the bed, turned around to talk to him on the bed and he started to fall backwards on the bed. His jaw clenched and his eyes shut, then he started to foam at the mouth, I didn't even want to think about what was happening. All I knew I had to get some help. I dragged him off of the bed and put him on the floor to try to give proper C.P.R. I called 911. "I think my husband is having a heart attack! I am not for sure, though. Please send an ambulance right away!" I screamed. They were on their way.

Marty Penate

Meanwhile, I laid my ear on Ralph's chest. His heart was still beating, but he wasn't breathing. I had to keep him breathing! I had to keep him breathing. I put my mouth onto his and started to breathe into his lungs. His lungs expanded and when deflating, the air just gushed out of his mouth like the deflation of a balloon and his lips were like the loose rubber balloon lips vibrating while exhausting. At first I thought it looked like a sign of life. I put my head down on his chest to hear his heart beat and didn't hear anything. I had never felt anything so eerie before. The stillness of his body was bloodcurdling. But after 10 minutes and no paramedics, I realized that the deflating lungs and movement caused by the air escaping was a sign of no life. The only life was the air I was blowing into him. The ambulance got to the house. The morons couldn't figure out which house. I actually had to stop doing C.P.R. and go onto the front lawn and yell at them over the yard wall to get over here! Unbelievable! They followed me inside. Now, with my husband just getting out of the shower and sweating terribly, he did not have time to put any clothes on. So, my poor Ralph lay there naked. I wasn't too concerned about dressing him. I just wanted him alive. But these men saw a naked, short, middle-aged heavy-set man. Then the paramedics looked at me, a tall slender younger healthy brunette. I actually had to look at one man in disgust because I knew exactly what he was thinking. I know one of them thought that he died having sex with me. The perverted old fart! No respect. Then they couldn't get him onto the gurney. Three men could not get my husband onto a simple roller bed. I know my Ralph was no little thing, but for 3 men not to be able to lift up 250 pounds! Then I knew he was doomed when they were more concerned that they may scratch the paint off the wall of my beautiful Victorian Manor than getting him out.

"Tear the fucking wall down if you have to! I don't care! Just get him out," I yelled!

I don't know when the older man left, but what started out as 3, turned into 2. There was the ambulance driver and the one that sat in the back with the patient. After getting him out of the house, they rolled Ralph into the ambulance on the gurney. We started off to the hospital. The sirens and the lights were turned on to get us there as soon as possible. Now, the paramedic in the back of the ambulance was having a problem with some battery pack. I do believe it was for the defibrillator to be used to get his heart beating wasn't charged. That's what they were insinuating anyway. The man in the back with Ralph needed some help from the driver to start the machine for Ralph's heart. So, the driver stopped the ambulance.

"Do you want me to drive the ambulance to the hospital," I asked in desperate disbelief? "I will!"

"If you don't hurry up and help me, he won't need an ambulance. He'll need the morgue," the guy in the back blurted to the driver!

"I am sorry Ma'am," the driver stated with empathy as he looked at me with his big sad eyes. The driver stopped the ambulance to help the paramedic in the back with Ralph. I couldn't believe it. They seemed to be trying to save Ralph, but I didn't know what they were trying to do, exactly. The driver was plugging something in to the wall of the ambulance where all of the other electrical outlets were for different machines. To me, it looked like the cockpit of a jet plane in the back of the ambulance. Within 5 minutes, the driver of the ambulance got back up front.

We got to the hospital finally. The paramedics rolled Ralph into the Emergency Room as I followed. The hallway was cold and sterile with the floor tiles perfectly aligned in a row. They were white commercial tiles that blended into infinity. The nurse made me stay out in the hallway and give her the administrative information she needed. It was a whirlwind of registration and everything. It felt so surreal. I went to the registration window, then to the waiting room. I sat down staring in to space, trying not to cry. The E.R. nurse came out to the waiting room.

She called my name, "Pam Garcia."

"Yes. I'm here. Is Ralph okay?" I asked, walking towards her. She motioned me to follow her. "Where are you taking me?" She wouldn't tell me anything. I didn't know if Ralph was alive or not.

"I think you might be more comfortable in one of our quiet rooms," the nurse strongly suggested in her white uniform so perfectly in place with a stethoscope around her neck.

"Oh, thank you." I replied like a zombie with my eyes wide open. When entering the small room, it looked very familiar.

"Oh yeah, me! This is what they put us in when my Mother died in her accident," I thought to myself. "This is the bad room, the worst room. The room I never wanted to see again. But here I am, waiting on news about the health of my husband, the father of my children. The best children in the world that deserved to have their father." My children were only 9 and 7 years old. My son, the spitting image of his father, was the oldest. My daughter, with her gorgeous long black hair and the pair of onyx stones set in the middle of her face to match, was her Father's Princess. This room that I inhabited for the moment had two, burgundy cloth wing back cushion chairs, a small cherry wooden table with a phone and a bible on top of it. The room was smaller than my walk in closet at home. This room implored death. All I could do was kneel down and pray to God to spare his life.

"Please don't let him die. He can't die! What am I going to do? I can't live without him!" Crying frantically, I begged to God and quoted the bible and said prayers to please let him live! "It's too soon! He is only 38!" I demanded he live! The big question already came to mind, "Why?" Are we just mortal? Do we have any purpose? Do we have Angels watching over us? Why would God take away such a good father from the best children? So many questions raced through my blank and numb mind at that time. All I could do was sit and stare into space.

" I think he had a heart attack," I said to myself. "What am I going to do now?"

Shortly after that, the doctor came into the room and told me the news. "I am sorry Mrs. Garcia. We did all we could." Ralph did not make it."

    I just sat there stunned. What could I do? Demand a recount? No. Then, within a split second, reality set in. I looked up at the doctor, screaming, "Why? Why? Why? What did I do?" All I could do is sit and just lay my face into my hands with my elbows resting on top of my lap. I cried and cried. I cried in to a state of hysteria. I almost couldn't breathe. My sister finally arrived, cradling me in her arms just making that shushing noise that didn't make a difference in what I was feeling. She felt like an extension of my passed mother, someone caring and holding me while I resumed the fetal position. I wished I could be in that period of my life right now, to a time when this has not happened. To any time in my life when I hadn't suffered any pain such as losing anyone so dear to me. A time when I was young and I could run and hug my Mom and kiss my Dad when I saw him home from work. Earlier in my life, I had no clue about any of these feelings I would endure. Learning the pain, when a true love breaks your heart, your chest really hurts. The grief of losing people you love the most, the ones you know that no one else could ever love you as much.

    The nurse came and asked if I would like to identify his body and take a last look. My mind in a state of shock, I agreed. My sister stayed behind to obey proper paper procedure. I walked into the room where Ralph lay on the table. His complexion was literally blue. I was in awe. He was on the table with a sheet draped over him. The slightly pale color Ralph was when we arrived, had ripened into a much deeper blue. Ralph's tongue hung out of the side of his mouth. It looked as though he choked on his own being and his throat and insides were squeezing and compressing and oozing out of his body. He didn't even look real. He didn't look like my Ralph. I couldn't look at him anymore. I couldn't help to think of what I could've done differently. I should have been stronger. I didn't even want to go dancing that evening. I should have driven straight to the hospital. I shouldn't have opened the window. I should have made him more healthy meals. I should have made him exercise. Now he is gone. The love of my life is gone now, forever. Who will I love? Who will love and take care of me? Then, as I think again through my own despair, my children, they love me.

I had to call people. Oh, all of the people I had to call! Oh my God! So many people I had to call. I had to tell his parents. I had to tell his parents they lost their oldest son. I phoned Isabel, Ralph's Mother. She couldn't believe her ears.

"What? Not my baby! No, no not my baby! How? When? Where are you?" She was screaming. What else could I expect from her? She is a very emotional person.

"We will be right there," she said.

My sister and I went back to the house. The sun had come up and shimmered and glistened across the lake just beaming into a new day. A new day had arrived. My children and my sister's 14-year-old daughter were still asleep upstairs, oblivious to anything that happened. I was just in shock. What was I to tell the children? How can I tell them their father passed away? Would they understand this? Do I tell them when they notice him missing? I was extremely distraught. So many thoughts were in and out of my mind and I could not grasp a single one of them. I made some coffee and sat in the breakfast nook and stared at the lake with sparkles of red from the sunrise made me feel sad. I collected myself to the best of my ability during the time waiting for the children to wake up. I finally accumulated enough courage to go up the stairs and awake both kids. We went into Serena's room and sat on her French provincial bed with the canopy hanging overhead. Her room had a lovely view of the lake with her bay windows on the second floor, the sunrise was a beautiful red glow with her pink and frilly, lacy curtains framing it. I sat them down on the bed. I looked into their big and innocent brown eyes laced with long fluttery lashes and regretfully told them that their Daddy had a heart attack last night.

"Is he at the hospital?" the oldest one, Rafael, asked.

"No," I said.

"So, he's home?" My youngest, Serena asked so intel-

They think I Killed My Husband!

ligently beyond her years.

"No," I replied.

"Well, where is he," my daughter demanded?

"Honey, I hate to say this to you, but your Dad didn't make it."

"What do you mean, didn't make it?" my daughter demanded again.

"Sweetie, he died," I stated trying to hold in my tears the best I could.

My son turned to me with those big brown eyes and couldn't keep his tears in either, and said, "But Mom, Dad's my hero."

I couldn't hold it in anymore. I just wrapped my arms around my kids and gave them a big, wet, group hug. I couldn't let go. We just held on, crying, not ever wanting to let go and we didn't. The tears kept falling onto our legs and didn't seem like they were ever going to stop.

One by one that day, the family rolled in. My sister stayed with me throughout the day. She made some calls for me. It was just so hard to tell people over and over again. All the people I called, I told them of his passing, the next question, out of their mouths were, "How?" I couldn't keep repeating it over and over again. Reliving the tragedy I wish never happened was too much to endure.

Friends and family coming over to console me was good. It also confirmed the terrible news that was being told. If they weren't here, nothing would be wrong. I would like to think so, but I had to realize he was gone. These people being here or not, had nothing to do with what happened. They are here because it did. If they weren't here, it still would be true and difficult to get through without them. I cherished every moment and every person.

My late husband's sister, Maria finally got in from out of town. She was my age and had long blonde hair and very pretty. She drove about 7 hours. We were outside on the front porch, overlooking the serene calm of the lake, gazing in silence.

She asked, "What really happened? Why did he get so

upset?"

"He got into a fight," I said.

"What? Are you kidding me? Why was he fighting," she asked angrily with disbelief?

I told her all about what happened.

"Ay, Dios mio. You can't tell my Mom. She will freak," she exclaimed!

"No kidding! I really don't want too many people to know about the details. You know what I mean?" I replied.

"You don't have to worry about me," she stated.

But, I knew better than that. Maria was a very nice person, but she was still one of the biggest gossips I had ever known.

After reliving the evening and telling her what happened, of course, I was crying. Crying so much I was out of control. We were both leaning over the wooden railing of the enormous wrap around porch. Our forearms resting on the top banister, looking across the green field and out onto the majestic blue lake. I could really feel as one with the universe and nature with auras around me. It could have been the absurd shock of everything I was feeling.

While I was bent over the rail, crying, I told Maria, "I tried to do all I could! I really did! I didn't even want to go out! He just lost total control! He insisted! I lost total control! I couldn't do anything more than I did!" Still crying, I had so much snot flowing out of my nose I had to get it out. I was too much of a mess to go inside. With no hanky, I just stood over the rail, placed my fingers at the end of my nose like I was holding it to jump into a pool, and squeezed all of the mucous out of my nose. A big glob of snot was dripping from my fingers about a foot long.

Maria looked over and exclaimed, "I really could've done without that! Yuck!"

All I could do was laugh at myself. It was pretty gross. But, I really didn't care. I couldn't move and didn't have a hanky, so I just made use of the grass. Oh, well. We did have a good laugh.

They think I Killed My Husband!

"I am going in now," Maria stated as she walked inside. I couldn't imagine why. (Sarcasm) I went inside too. I needed a tissue anyway. I never knew I had so many people that cared as I walked into my home. I couldn't even think clearly.

     My brother was even coming in from Virginia. He is a tall slim man with short blonde hair with a handsome face and hazel eyes. He has only one child, a little girl, but she is completely grown. He and his wife have been married for 30 years. I was glad he was coming. He and I were always close. I knew he would help me out. Knowing my brother is coming, made me remember that smoking some pot would be beneficial right now. My brother gave me my first hit from a joint. I had to go to my bedroom to get some privacy for a minute. I had to go in the bathroom to smoke a bowl. Marijuana is such a good thing right now. Soothes the spirit. Even then, I missed Ralph so much. We had so much fun together. We were as one. I feel like I have lost a part of myself. I knew I had to start a mission in search of the other part of myself I lost. Logically, it would be an impossible mission and I knew it would never be accomplished. But, for some reason, I am compelled to try. I had to try. My mind knowing this is really stupid, buy my heart was so broken, it felt like there was a piece was missing and I had to find it to survive. The ongoing mission starts.

Chapter 2

Getting back to work

The next morning I woke up and got into the shower. My brother was staying with me. He had made the coffee already. I finished my shower and put on my robe. I could smell the coffee all the way in my room.

"Thank you." I said taking the coffee mug from my brother. "Now, I have to go into work today and tell them the CEO and founder of this business is dead."

"Would you like me to come with you," my brother asked?

"No, I will be fine. I have to go in and try to salvage this or sell," I replied. My drive to the office seemed like the shortest drive I ever made. I had a business of being a jewelry importer/exporter and some gold plating jewelry and emblems for manufacturers. There was so much that Ralph did that was totally different than my tasks. My thoughts were far from tame. My husband has just died. What in God's name was I supposed to do? I thought and thought. I really ought to sell the business. I am tired. It's exactly what put my husband in an early grave. I have a good chance of living a long, good life. I always believed in taking care of myself, and it shows. But, how do I accomplish selling the business? To whom should I even think about selling it? Would anyone be interested? Would they try to bring the company to even a higher level? Would they destroy it? I didn't care as long as I had my money.

I walked into the office. I was showered and dressed

to a tee. All in black, of course. I had several black outfits, so no one was alarmed at all. I had my glasses on, with my face all made up underneath. I hid my tear-swollen eyes the best I could with lots of pencil eyeliner and waterproof mascara. So, I appeared as my usual self. So, I thought. I made the necessary business phone calls first thing in the morning. The phone calls I put off until Monday, that I should've done Friday. Not saying anything to our present customers yet, I carried on like a little trooper, just as if nothing had happened. How I hated to deal with the daily financial pressures of this business. I choked down the swelling and the tears until I felt my head bursting. I told the managerial crew and my administrative office employees about Ralph's passing. They were stunned! It was almost unbelievable.

After telling them, the only thing they could ask was, "Why are you here?" They were right. Shouldn't I be in some sort of mourning? I am. I most certainly am. Why am I working? There is no reason for me to be at work. I had to go home and let some of this sink in. I had to stay at the office to keep myself going though. Working kept my mind off of the whole situation. With the environment I was in, I seemed to be able to handle the red tape of the funeral services and insurance settlements better.

The children were with my sister for a couple of days after school. So, they were with family while I worked and I picked them up on the way home. Everyday after work, I arrived at my sister's house and she had cooked a big home cooked meal. Of course, we stayed and ate. My brother was always there too hanging out while I was at work. It was quite a good time. My original family was together again, at least what was left of it. Our parents have died already too. Our father was taken with cancer and our mother passed on in a fatal car accident. Now, at the age of 31, I had lost my husband too. I have done what life is required of us. Be our parent's children until they die. I have children of my own, live a good life with my soul mate until death due us part and I did. What else is there? My Grandchildren I guess. Can there be love after death? Could I fall in love again? All I can think about is my Ralph. I catch myself talking to him as though he was still here. He always had good advice. When my Mother died, he had so many wise things to say. Some words were pretty harsh, but true.

I could hear him tell me to get up off my ass and get to work, "All of the moaning, groaning, crying and complaining was not going to bring my Mother back to life, nor him." I give the most credit to him for helping me get through his own death.

I would start to cry and ask God the almighty question, "Why?"

Driving home from work for the first week was pure hell. The theme from the movie about this big ship was on the radio non-stop. I heard that song every hour on the hour. I remember last month when I went with the children to see that movie. I came home that day so depressed. Ralph telling me that he didn't care to see the picture.

He told me, "I can tell you how it ends. The ship sank."

"Ha-ha. Very funny," I explained to him in our bedroom when I arrived home after the movie how depressing it must be to lose the love of your life before you had a chance to live your lives together. We actually discussed what he would do if I died.

Ralph told me, "I'm sorry. I would miss you and still love you, but you are not here. I would want to marry within a couple of months."

I couldn't believe he said that! "A couple of months? You would get married within a couple of months?" I asked him.

"I like being married and would want to get married again as soon as possible. I would want you to do the same if it were me," he told me.

Hearing that song was all it took to get me into a state of hysteria. Crying like a mad woman. Cursing God for taking my children's father, cursing my late husband for not taking better care of his body, and blaming all I thought should be blamed. Onlookers wondering what could be troubling this sophisticated woman driving her new Corvette convertible, what problems could she have? If people only knew, but what do I know? I have food in my nice, big refrigerator and I am driving home from my own business in a Corvette convertible to my $3 million dollar Victorian Manor on the lake. I know things could be worse and there are others much less fortunate. But, I owned nothing! Everything was leased or purchased with a loan for tax purposes with the income from the business. The world I was living in seemed to be crumbling. My little picture perfect suburban life, now a single parent household, everything was up to me. I had to go to the banks and get everything squared away and see how much I did have.

The following day I went and did the necessary errands to the banks and one bank, I discovered Ralph had a safety deposit box without me!

"Why would he get that secret box for?" I asked myself. I showed the woman his death certificate so, I may obtain its contents. I also asked if I could see the sign in log to see if and when Ralph had signed in. I looked at the logbook. I noticed he had been inside the box just before he died. He never mentioned going to the box to me. I signed in the logbook, then the teller and I proceeded to the vault where the box is located. The teller escorted me into a private room where I could view the contents of the box. I sat down and opened the box.

"How strange," I thought out loud. The box contained several amounts of jewelry and some gold. I tried to close the box back, but something seemed to keep it from closing properly. I looked way inside the empty box and shook it and out fell a key. It looked like it may have been another safety deposit key.

"Aw, how sweet. He was storing all of this jewelry to one day surprise me. But, this is weird. I wonder what this key is to and where?" I wondered and had to find out. I gathered everything from the box to look at later at home. The teller came back when I called her to help me and I just closed out the box and left the bank. Something told me I couldn't share this information with anyone, yet.

When the time came to go to the Funeral Wednesday, I rode with my sister and my brother. I needed all the support I could get. My children were a great support too. I don't know how I could have managed without them. I tried so very hard to be strong for them. I cried in front of them, but I did not want to break down into a crying frenzy in front of them. I left those for nighttime, while in bed, trying to talk to whoever would listen. The service was lovely. Ralph had requested to be cremated. So, I had a lovely portrait out for viewing. It was as lovely as a funeral could be. I called the funeral director and they took care of everything. It seemed the whole town was there. Over 400 hundred people came to pay their respects.

The Saturday following the Funeral, also exactly one week since Ralph's passing, my brother left. He was back home in West Virginia. No, one but the kids and I are living in the house now. After the kids went to sleep, the house seemed so big, empty and I felt extremely lonely. It was so quiet, almost eerie. I was drained physically, emotionally and mentally. I went to my room and got ready for bed. I turned off the lights so the only illumination in the room was from the glow of the television. I had the volume down low so I could fall asleep easier. I laid in bed watching television and started to drift off to sleep. My legs and entire body started quivering and shaking uncontrollably. I thought it was just nerves, but I was still so exhausted. My eyes seemed to shift back and forth and everything started to go gray. Then my arms and legs felt extremely heavy and tense. Meanwhile, I started to feel a cool sensation enter my body through the bottoms of my feet. As I sensed this coldness flow up my feet, into my ankles and up through the core of my legs, it felt like the calm of the coolness soothed my inner being. The portions of my body that were once shaking became serene and motionless as the coolness slowly moved up my legs and through my hips. This calming feeling engulfed my entire body working its way up and through my torso, stretching out my arms to the side of the bed so I was like a horizontal "T." I felt so peaceful. My eyes still open, but could see nothing but black and a blue shadow forming the face of Ralph! I blinked hard and I could still see him. Not a mortal view, like a ghostly fog forming the shadows of his face. These shadows were darkening and seemed to envelop my entire being. The next thing I know I was entering the bedroom from the hallway. I looked up and saw Ralph sitting on the bed with his legs folded wearing nothing but his underwear!

"Ralph!" I exclaimed. "How can you be?" I asked.

"I'm back!" Ralph sternly stated.

"Huh?" That was the only thing that was capable of coming out of my mouth now that this whole situation registered in my brain. Seeing a sight so familiar to me and to see it again with such joy and excitement from my heart was undeniably love. I want him to be with me forever. I don't want to be without him. I thought to myself with such a smile and light about my face.

Ralph looked up at me and stated with such arrogance and confidence. "Fuck this dead shit. I'm back."

"But how?" I questioned happily. "You were embalmed already."

"Don't worry about it. I'm back." He said like a gangster from a movie.

"Well, Baby, I am glad you are back! No one wants you back here more than me!" I commented like a schoolgirl and her boyfriend is coming back to her. "But, what about all of the people I have told you were dead? What are we going to tell those people?"

"Fuck them! I'm back and I'm not going anywhere. I'm here to stay!" Ralph said with such love and passion for me that the feeling in the air was overwhelming.

"Oh, Ralph! I love you!" I said as I ran over to him with my arms out to give him a huge hug. I fell on top of the bed, embracing a pillow then rolled over to suddenly open my eyes with a start. I lay there in the dark cold room, alone. I was shivering and felt cold. I tried to go into my state of mind that

I was just in. I stared at the ceiling, seeing if everything would go black again. It did not. Laying on the bed, longing for my love, I cried and cried.

"Come back! You said you were here to stay!" I screamed angrily. "You have to come back!"

All I could do was cry and think. I couldn't figure out what just happened. I was so cold. I wasn't shaking anymore. It was so real. I spoke to Ralph. Maybe it was stress from everything I had gone through this week. Maybe Ralph came to me. His spirit was in denial that his body was deceased. He needed to tell me that he wanted to be here with me. Some people talk about their 'out of body' experiences, maybe I had an 'inner body' experience. In séances the medium is the tool the spirit uses to speak to their loved ones through, why couldn't Ralph just talk to me direct? Trying to evaluate exactly what happened, I feel it was Ralph's spirit that entered my body through my feet and making his way up and into my body, then finally into my brain. At that point, that is when I saw his face and then seemed like a dream. Could Ralph actually enter my mind and create thoughts and visuals telepathically? Is that how the spirits enter our physical bodies and activate the dream sensors in our brain to communicate, or maybe it was nothing more than a dream?

The next morning I woke up very groggy. My legs felt as though they had lead pipes attached. I was so numb from everything. I felt I was on tranquilizers, but I wasn't. I was still so drained and exhausted. I had to get back to the normal ways of life, if I could ever think of it as being "normal" ever again.

Monday morning came and I had to get to work. My feet felt like concrete bricks tied to my ankles as I walked from my car to the doorway into the building. My mind had to remain clear. I had to evaluate everything and improvise the best I could. I needed salespeople. I put an ad in the newspaper for salespeople first thing in the morning. Everyone was so quiet at work. Everyone was very supportive. My employees were a little too kind. That just reminded me more of this sad situation.

They think I Killed My Husband!

I stayed on the phone in my office and spoke to my clients and talked as if nothing had happened. I didn't want them to worry about the service that we were going to provide. I was in a state of denial. I was living my life like my husband just left town for a few days. How I wish that were true. That's what it felt like. I knew it wasn't, so I did have my sense of reality to some degree. I kept the radio playing in the background for some cheerful noise.

Later that week, I had set appointments for interviews with the responses from the ad in the paper. Cynthia, an older lady employee, recommended a friend of hers to be a salesman. Cynthia had short blonde hair and was thin and still dressed very sharp. She said she told him to call and make an appointment.

"What's his name?" I asked.
"Roberto," Cynthia responded.
"OK, what has he done in the past?" I inquired.
"He has received awards for the most sales in a month from everyplace he has worked," Cynthia exclaimed!
"Have him call and I'll make an appointment with him," I said.
"Great, I will make sure he calls you, Pam." Cynthia replied.

Roberto called me and we set an appointment for later that day. I interviewed several people through out the day before I met with Roberto.

The time finally came for Roberto's appointment. He arrived a little early. I saw Roberto sitting outside my office door.

"Oh my God! What a hunk," I thought to myself. He was a picture health. Roberto had blonde hair that glistened like gold when the light hit it. His eyes were big, bright and blue. They looked like pools of water. His face was a handsome face. He looked like a young Robert Redford, maybe even cuter. His body was toned and taught. Roberto's skin was a nice bronze tan color. I asked him to come into my office. I held the door

25

open as he walked in ahead of me. I couldn't help but to check out that derrière! It was as nice as I thought. Then I caught myself. I was still not ready for anything like that.

As the interview proceeded, I discovered Roberto was a very nice person and felt I may be able to trust him. He was my age. I don't know why that would matter, but it seemed to benefit. I felt most comfortable with him. Roberto was very eager and seemed very sincere. Another employee of mine also recommended him, so I took that into consideration. He told me of his goals and about his personal life. He told me he was engaged. I was even happier to hear that. I had to keep it a professional relationship only. Roberto was hired.

I would sometimes just sit and look at him sometimes when he was in the office. He was so pretty. Still a manly man, Roberto was simply a beautiful man. I found myself thinking, "What am I becoming, so soon?" I am a female executive, CEO of a business, hiring cuties to work for me. He was very qualified and I thought I could trust him, but he was easy to look at.

A few weeks later, my attorney stopped by the office to see how I was doing. Jack was always a great guy. He had his faults. He used to have an office in my office suite about a year ago. I remember one weekend last year, he disappeared. The next Monday morning, his wife, Ramona, called to see if he was at work. He wasn't at work either.

The next Tuesday morning he came into work and my husband asked him, "Where the hell were you yesterday?"

Jack replied, "Why?"

"Because your wife called looking for you and you didn't call in either," Ralph told him.

"I was smoking crack all weekend. I took my check and smoked most of it," Jack responded.

"What? Are you retarded or something? I can't believe you, man," Ralph yelled in disbelief. "You must be on crack!"

Then later, Ralph told me about it. I never said or inclined anything to Jack that I knew of his awful secret. I know everyone makes mistakes and has to release their stress. I know there are more productive ways of doing so, but I made no judgements. I was glad to see him. He came to see how I was doing.

"Can I do anything?" he offered.

"I'll let you know, thanks," I told him, abruptly looking up at him then back down at my paperwork.

"Show me around the new office," he demanded.

"Fine." I took him on a short tour. I introduced Jack to some of the upper management there. When it came time to introduce him to Roberto, Jack just smiled and told him it was a pleasure to meet him.

Then Jack turned to me and snickered, "Well, well, I can see Ralph didn't hire him, did he?" I just couldn't help but to have a shit-eating grin on my face and all I could muster is a shake of my head and a little giggle.

"How could you tell?" I requested sarcastically.

"Um, hummm, he's a pretty boy, Pam." Jack scolded with a sneeringly happy look on his face. I just smiled and went back to my office and sat down. Jack followed me in. He closed the door and sat down in the chair in front of my desk. We proceeded to catch up on old times. We talked about some of the wild and crazy stuff Ralph did. We laughed, we cried. It was a very nice visit. He was also there to ask me a favor. He admitted that he needed me to be a character witness on his behalf. The State Bar had disbarred him and suspended his license to practice law. He had to appear in court regarding this matter next month. Jack needed me to go and say a bunch of good things for him. I was happy to do it. Jack was a good man at heart. He was honest. He needed a former boss to go in and report on his work habits.

"Sure, Jack. You always were a good worker. I would be more than happy too." I said with sincerity.

"Great Pam. Thanks! I'll let you know when the court date is. I should find out this week. I better go and let you get back to work now." Jack said getting up and walking out of the door.

"Okay, Jack. It was so nice seeing you again," I exclaimed! "Call me!"

"I will," Jack assured me as he left my office. I quietly returned to my work and my radio listening.

The week went by and the dreaded weekend was upon me again. I just stayed at home. I mowed the yard, and washed the cars. Then I realized something was missing, the boat, my 32' Sea Ray. I forgot all about it. Ralph took it to a boat shop to be repaired. He never told me which one!

"Oh, man," I thought. "Where is my boat?" I had to think where had Ralph taken the boat before. I drove around town by all of the boat repair shops. I asked some people that Ralph associated with regarding the boat, they hadn't seen it nor did they know where it might be. I went back home to rethink of where it might be. I stood outside in the driveway trying to remember places Ralph took the boat.

"I can't believe I don't know where my boat is. I hope someone calls me when it is done. How unbelievable." I thought. "How can I not know where my own boat is?" I looked up and yelled up at the sky in a fit of rage to Ralph, "Where is the boat? I can't believe you are not here to take care of the boat! Why aren't you here?"

I walked down by the lake and out on the dock. The sun was finishing the day by sinking into the horizon of the lake and the land. The sky was red and reflected on the lake. The lake and sky were made of streaks of red and orange with the black shadows of the trees on the banks separating them made the sky look like a big orange sunburst. It was beautiful. It was as if I was looking at the world through a ruby. I couldn't understand how a God that can make something so beautiful and cause so much pain at the same time. It was like looking at the mirror image of my pierced, bleeding heart that was bursting with pain everywhere. My heart was truly broken.

Work continued on throughout the weeks. Roberto was doing well. I could talk to him about almost anything. He was a good a man and very much in love with his fiancé. He was telling me about a friend of his, Dennis that was coming in from out of town.

"Really?" I said.

"Yea, it's his birthday on the 15th of this month. We are going to have a Birthday party for him at my apartment complex by the pool on the 20th," Roberto told me.

"My birthday is the 20th of this month," I stated.

"I want you to come. It would do you some good to get out and meet some new people. We can celebrate your birthday too," exclaimed Roberto.

"Great! It will be good to get out. I would hate to be alone on my birthday" I revealed.

So that was something to look forward to. Later on in the week, Roberto's friend Dennis called for Roberto. Roberto was busy and the receptionist was out to lunch and another employee had called in sick, so I answered the phone. At the other end of the line I heard a deep, sexy voice.

"Hello. May I speak with Roberto, please?" he requested.

"May I tell him who is calling?" I asked.

"This is Dennis. An extremely good friend of his," Dennis said.

"Oh, he is a little busy right now." This is Pam, is there anything I can do for you?" I asked.

"This is Pam? Well, I guess I can talk to you then," Dennis suavely said.

"I guess you can," I replied.

"Roberto has told me about you," Dennis flirted.

"All good, I hope," I joked.

"Oh yes. It's all good. Has he told you anything about me?" Dennis questioned.

"A little bit, not too much. Just that you two lift weights and work out together," I responded.

"You mean he didn't tell you how cute I was? Wait until I see him," Dennis said over the phone.

"No. How cute are you, Dennis?" I asked with a snicker and a smile.

"Extremely. I have this big broad chest and shoulders with something else big to match," he said with a tease.

"That was a little more information than I cared to have, Dennis." I abruptly exclaimed.

"Sorry. So are you coming to my birthday party?" Dennis asked me.

"I sure am!" I said with a flirtatious smile on my face. "It's really my birthday on the day of your party. It'll do me some good. I haven't had a good time out in a while."

"Great!" Dennis happily exclaimed. "Maybe we could hook up before then. Is Roberto available yet?"

"Let me check. Yes, he is. It was nice talking to you Dennis. I can't wait to meet you."

"You too." He said goodbye and I transferred him to Roberto.

It was fun to flirt. I was feeling so guilty though. I never did anything or said anything like that to anyone in so long. I didn't even like to look at another guy while married. Ralph would get so jealous. If I looked at someone and actually made eye contact, Ralph would definitely let me know how sleazy it was and so obvious that I must have wanted the guy. All I did was look. If the guy noticed me looking at him then looked back and maybe gave me a smile, oh, my God! Ralph would go ballistic! He loved me so much. He was so worried about losing me to someone else. But, I would never do anything to hurt Ralph. I loved him more than he knew. However, I was going to have to get back into the game sometime, even though I didn't feel like it right now.

I ran the company for a while then after the news got out of Ralph's death, some friends of ours were wondering what I was going to do with the business. Frank, the man that owned the company I was leasing the office equipment from, asked me if I would like to sell the business. I told him I most definitely would for the right price. Work was so hard right now. My mind and heart was not in it. I didn't want to keep living Ralph's dream without him. He mentioned that he might have a buyer. He would get back with me.

They think I Killed My Husband!

Work went on as usual and the children were in school. Life went on as always. I had a meeting with the lawyer of the estate. I couldn't believe settling an estate could take so long. The insurance is a cash settlement for accidental death insurance and there is also several credit life insurance policies that will pay off all of the loans that had this option. The lawyer told me that all of the major property had this and the cars and the cash settlement is over one million dollars.

"There is one problem," The lawyer told me. "The insurance is having the cause of death investigated. Before the insurance company will pay, they are making sure the cause of death was truly a heart attack, a heart attack with natural causes."

"What do you mean, Tom?" I questioned. I was almost in shock. I was suffering so and to think someone would think I wanted this to happen! I couldn't believe it.

"It's just routine since he was so young." Tom responded with sympathy. "They'll just do an in depth autopsy and then the results should show by natural causes."

"How could anyone think I would do such a thing as killing my own husband and the father of my children? Haven't I suffered enough?" I yelled. "But, wait a minute," I thought out loud. "Ralph was already cremated."

"Before cremation, the crematory has tissue samples and blood samples saved in a lab per request of the insurance company," Tom educated me.

"I did not authorize this. How could this be? Is this normal procedure?" I questioned diligently.

"It's normal when a big estate or big insurance settlement will be involved or a crime has been committed. The police may have authorized it." Tom quickly returned my argument.

I wanted to get away, go on a long trip somewhere far, far away. But, I couldn't. I had to run the business. There was no one else to make sure everything was done correctly. I had to take care of business. I was all alone. Later in the week, Frank called me at work. He informed me someone would like to buy the company.

"How wonderful!" I exclaimed to Frank. I wanted to get out of this business so bad!

"It's not a whole lot, but you could really do a lot with it. Invest the money right and you won't need to work." Frank advised sincerely.

"How much?" I inquired.

"I know you might want more, but given the situation, I know someone that wants to offer you $8,500,000.00 for it. That is gross, and whatever debts you have will be paid out of that amount. So, Pam, you would pocket the net. Do you understand?" Frank stated.

"You know that the business is worth more than that!" I told him indignantly. "I need more than that. My house needs to be paid! What am I going to do? I have worked my whole adult life for everything I have! Isn't there anyone that will pay more?" I asked in desperation.

"Well, not at the moment. Everyone knows that you have lost your husband and it is only a matter of time before the whole business collapses and you lose everything," Frank told me.

I wanted out. I could pocket over $1,400,000.00. The life insurance company wasn't paying anything now, since I was possibly being accused of murder, I needed the money. That would be about three year's worth of income that I had been accustomed to.

"When can we do this?" I asked without hesitation.

"Let me get back to him and find out how soon this can be done," he replied.

It was a Wednesday and I sure didn't feel like celebrating, but I needed a drink. Dennis called me later that day. He asked me if I wanted to meet Roberto and him at Bahama Winds later for some drinks. Bahama Winds was such a meat market during after work hours. I hadn't been there yet, but I quickly found out. I met Roberto and Dennis for some drinks after work. I met Dixie, Roberto's fiancé. She was an adorable, petite, beautiful Hispanic woman with hair and eyes as black as pools of crude oil. Roberto appeared to be so happy with her. I was very happy for him. I was so confused though. Roberto was the same age as me and he is just starting life with his partner of life. I, on the other hand, was done living my life with my life partner. Seems so ironic. I have already lived my life by the age of 30. I went to college, got married, had 2 kids, boy and a girl, and buried my husband and my parents. I'm done. I'm 30 years old and a widow. This is so not right. I had the issue that the insurance company initiated in the back of my mind. I was going to relax and take it easy. I really needed a little break. Work was starting to get me stressed along with dealing with the whole situation of Ralph's death. I thought of my kids. My children were so great. They were doing wonderfully. Thinking of them usually soothes my mind.

    I was having such a good time for now. It was wall to wall men. I caught a glimpse of some men looking at me. Some even gave me that certain look when I glanced over their direction. The kind that told me I looked good. Dennis was giving me a little bit of attention. He was also looking at other girls too with that flirtatious look. He was also trying to see who and how many women would give him that look back. He was so handsome. I felt guilty feeling the urges I was feeling. Dennis had a nice tight ripped body. He had on a black shirt with a black pair of jeans. He had the outline of the perfect male body. Not over pumped, but pumped. He presented nice broad shoulders and a thin waist. His nipples were sticking up and showing through his T-shirt. His blonde hair cut short and slightly preppie but with a surfer look. Dennis had gorgeous blue eyes and a beautiful golden tan and a scrumptious tight ass. I wanted to flirt and have a good time. I also wanted to respect my husband's recent death and be a respectable widow in mourning. I guess I completed my flirtatious actions by talking and laughing at all of the stupid jokes. The couple of Margaritas helped considerably. It started to get loud at the Bahama Winds Club, so we decided to go to the Bicycle Club. It was another club not far from where we were. We went to the Bicycle Club. I followed Dennis in his Mercedes coupe driving my Corvette convertible. We all met out front of the club. I followed everyone up the sidewalk into the foyer of the club. Dennis pulled some stunt as we walked in. He told everyone to start leaving the club. I turned around to walk out, in a confused state of mind, not to mention a little intoxicated. There were other people walking into the club as I was trying to walk out into the foyer of the club.

"Okay, everyone put your hands against the wall!" Dennis shouted.

Confused, I stopped and looked at him with a queer look on my face. He took my hand and spun me around so I was facing the wall.

"Come on, put 'em up on the wall and spread 'em!" Dennis commanded as he took his foot and separated my legs and pressed my hands on the wall. I had no idea for what purpose he was doing this. Then he started to frisk me. Now I had an idea of why he was doing this. I liked feeling his hands skimming up and down my body. His hands ran the length of the inside of my legs and around the curvature of my ass and back down the outside of thighs and calves. I got so hot and horny, I could feel my cum oozing onto my panties. I was so excited physically. My mind was not really excited. I was always thinking of Ralph. So, why was I so horny? I liked the fact he wanted to feel me up that bad. Then my mind came to realization. I suddenly realized that the strangers walking into the club were staring at me in a most peculiar way. They must think I am some fugitive being captured by this policeman dressed all in black!

"Oh, how funny!" I thought. I had to go to the Ladies Room to clean myself up. I had cum all over my panties. I went back and sat down where Roberto, Dixie and Dennis were sitting. We ordered another round of drinks and some appetizers. I felt like I was in a daze. Like in another dimension sitting around the table talking and having a good time. I wasn't used to being out anywhere without Ralph. Roberto danced with Dixie a few times. Dennis didn't ask me to dance. I was a little disappointed, but thought he may not know how to dance.

They think I Killed My Husband!

"Do you know how to dance?" I asked Dennis.

"Oh, of course I know how to dance. I just don't want to right now," he blurted with a smart-ass smirk.

"Oh, okay," I stated. "I guess I'll have to go ahead and dance by myself!" I exclaimed. So feeling no pain from the alcohol I had already consumed, I got onto the dance floor and proceeded to dance. I love to dance. I am very good at dancing. I never danced professionally, but I can clear a dance floor. So I was dancing and getting into the music. I was feeling the music just go through my body and vibrate out in the rhythm of the beat and cause my body to move to the sounds flowing in and out of my body. I was dancing like no one was watching.

Suddenly, a nice looking Latino started to dance with me. He took my hand and twirled me around to the salsa beat. It was wonderful. I was spun around like a professional dancer! He even dipped me! We were dancing like we had been dancing for years together! What a great dancer this man was! He pulled me close holding both of my hands with his. I was dancing with him with my nose touching his and his hands holding me there. I danced the best I could dance, which was pretty damn good. I thanked him and said I needed to get something to drink. I did work up quite a thirst. I sat down at the table where all of my friends were.

Roberto looked at me and said, "Pamela Garcia! I would have never guessed!"

"What?" I inquired with a guilty but innocent look on my face.

"That was great!" Roberto exclaimed.

"Thanks!" I replied.

Dennis was quiet. I hope I didn't do the wrong thing. Ralph would have been so furious if I danced with anyone else. I wasn't sure what the rules are. Were we out on a date? No, I confirmed. He didn't buy me anything nor did he pick me up and take me anywhere. He was looking and flirting like a dog with other girls right in front of me over at the other club. I came to the conclusion that what happened was purely spontaneous and extremely enjoyable. I haven't danced like that with

35

anyone! It was fabulous! I ordered another drink to quench my thirst. Shortly after getting my drink, the young Latino dancer asked me to dance again.

"Sure," I said.

"What is your name?" I asked my Latino lead man.

"Gabriel." He told me.

"Where did you learn to dance like that?" I asked with a smile on my face looking into his dark brown eyes.

"I am a dance instructor," Gabriel said.

"No wonder you dance so well! I love the way you dance! I have never danced so smooth. At least I haven't danced with someone so connectedly," I exclaimed.

"You dance very well," Gabriel commented.

"Thanks. You make me look great out there!" I retorted. After we danced some more, Gabriel walked me back to the table. Everyone else was ready to leave.

"Pam, we are going to go," Roberto said as he and Dixie were getting up.

"Yeah, the boss lady, Roberto says is a real bitch if you are late." Dennis added.

"Ha-ha. Come you guys. You all are going already?" I asked wondering why they were cutting out so soon. Dennis looked at me and told me he would tell me later. Perplexed, I agreed. I needed to get home too. We all started to walk out of the club to go home. Dennis walked out with me. I didn't think anything of it. I thought he was just being a gentleman. He gave me a kiss when we got to the Corvette, and I got into the car. I saw Dennis get into his Mercedes and drive away. I got into my car that was still in the parking lot. I was fumbling through my purse to find my makeup and my marijuana. I smoked a quick toke from my pipe and dabbled a little more makeup on my face to freshen up a bit and to look straight.

As I was putting on my lipstick, a shadow covered the side of my face. I looked over my shoulder and just to my left was a man! I screamed! It was Gabriel. He wanted to see if I would go out with him sometime. Just then, my cell phone rang. It was Maria, my late husband's sister. She was calling to see how I was doing. I was a little tipsy, with a strange man I was dancing with standing outside of my car. This is not a good time to be talking to such a self-righteous divorcee'.

"Where are you?" She demanded.

"I went out with some friends. I really needed to get out a little," I said with a guilty tone to my voice.

"Oh. Where are the kids?" She demanded with an attitude.

"They are at home with a sitter." I reassured her.

"Whom are you talking to?" She had to ask.

"A friend." I said. "I need to get going home. I was just leaving when you called. May I call you back, Maria?"

"Of course, call me when you get home." She said.

"Thanks. I will," I agreed. Now back to this man still standing beside my car, "I really did have to go."

"I would like to see you again." Gabriel assured me.

"Here is my card. Call me so we can go out this weekend. Please?" He pleaded. "You are so beautiful."

"OK. I will. Thanks! I had a great time! You are such a wonderful dancer." I claimed. He helped me put the top down and I drove away with his card and phone number in my purse.

The night was wonderful. It was May and the weather was dry and warm. I drove home with top down. I had the radio on. The music was fast paced dance music. The wind danced through my hair in step with the stars above. I felt as if I had no problems at all. I had so much to deal with and had already dealt with a lot. I was thankful to know I could still have a good time while having so many confrontations. My mind was focused on the road. I integrated the music with the highway. I was definitely going a little past the speed limit. I was at a comfortable speed though. I didn't want to slow down. I noticed a Mustang beside me. The driver revved up his engine and then slammed on his brakes. Giving me a signal that he wanted to race a bit. The Mustang swerved into my car! I gunned it. I was accelerating as fast as I could go in my Corvette. He quickly accelerated his Mustang. He started towards my car again! I had to quickly whip his ass. I accelerated as fast as I could. All he could see was the back of me. Then I realized how fast I was going and how incredibly stupid I was being.

"I'm doing 93 in a 45! I am going to get a ticket," I said to myself slamming on my brakes. The Mustang sped past me and kept on going. He didn't slow down at all! We were getting into a congested area too! I started to go the speed limit since the highway was at the part where it went through the middle of town. I am hearing this funny sound coming from somewhere. I couldn't figure it out. I turned down my radio and looked up into the rear view mirror and saw a police car behind me with the lights on!

Then I hear, "Pull over to the side of the road, please." This was being said over a speaker outside of his car.

I looked down at my speedometer. I was not exceeding the speed limit. With a confused look, I obeyed the officer and pulled over into a drug store parking lot. I made sure I had everything put away that I needed to have away. I stayed in the car. I was looking for the registration. I forgot where Ralph kept it. I knew it was in the glove box or somewhere in the car. I just didn't know where. I was looking all over inside the glove box. I looked in the owner's manual, which had a zippered book cover made of leather. I unzipped that and looked inside. I flipped through the pages and found it. While I had my head down looking for this registration, the policeman walked up to my car to ask for my driver's license and registration. I raised my head and looked around the parking lot. There were 5 police cars around me and all with their red and blue lights on! I gazed around the back and sides of my Corvette convertible and saw nothing but red and blue rotating lights! It looked better than the disco I just left!

"What is this?" I exclaimed. "This is ridiculous! You guys are making this look like some huge drug bust!"

"Driver license and registration, Ma'am?" he demanded.

"Here," I sighed. "I wasn't speeding. Why are you pulling me over?" I asked, worriedly. I was a little nervous. I had been drinking a little and did have marijuana in my possession. They checked out my license and came back to ask me a few

They think I Killed My Husband!

more questions.

"Do you know how fast you were going about a couple of miles back?" The policeman inquired.

"No, not really. How far back are you talking about? What about the other guy that was trying to run me off the road?" I wanted to know, trying to act as though I hadn't been speeding.

"Well, we received a radio from our Sergeant that was pulling up to the road you were racing on. Were you racing with a Mustang, Mrs. Garcia?" He asked.

"I will be completely honest with you. I did go a little fast back there. Then I realized how fast I was going and quickly slowed down. The Mustang kept racing through town! I slow down and do the right thing and I get stopped. But the other guy, since he didn't slow down, gets away," I defended.

"We don't have an actual reading of how fast you were going. The Sergeant knew you were speeding and radioed ahead. That is why everyone else is here too. Since we don't have evidence recorded of how fast you were actually going, I am going to let you go. Just please drive more carefully," the officer warned me sternly.

"Thank you," I said graciously. No doubt I was gracious! I thought I was being carted off to jail when I saw all of those cop cars! Five cop cars with all of their lights going in the middle of town, I felt like tomorrow's cover story for the newspaper! My heart was still beating so fast. I can't believe how lucky I am. I didn't think I would say that anytime soon. I felt like the unluckiest person in the world. This would have been nothing to get out of. I would get through it.

I arrived home. I was so glad to see my kids. I went upstairs to tuck them into bed. I made sure they brushed their teeth before they lay down for the night. I gave them each a big hug and kiss and told them what happened and about all of the cop cars. Their eyes got so wide with excitement and surprise. I told them it was innocent situation. I shouldn't have been speeding and I was caught. They loved the story and also understood that people shouldn't speed and I did something wrong. I hope they could learn from me.

The morning was nice. There was a slight fog hovering over the lake. It looked almost spooky. I loved to sit and drink coffee in the morning looking out at the lake from my breakfast nook. I always had my brown coffee in a black and white checkered mug. It matched the black and white tile of the kitchen floor. I loved my bright beautiful kitchen. The Victorian décor was so comforting. I had to get the kids up shortly for school. They have been so wonderful through all of this. They come and make sure I am doing okay. They are such wonderful children. It is not fair that they must go through the rest of their lives without their father.

    I went upstairs to wake them. I bent over and kissed my daughter on the cheek. She opened her eyes and looked at me and smiled. She sprang up in the bed and gave me a huge, incredible hug! We stayed locked in each other's arms for a couple of minutes. I could feel my eyes start to swell and get wet.

    "I love you," Serena said.
    "I love you more," I replied.
    "Nuh uh!" She muttered.
    "Uh, huh," I replied.
    "No, I love YOU more!" Serena retaliated.
    "Okay," I said.
    "But, I love you MORE!" I added with a giggle.

    I went to wake up my son. I went to his room. Their rooms were both upstairs. His bedroom had a flat window in the front of the house where he could overlook the lake. My daughter's window was a bay window and had a wonderful view of the lake. We watched the Christmas boat parade from her room. The view was awesome from the second story. By day, you could see the green stretch of grass that went to the blue of the lake that matched the sky. At night, to see the boats lit up on the lake and the reflection of these lights on the water was such a pretty sight to see for Christmas without leaving the comfort of your own home. It was lovely.

They think I Killed My Husband!

They went to school and I went to work, just another day. The weekend came and none too soon!

The day started to get hot and the sun was high. The grass needed to be mowed. The gardeners were on vacation for a couple of weeks. I asked the kids if they would like to take turns mowing on the riding lawn mower. They were so excited. This was the closest they could get to drive anything at their age. My son loved to drive. In the past my husband let the kids drive the boat a little ways in open water. My son started the job of mowing the lawn first. He mowed the back yard and part of the front by the lake. Now it was my daughter's turn. I helped her on the mower. She had sunscreen on and her black sunglasses on to protect here eyes. She looked like a miniature teenager on the riding mower. I helped her get started mowing and told here where I wanted her to mow. The part that was left was the big open area of the front yard. It was just a big, flat plain, just ride and mow. My daughter made it off to a great start. I stood outside and observed her for a few minutes and went inside to do some cleaning. About ten minutes later, I went to the front living room to look out and see how Serena was doing. She looked like she thought she was the coolest person in the world. She was so pretty with her long brown-black hair flowing in the breeze. Her dark sunglasses just confirmed her "coolness." Looking more closely and observing her mowing tactics, I had to start laughing hysterically. She had left tracks in the yard that were so crazy, it looked like Picasso was mowing the lawn. The shaven path left from the lawn mower was too funny. She was mowing with such a professional attitude and left such an unprofessionally mowed yard, it was to laugh. I had the most unique design left in my yard. She was mowing aimlessly. No pattern in the way of mowing. She didn't mow in a perimeter spiral working inward, just a round and crazy eight style. I ran out and stopped her.

"Let me finish," I asked.

"Why? I can do it," Serena confirmed.

"No, Honey. Look at what you did. My yard looks like Picasso came and mowed," I said with a laugh. "But, thank you. You did good for a beginner."

"What is wrong with it?" Serena asked.

"Well, Sweetie, nothing really. But, you can get more mowing accomplished if it's done with organization," I said.

"Watch me and you will learn."

A little hurt and confused, she got off of the mower and let me finish. I finished up the yard. It didn't take long. We later rode our bikes up the road along the lake to the Ice cream shop and got ourselves a treat.

A friend of mine came over later. It was Sherry. I wasn't expecting her. She was at my back door and I opened it. She was almost in tears.

"I just found out." She said with open arms turning into a tight hug. " I am so sorry."

"I know. Thank you," I gratefully said.

"I just finished working. Look what I got as payment." Sherry said holding out her hand with a little baggie in it. The little baggie had some white powder in it.

"Is that what I think it is?" I questioned.

"Yes. Do you want some? I don't know if I should or not. I might be able to sell it."

"Screw that!" I said. "Let's do it. I need a little release. I can't think of anything else better to do than to chill here, watch the big screen and relax."

"Great!" Sherry exclaimed. "I was hoping you'd say that."

We went to my room and did a couple of fat lines. The kids were upstairs watching movies in their playroom. Sherry and I went to the Family room and watched some television. Sherry and I talked about the good times and laughed and cried. Sherry was a single mother. She has two children, which were with her mother at the moment. I told her of Serena's lawn mowing experience. Then I asked her if she knew of any boat mechanics around here that Ralph might have taken the boat to. Sherry worked in the auto industry. She also worked for me on occasion in our business. She told me of a couple of places that I haven't been to yet. One sounded familiar, so I would look tomorrow to see if it was there.

"I can't believe you don't know where your boat is! Are you sure you are not really a true blonde?" Sherry asked me while laughing. We talked to the wee hours of the morning, as this stuff will make one do that. We had a great time. I had to go to a party tomorrow. It was my birthday tomorrow too!

"It's my birthday!" I told Sherry. "I am going to a birthday party too!"

"Oh, really? Where?" She asked.

I told her it was the pool and clubhouse of the apartments where Roberto lived. Dennis is having his birthday party there.

"Cool. Is Dennis cute?" She inquired.

"Oh yea. Extremely," I said.

"Well, good. It will do you some good to get out and meet new people," Sherry commented. It was getting late and we went to sleep. Sherry just crashed on my couch. I went to bed, anticipating on the fun of tomorrow.

Tomorrow came and I was ready. I called for a baby sitter earlier in the week so I was sure of having that covered. I got in the shower to wake up and get ready to go to the pool party. I packed a little bag with extra panties and sunscreen and makeup and a towel. I was excited about going. Dennis was so cute. I missed my husband so much. I missed having constant love and attention. I guess I needed to get attention some how. I had to find it elsewhere.

I headed to the party. I was in my Corvette with the top down. It didn't seem like my corvette though. It was still Ralph's Corvette. I can't seem to say with a feeling of truth that it was my Corvette. I had a short dress on with my suit jacket over that and high-heeled 'Nine West' sandals on. I had my Chanel purse and my Chanel sunglasses on. I was the epitome of a fashion victim.

I was a little lost with the directions. I called Dennis on his cell phone from my cell phone to talk me through the directions while driving. I arrived at the party. Dennis was waiting out in front for me. Dennis had on these skin-tight black spandex shorts that flattered his perfect muscular tight ass. He was tan and his hair had blonde highlights that accented his blue eyes.

"*How sweet,*" I thought.

"What a Sweetie. You didn't have to be out front to meet me," I said.

"I thought I could help you carry your stuff. Besides, we need more ice and I need you to take me to Albertson's to get more," Dennis replied.

"Oh, OK," I said, as Dennis got into the car.

"So, what do we have here?" Dennis inquired while looking at some of the stuff in my open bag. He pulled out my gold leather headband. I use that to just pull my hair back and not have to do anything to it. These are very handy when going to the beach or swimming.

"I like this," he commented.

We got onto the road heading towards the grocery store, when Dennis asked me to see what she's got. He was talking about the car. I gunned the engine a little and just for a short while, then I slammed the brakes to get the car at a normal speed extremely quick.

"How's that? Do you want to drive?" I asked.

"No. That's OK," Dennis answered quietly.

I must have given him a little start. He looked like he was a little in shock. He was stiff.

We made it to Albertson's Grocery store to pick up more ice. He had on his short black combat boots and a loose tank top tee shirt with little spandex workout shorts. He had the most gorgeous legs on a man I had ever seen! I just drooled as I watched him go into the store. The curve of his tight buttocks in the shiny, black spandex shorts looked so delicious. His tan legs were so smooth, muscular and shaven, I just wanted a taste. I couldn't look like a slut though. I had to play it cool. I was out of practice.

"*Wow!*" I thought to myself holding a drool cup under my chin.

Dennis made it back to the car with the ice. He put the

ice just behind the seat. He had my pool bag between his legs. He picked up my headband again. He put it on his head. The gold leather matched his gold hair. He started speaking with a lisp and talking about how he loved his tiara. He was confident enough with his manhood that he actually walked me to the party wearing this headband. He was a pretty man. But, no question a man. With the headband on, it created an illusion of a tiara, he was funny right now to look at.

As we walked onto the pool area, some of Dennis's friends were there waiting to greet him. One friend saw him and couldn't resist singing to him these words to the tune of "Mighty Mouse." "Here he comes to say he's gay!" Steve sang with an operatic voice.

I just busted out laughing! I thought I was going to hear "Here he comes to save the Day!" That was too funny. Dennis took off the headband immediately.

"Ha ha ha. Very funny," Dennis said. He looked over at me and saw me laughing then when I realized he saw me, I shut up very quickly. I was still trying to contain my laughter. Everyone gave me a warm welcome, except some of the other women that were there. I was starting over. I didn't have many friends or acquaintances yet, none of my own anyway. The married friends I had with my late husband were not really calling on me to do anything. Who wants a third wheel around anyway?

Dennis put my stuff behind the bar in the pool area. Steve was bartending. Steve was a little bit chunkier than Dennis and Roberto. He had a goatee and mustache with dark hair that made him look like a WWF wrestler. He was getting everyone beer from the keg. I talked with Roberto a little and looked around for Dennis and he was in the pool. He said he already drank some moonshine a friend of his brought from Tennessee.

"Come on in, the water's fine!" Dennis yelled.

"I'll be right there!" I exclaimed as I jumped in.

Dennis came and put his arms around me. It was pretty cool. I was facing Dennis and I had a strange man's arms around me in the water. It was such an arousing feeling to have nothing but our swim suits on with his fingers touching the sides of my abdomen. He turned me around and grabbed me from behind. He crossed his arms around my torso and pushed my ass into his groin. I was sitting on his lap in the pool.

"Do you like that?" he asked.

"Yes. It feels nice." I answered.

"So do you want to go upstairs and have sex?" Dennis asked me.

"Are you kidding me?" I questioned.

"No, I am so horny. I had so much hooch. I may have to pass out later," Dennis added.

"So, you think I am going to just go and have sex with you. You didn't even shave!" I commented. Dennis shaves his entire body. So he had a chest full of razor stubble.

"If you don't, I'll have to find someone else." Dennis came back and told me.

I was appalled. I had been married too long. I couldn't believe what was being said to me. What an asshole! I told him I needed to get another drink. I got out of the pool.

I did get another drink. I also saw Dennis flirting with one of the other girls that was at the party. Holding her the same way he held me in the pool. I just started to talk to Roberto and some of the other guests at the pool. Roberto introduced me to a friend of his that had arrived recently. His name was Aaron. He was a tall nice looking Panamanian. He looked like a Caucasian Lionel Ritchie. Aaron was at least 6 foot 4 inches tall and very muscular.

"Nice to meet you," I stated. We started talking a bit. He seemed very nice. I talked with him a little while and we walked to the weight room of the complex and goofed off with the weights for a few minutes. The day was coming to a close. Aaron needed a ride home. He came with a friend that lived in the complex and his friend went home and is probably asleep. Since I was leaving and most everyone there lived at the complex, I agreed to take Aaron home. I did not know the intentions of just taking someone home. I thought that taking

They think I Killed My Husband!

someone home meant taking someone home. Aaron and I were getting a little friendly on the pool side. We had engaged in a few kisses. I was feeling a little tipsy from the beer.

    I drove Aaron home. He asked me if I wanted to come in and see his place. I said I better not. I now realize that something more may happen and I am not ready for it, I didn't think. Apparently, I had to be made ready. I got out of the car. The top was down and I was leaning against the side of the Corvette just over the back tire with my butt resting on the fender. Aaron started to kiss me. He was such a good kisser. Aaron lifted me up so I was sitting on top of the car. I was still wearing my swimsuit and had my jean dress over it. The car was in the street in front of Aaron's house. I had in my pocket the remote and key to the Corvette. The Corvette's remote was a sensory remote. You didn't have to push any buttons. The sensor would be in close range and would automatically unlock the doors and lock the doors when you walked out of range. Now, when the doors locked this would engage the alarm and the horn would honk letting you know the alarm engaged. I was so tipsy and now unaware of anything around me being so caught up in the passion, I didn't care. We were kissing such delicious kisses. Our tongues were playing with each other. We were breathing each other's breath. We started to fondle each other with a hot, desperate desire. He put his hands on the outsides of my thighs and slid his hands up and pushed my dress up to my hips. I had my hands around his body and ran my fingers through his hair. Aaron unzipped the front of my dress and started to kiss my chest and caress my waist with masculine gentleness. He put his arms around me and then he slid his hand down and put it under my ass. He lifted me up just slightly and shifted me closer to him. I wrapped my legs around his ass to hold him closer too. I was kissing him so passionately. Our tongues wrapping and intertwining each other, I was so hot! I felt Aaron put his fingers in my pussy. Then all of the sudden I felt something much bigger enter my hot wet pussy. My eyes opened wide! What a big surprise! It felt so good! The idea of having some strange dick

was even more erotic. I had no other man in 13 years. It felt so good. I didn't care where we were or who was watching.
Not realizing we were in the front of his house, in the street, on top of my corvette, I started to hear a horn honking. With every thrust of Aaron pushing inside me the Corvette would honk. Then, I would hear a click, the doors unlocked. Then I heard the honk, the doors locked again. We were fucking and the car was on automatic with the doors locking and unlocking. The horn was blasting to the beat of our passion. I didn't care. I was oblivious to anything around me.

"Can't we please go inside?" Aaron asked.

"No, not now!" I demanded. I didn't want to stop now! Not for anything! From the moment I felt that big hard cock enter my hot wet pussy I didn't want anything else! The air was warm and humid. I hadn't felt anything so wonderful in so long. Ralph was a great lover, but size does matter. Aaron was huge! I could feel him so down deep inside of me it hurt. I felt the kind of hurt that feels good. We kept grinding and pumping as his big rod slid in and out of my pussy. I had my arms back over my head lying on the car. I realized the car was honking from the remote I had in my pocket. I took the remote and threw it on to the ground. It worked. The car stopped announcing to the world to look over here at the couple having sex.

Aaron whispered to my ear, "Put your arms around my neck."

I opened my eyes and looked at him and said with a sigh, "Okay." I put my arms around his neck and he told me to hang on tight. So with my long muscular legs wrapped around his hips and my arms locked around his neck and Aaron leaning on top of me, he stood up with me still hanging on! I was mounted on his dick! I felt like I was in midair. Aaron had his hands underneath my ass so he had full control of me. He started to thrust his hips and move me up and down with his hands. My legs clutched his hips and my arms around his neck I could still keep kissing him with long wet passionate kisses while bobbing up and down on his big hard cock. I was getting the shit fucked out of me! I loved every second. I could feel my warm love juice oozing down the sides of my pussy lips and my ass. It started to mix with the hot sweat that was pouring out of our bodies. He started to cum! It was incredible! Then I started to get loud with emotional and passionate groans of lust. That was something I don't think I had ever done!

I don't know how long this lasted but I do know that the sun was going down when I brought Aaron home and it was totally dark when I decided I had to go. I drove home in the cool night air with the top down and smile on my face. I was feeling so guilty, but excited. Stimulated even. (Ya think?) Aaron was so nice. But I can't settle for the first guy I come across. Aaron called me later to make sure I made it home all right.

I anticipated facing Roberto the next day at work. He called in sick, however. I was a little relieved, but it also meant I had to stay late and work. I really depended on Roberto to be in to do his job. I was at the same party and I made it to work. Dennis called the office to speak to him later that afternoon.

"Roberto isn't here today. He called in sick." I reported to Dennis.

"Sick? I highly doubt that," he retaliated.

"What do you mean?" I questioned.

"Well, remember that thing I was going to tell you later about Roberto?" Dennis asked me.

"Yes." I said, with continuance in my voice.

"Well, Roberto has had trouble in the past with alcoholism. I am afraid that he may be slipping a little."

"Oh great!" I said with sarcasm. "He seems to have everything so together, his engagement with Dixie, his job, his mind, everything!"

"Well, there is a long story about Roberto and me and Dixie. They almost called off the engagement because I let Roberto have sex with one of my girlfriends and now he doesn't want to let Dixie have sex with me and she wants to." Dennis confessed.

"So, what does that have to do with me or my business?" I inquired.

"Well, if Dixie calls off the wedding because of this disagreement, I'm afraid Roberto will go off the wagon for good." Dennis stated.

"So, Roberto called in sick today because he was hung over and depressed?" I asked, pissed off and disappointed. "Where did you disappear to yesterday? Did you get laid or what?" I questioned Dennis.

"Huh? Oh no. I asked every girl there if she would have sex with me and none of them would. I had to go and lay down in Roberto's apartment. That moonshine kicked my ass. I fell asleep," he told me.

"You actually asked every girl there if she would have sex with you? I know you asked me, but I sloughed it off like you were too messed up and I couldn't take you seriously. That's probably what everyone else was thinking too. I can't believe you asked every girl there that question! I surprised you didn't get slapped!" I added.

"Yea, me too." Dennis confessed. "I was pretty messed up."

"I wondered what happened to you. I got a little tipsy too. I met a friend of yours that didn't make it to the party until later after you disappeared." I told Dennis.

"Oh, really? Who might that be?" Dennis asked.

"Aaron. He is really nice. I had to give him a ride home." I confessed.

"Oh yeah, Aaron is a great guy! He'll do whatever he can for you," Dennis bragged about Aaron.

"That's good to know," I said.

"Well, gotta go Honey! I'll talk to you later and find out the scoop about Roberto for you too!" Dennis said goodbye.

I went back to work and finished up the work I needed to finish. I had to stay late and I called my sitter to stay with the kids a little longer than usual. That was no problem. I hated to have to deal with all of this right now in my life. I wish I could just stay home and mourn properly.

"This situation is for the best." I would tell myself. "I may go crazy if I didn't have something to keep my mind off the fact of how much I miss Ralph."

They think I Killed My Husband!

I received a call later in the week from Frank. Frank said that the person he was talking to about my business wanted to buy it from me for $8,500,000.00!

"When can we do this?" I asked with great anticipation.

"When do you want to?" Frank asked. "He would probably want you to stay on for the first six months and pay you the balance as a minimal fee for training and transition purposes. That is why you would get the extra money."

"I have no problem with that. Set it up and I will adjust my schedule. I really don't want to do this any more. I do want out. I need to relax and mourn like a respectable widow should. But, don't make it sound like I am desperate. He may think the business is no good. It is. You know that. I just don't want to do it anymore without Ralph."

"I understand," Frank admitted. "I'll get it done."

"Thank you so much, Frank. If there is anything I can do for you, just let me know," I told him.

Frank was a very handsome man. Frank was extremely wealthy too. He would cruise the town in one of his Rolls Royces. He had a very successful business similar to ours but in a different market. He tried to help me out with some business advice. Some advice I took and other advice I didn't take. All of the advice he gave me was for the best.

The weekend came and went. I spent most of the time with my kids and mowing the yard, now with money becoming short. I spent some time at my sister's house. She was under going a new project for her and her family. They were building a new big beautiful house on a lake, just 10 minutes from me, right outside of town. My sister has been such a dear through all of this mess I have been going through. I didn't say anything about the sale of the business. I learned from experience never to talk about something that is going to happen, wait until it is done.

Later, I called Frank back to inquire about the possible meeting. Frank asked if I could meet with them later this week.

"How about Thursday at 2:00?" Frank asked me. I told him that would be fine. I wondered if I should bring my lawyer to this meeting or wait to see what they proposed and take the offer later to my lawyer.

"Should I bring the financials?" I asked Frank. "He would probably want to see those before even giving me any proposal in writing."

"Absolutely!" Frank remarked. "I thought that was something you knew to do without me telling you."

"Of course. I just wanted to confirm with you that it would be beneficial to have it on hand. I'll call my accountant to make this available to me, so I may have it if necessary," I commented. I couldn't wait! Wow! I can sell my business and go on with my life? As meager as it may be, I can live simply and raise my kids conservatively. Just a little idea that Ralph and I started a few years back should be worth more than eight and a half million dollars! I felt sad of how hard I had to work to get this money. I was literally selling Ralph's and my dream to someone else for practically nothing so I could get by until the insurance was satisfied. This meant the realization of Ralph being gone. It was like another nail in his coffin. But I had to raise the children by myself now. I didn't have a nanny while I ran to the store. I needed to be financially secured to enable myself to have the adequate amount of time for my children. I needed money also, right now since the insurance companies were giving me a hard time with the cause of death. The insurance companies haven't called the police detective or me. This left me a bit curious.

I arrived home later that day. My housekeeper was still there. She apologized for being late and she was going to work late to make up for it. I told her that was fine. I asked her if she had time to take a break and go outside and burn one with me.

"Oh, sure. I have time for that!" She said. "Are you doing okay?"

"Yes. Just a little more stress to add to what I already have. If you are going to be here for a little while, do you mind keeping an eye on the kids while I go to the store?"

"Of course not," she replied.

So, we went outside to burn a joint together and I told

her a condensed portion of what I was going through with the insurance companies and the police. I didn't tell her that I might be selling the business. Not that she would say anything. I just didn't want to say anything to anyone right now. She told me that if I needed to cut her hours back, she would understand.

"I don't need to do that yet." I responded. "But, thank you though." Rita was a good person. I trusted her. She reminded me of a female version of my older brother. She was thin with long dark hair and always exercising. Her daughter worked for me for a while at the office. Rita was a very hard worker. Everyday she cleaned my house. The way she would clean my kitchen floor, she would actually wipe down my floor on her hands and knees like one would wipe down the counter top.

We finished the joint and I told her I was going to the store and would be back shortly.

Going to the grocery store high was not a good thing to do. It was fun though. I ended up buying everything I could think of or just happened to walk by. I got a call from Aaron on my cell phone while at the store.

"Oh, hi!" I answered. "What are you doing?"

"I'm calling you." Aaron countered. "What are you doing Thursday?"

"I don't know yet. What did you have in mind?" I asked.

"I have some tickets for the House of Blues. Would you like to go? A friend of mine is playing there that night."

"Sure! That sounds great!" I exclaimed. "What time?"

"The concert starts at 8:00. Why don't you be at my place around 7 or 6:30? That'll give us some time to relax before hand."

"Relax? I guess I could use some relaxation." I warned him.

"Great! I'll see you then. Do you remember how to get to my place? You were pretty out of it when you were here the last time," Aaron made me aware.

"You'll have to give me directions again. I am sure looking forward to it!" I exclaimed excitedly.

"Thursday could be my lucky day!" I thought to myself. I had a meeting with Frank and this so-called buyer and I had a hot date that night!

Life went on as usual for the next few days and finally Thursday came. Roberto had been at work the rest of the week like I had hoped and expected. He confirmed Aaron's good character. I went to my meeting Thursday while Roberto held down the fort. I met Frank at his office. Frank had a beautiful office. It was filled with vases from the Orient. The floor was made of marble and the paneling was rich cherry wood. His desk was black lacquer. The furnishings were similar to Chinese black lacquer furnishings. I sat down on the big black leather chair. He had a couple of chairs in front of his desk.

"We can go into the conference room when Don gets here," Frank told me.

I was a little early. I didn't want to louse this up because I was late. I am rarely late for an appointment anyway. I hate to be kept waiting and I wouldn't want others to wait on me. I would have to say that being late was one of my pet peeves. I can't say that I have never been late, but I can say that I have never kept anyone waiting longer than 20-30 minutes. The reason for such tardiness from me was due to an unusual situation. My car broke down or I was stuck in an awful traffic jam would be an example of a reason that may make me late. My time was valuable and I respect other's time. There is no reason that someone can't have professional courtesy to let the other party know they were running late. That is my reasoning. Don made it right on time. I was glad of that. We all sat down at the table in the conference room and proceeded to the meeting at hand.

"Why do you want to sell your business, Mrs. Garcia?" Don questioned. "Frank had told me a little of your dilemma, but I would think you would want to keep it for the income."

"Yes. The income is a good income, but I have to remain working for this income to remain at the level it is. If I were to not work and rely solely on employees to keep me in business, I would be out of business within 2 years. Good help is extremely hard to find. Even if one has good help, it is not the same as the check signer making sure everything is up to par. My husband and I originated this business and it would be very hard to continue it without the proper management."

"So, Mrs. Garcia, are you trying to talk me out of purchasing your company? If you are, you are doing very well." Don retorted

Frank cut in, "No, Don! This would be a great business for you. It's right up your alley and with more capital to invest in this company, this business could really be so much more than what it is now. Don, right now it's an infant. You can make it grow to a giant!"

"Yes, Don. I agree with Frank. I could stay and train and make sure it goes in the right direction after the change of ownership. Right now, under the circumstances I have been dealt, I don't want the responsibility."

"I understand completely." Don stated coldly.

"Yea, sure," I thought. I knew I had better keep my mouth shut. This man was ready to hand me a big chunk of change for my business. All I had to do was just work a little while as a consultant.

"Do you have the financials? I would like to see them, please." Don requested.

"Sure, right here. We grossed almost $20,000,000.00 last year. I am predicting $22.4 million this year." I stated.

"Really? I would like to offer you a sum of money right now that would be very beneficial for you." Don informed me.

"What is your proposed offer?" I inquired.

"I have it here in writing, Mrs. Garcia. I hope it is what you were expecting." Don said.

I took the proposal and scanned it carefully. I saw the $8,500,000.00 figure. I read more closely. The proposal stated that I continue working for one year without pay and I would have to pay off the debts with the gross amount and he would have it debt free and I would have less money. I also don't work for free. I was used to bringing home over 7 figures a year for our personal bills and household funds. Now after one year of working and losing money, I would be down to a mere $3,500,000.00 after taxes probably. It sounded good if I never had anything. I came from a good family. We didn't have much then. I know how it is to have nothing. But, I now know what it is to have worked my ass off to acquire something for myself. I wasn't about to give it away.

I retaliated. "How about $10,000,000.00 and you pay me a salary of $300,000.00 for two months and you pay the debts at the time of the acquisition. If I say so myself, Don, that is one hell of a deal. The company grossed over $22,000,000.00 last year. If I were to wait and sell it, I would have an asking price of only $12,750,000.00 and take over all the debts. But, I don't want to wait. My husband is dead now. I want out now. I will stay for 3 months and that is it!"

I walked over and I threw the proposal in the trash for dramatic purposes. I leaned by the door of the office and looked at the gentlemen, waiting for a reply. Don looked at me in total amazement. Frank just looked at me and smiled.

"I told you she was one tough cookie, Don," Frank confirmed.

"Mrs. Garcia, I will accept your offer after reviewing your financials more thoroughly and I will get back to you by Monday. I admire your confidence and strength. Not many women would be able to keep up with everything considering the circumstances. In which, I have not given you any sympathy of. I am truly sorry for your loss."

"I will be looking forward to your call Monday, Don. No matter what your decision, I would like an answer." I demanded.

"Indeed you shall." Don replied.

Don took my financials and all the other information and left. He did leave me his card so I may call him with any further questions. I did the same for him.

"It went very well!" Frank exclaimed. "I don't think I ever heard him say he was sorry to anyone!"

They think I Killed My Husband!

"Why does that not surprise me?" I asked Frank with a touch of sarcasm. "Do you think he'll buy? That's all I care about." I continued trying not to cry and to remain strong and calm on the outside.

Frank told me honestly, "Since he knows your situation, unfortunately that is not in your favor. He may come back with a little less offer, but I think he might alter your proposition of the work schedule and salary."

"Good. I hope you are right about that. I don't want to work anymore at all! Two months will seem eternal when I have so much more I could be doing." I told Frank anxiously. I looked at Frank and thanked him for everything he has done for me. I told him if I could do anything for him, to just let me know.

I stared at his handsome face and really thought "Anything! I would like to do anything!" But, Frank was a married man. However, Ralph had mentioned some times where Frank had invited him to go along with him and a couple of other young girls for an afternoon of fun in his Rolls Royce, but he never went. I am sure that I wasn't a bimbo that would go either. So, I just kept my thoughts to myself.

Thursday evening came. I had a date. I was to meet Aaron at his house in the city. He had given me directions earlier that morning. I arrived at Aaron's house. He was waiting for me outside.

"Do you mind if I drive?" Aaron asked me.

"No, not at all! That would be nice." I verified.

I got into Aaron's car. He had an economical car. It was okay. But, it wasn't my 'Vette. I didn't want to hurt his feelings by suggesting he drive my car. I just sat and appreciated being driven around for a change. We went to a local pub first for a couple of drinks. I ordered a beer and Aaron ordered the same. Aaron excused himself to the bathroom. He came back and handed me a little baggie with some white powder in it.

Acting like a naive little girl, I asked, "What's this?"

"It's coke. Would you like some?" Aaron asked.

"Okay. Looks like a plan to me! I had a great meeting

and would love to celebrate!" I went to the bathroom. I came back and told Aaron it was getting a little late if we wanted to make the show.

Aaron agreed and we left to go to the 'House of Blues.'

I had a good time. Aaron is a lot of fun. The processed fun in the little baggie was a release too. We made it back to Aaron's house. He had a little bit of coke left in his pocket. We each took a couple more hits and went to his bedroom. It was so erotic. One more quick rush seemed to go like an ice fountain through my veins. Ironically, I was so hot and horny for him. I was having such a good time. We seemed to have a lot in common, great sex. The room was dark and cool with the cool light of the moon invading the sheer curtains. We started kissing and made our way onto the bed. Aaron was kissing my mouth and rolling his tongue in and around my mouth. He played with my tongue as I played with his. His hands swept across my torso and pulled me closer to him. Our mouths locked together with my hands grasping his hair for more. He was sliding his hands up the sides of my body and taking my shirt off with them. My shirt was around my neck and I held up my arms so he could remove my shirt completely. Once my shirt was off, Aaron started to kiss my chest. I leaned back with pure pleasure. He moved his mouth around my tanned upper chest just above my bra. Tasting me like I was a great big ice cream cone. Aaron swirled his tongue all over my soft skin of my chest and down to my breasts. While he was doing this, he was managing to unhook my bra in the back. I just relaxed and my head fell back with my eyes closed. My bra became unhooked and he took it off of me. While still licking my breasts with his tongue, he then sucked my nipples. They were getting so hard. I got goose bumps all over my body. I started to moan with ecstasy. I could feel the love juices flowing, getting myself wet on the outside. I lay back on the bed so I would not stain the sheets. Without saying a word, Aaron climbed on top of me and started to kiss my mouth again. Aaron was such a good kisser. I ran my hands through his hair. I pulled him closer to me. He was trying to undo my pants. I knew what was next. I helped undo my pants. When he saw I was taking care of undressing myself the rest of the way, he started to undo his pants too. I saw that big dick he had. I felt it the last time. But, I sure didn't see that monster! I had to suck on that one. I put my warm wet lips onto the tip of his cock. I swirled my tongue a little just to give it a taste. I took my tongue down the front side of his hard genital. I licked it going down like I was licking an envelope. Then going up, I skimmed my tongue along the front of his cock like I was trying to keep an ice cream cone from dripping. I went up and down a few times with my tongue. Teasing him a little bit with the anticipation of when I would actually take it all into my mouth. I engulfed the huge penis as far down in my mouth as I could. I could only manage about ¾ of his 9 & 1/2 inches! He was good and hard. He asked me to stop before he came in my mouth. I lay back on the bed and Aaron climbed on top of me very quickly. He inserted his big dick inside my nice wet pussy. He stroked me in and out. I could feel everything. I even felt the pressure of him rubbing against my pelvic bone. That felt so good, a big hard cock fucking my tight moist pussy. He asked me to grab his neck again. I did and Aaron stood straight up! He was holding me in an upright, vertical position. I had my legs wrapped around his waist while my pussy was pounding up and down. Aaron was still inserted in me and he began thrusting and pushing in and out with his cock. We started fucking so hard and he thrust so much that the ceiling fan interrupted us. Aaron actually thrust me up so high I hit my head on the ceiling fan!

"Ouch! Shit!" I yelled.

"Are you all right?" Aaron asked.

"Yes. Don't stop now!" I screamed with laughter! We fucked for hours. Three hours to be exact. I was soaked in sweat. I looked up at Aaron. He was soaked in sweat too. His hair was completely wet and dripping! We fell onto the bed and rested a bit in each other's arms. It was so nice to cuddle and feel a man next to me. I told Aaron I had to go. The kids were at home.

I got dressed and gathered my stuff. Aaron got dressed

to walk me out to my car. He gave me a kiss good night and shut my car door. I drove home and felt so good and yet so guilty.

"It hasn't been long enough since Ralph's passing," I thought. I began to cry and ask myself how could I do this? It wasn't the same. I didn't even have an orgasm, at least not the great kind where I release so much tension. Ralph knew what I liked. He knew exactly what I loved. I started to cry. I wanted him to have the sex with, but I didn't want this guy. Although it was great sex, I wasn't in love with him. He was just a fuck. A great fuck, but it didn't mean anything. It wasn't the same. I was so confused. I did enjoy the night so incredibly. Maybe it was the drugs. My mind wasn't at its best right now either. I was hurting still. My heart literally ached.

The following Monday, Frank called and asked, "When would you like to have a meeting with Don and myself?"

"You tell me." I answered back.

"Don has his accountant and attorneys looking over the financials and the other information you gave him. I need to call and see when he would like to meet. I would like to know when you might be able to meet him, so I can try to get this done," Frank told me.

"Anytime next week will be fine with me," I said.

"Great. That will make it easier. I'll let you know when next week." Frank told me.

"Great! Call me when you know." I demanded.

"I will. Bye now." Frank closed.

"Bye," I replied.

A few days later, the police called me in for questioning. I can't understand why people would put other people through such torment. Hadn't I suffered enough? I lost my husband, now I had to convince people I would never even think of doing such a thing as murder? I am innocent until proven guilty. Why do I feel I have to defend myself? I didn't do anything. The insurance company is really being a bunch of total jerks. They just want to be really sure that the cause of death was purely natural.

They think I Killed My Husband!

"I'll need to call my lawyer and have him with me," I retaliated to the officer on the phone.

"We'll allow that. Have your lawyer call us in the next 24 hours to let us know when he will be available," the officer commanded.

"Will do!" I said and quickly hung up the phone. I don't know if I can get through this. Ralph was my rock. He wasn't here anymore and these people have the inclination that I may have killed him! People can resort to such low depths to not pay out the money or prolong the situation somehow. Here I am with two children and a company to run, and I have to deal with this too!

I went to see Tom, my estate lawyer and he tried to reassure me that it was purely standard when there are any benefits to pay.

"He was very young. They just want to make sure that the sum to pay is justified. No one is really accusing you of anything. They just want to ask you questions. The detailed autopsy is to also make certain there were no outside substances in his system inducing the attack. Your husband wasn't taking any drugs was he?" My lawyer, Tom asked.

"No. He was just drinking that night. But he does smoke cigarettes and the policy was written up with this information. He did smoke some pot earlier in the week. He didn't smoke everyday, but occasionally enjoyed it. It takes 30 days to get tetrahydrocannabinol out of one's system. I know that. There may be some traces of the THC in his blood still. Will that go against anything if they manage to find that?" I responded

"Not likely, but I'm no doctor or insurance agent. I wouldn't think it would instigate or initiate a heart attack, especially if he wasn't smoking that night. Was he snorting or doing cocaine?"

"No! He was too scared to. We did earlier in life, but when Ralph started to get anxiety attacks, he was to scared to!" I yelled.

"Okay, Pam. I believe you. It is a good thing. If they found traces of coke that could be reason enough not to pay.

You'll be fine. Since it was due to natural causes, you should have nothing to worry about," Tom confirmed.

I left feeling a little bit better. I didn't feel so much like I was being picked out from among everyone to be made an example of. According to Tom, this is routine. I wasn't taking it so personally. That was a great weight lifted off of my shoulders.

I went home and gave my kids a big hug and kiss and cooked some dinner for us to eat. I didn't feel much like eating though. Why is it when you feel sad, you aren't hungry? When you are depressed, you want to eat everything? I even felt like wearing black. I wore black everyday. I dress how I feel and that is how I felt. I didn't dress in black because I was expected to. The dismal color matched my dark feelings at that time.

Later that night, I called Sherry. Sherry was turning into a great friend. I don't know what I would have done without her. Sherry had two kids and lives with her boyfriend at that time. He was older and she became close to him after her divorce from her husband. Her ex-husband was in jail. Her children had lost their Dad too, until he is out of jail anyway. Sherry was leasing one my other houses from me. She always paid on time. She was a responsible person that way.

"I'll get the check to you tomorrow," she stated.

"Oh, I'm not worried about it," I said.

"I know, but I am," she said back. "It's the first today. I would have been by there tonight, but I had some errands to run. Get a sitter. We are going to Par-tee!"

Chapter 3

Life after Losing It

The following evening Sherry came over with the rent money. I was dressed and ready to go and the baby sitter was already there. I had on a short mini jean skirt with a nice tank top and heels. Sherry had on pretty much the same thing with a yellow halter-top on instead.
"Do you have any floss? I ate some ribs and need to get the pieces that are stuck," Sherry asked.
"Sure. I have some in my bathroom. Go ahead," I told her pointing towards my bedroom suite. I followed her into my bedroom suite to get the floss for her. We got to my suite and I went into the bathroom to retrieve the floss from my vanity drawer.
"I have something for us." She said and held out her hand that held a little baggie with something white in it. I walked over and shut the bedroom door.
"Cool!" I gleamed. "Here's the floss. Let me go and get a plate."
We did a little bit of extra curricular activity in the bathroom and went on our way to the city to dance. We took the Corvette convertible. The weather was warm, but the night air was just a little cooler, just right for going fast in an open car. On our way to our destination, we were the recipients of quite a few gawks and honks. Sherry got a call from her boyfriend. He was informing her that he just got home from the races.
"Guess where I am?" She questioned her boyfriend. "I

am with Pam in her Corvette with the top down heading out to go dancing!" She yelled over the wind whirling around her head. She started to giggle and told him she'd be good, as she pushed the "End" button on the cell phone.

"Oh! Pull over and let's get some booze," she suddenly ordered! I had to slam on my brakes, squealing to make the turn to the parking lot. I instantly pulled into the liquor store, since she told me while we were right in front of the store at the time. It was on the left, so I had a little bit of play and scooted into the left turning lane. The truck behind us sped by and honked his horn in several short repetitious blows. Sherry held out her arm and waved to the trucker as he drove past. I just looked and had to laugh. She did too. We went to the store and purchased what we wanted.

We arrived to our destination and immediately went to the ladies' room. After we fixed our hair and powdered our noses, we were ready for anything. I haven't been to a full blown, nothing but a club, club, since Ralph's death. I had been to bars that were also restaurants, but not a huge disco. The place was jammin'! It was a huge open room with the dance floor in the middle and a balcony surrounding ½ of the dance floor. The décor was very luminescent. Grand pictures hung high on the wall. Art deco style furniture splattered about the VIP section. The carpet was black with color confetti print, which glowed in the black light. There were men everywhere. I really didn't care though. I came to release some stress by dancing, nothing else. Sherry started to go towards the bar.

"Where are you going?" I asked, walking behind her.

"I am going to get a drink!" She yelled over the music looking at me like I was stupid. "I am in a bar and I am going to get a drink!" she explained.

"Oh, then get me one too. Here's some money." I requested as I was fumbling for some money in my purse.

"Don't worry about it. I'll get it. You can get the next round," Sherry stated.

"Okay. I am going to go and dance," I enlightened her.

They think I Killed My Husband!

I went to the dance floor and proceeded to dance. I just listened to the music and could feel it pumping through my veins and through my heart. I closed my eyes and danced like there was no one else in the room. I was feeling the buzz from the blow we did earlier. It was nice to escape for a little while. Ralph loved to take me dancing. He would watch me dance for hours. I get such a feeling like no other while dancing. I just let everything go. There is no holding back. I bend, swirl and get my arms in the action too. I use my entire body to move to express the rhythm and emotions of the music with my body. The people on the dance floor usually clear some space for me. A few guys would start to dance by me to make others think they were dancing with me. These guys are usually the dwebes of the crowd. I would just turn and make sure my back was to these men. Once in a while, a cutie would dance near me. But nine times out of ten, their girlfriends were dancing near by and oblivious to their boyfriends' flirtatious moments or the girl would give me dirty looks and quickly get her boyfriend off of the dance floor.

Sherry came to the edge of the dance floor with my drink. I walked over to get my drink. I was uncommonly thirsty by then. We talked and walked around for a while. Another song came on. I raced to the dance floor.

"I am going to walk around and get another drink." She yelled over the music. I gave her the "okay" hand signal and kept dancing. A really cute guy came from behind me and picked me up and lifted me onto one of the dancing platforms. I turned around with an expression on my face that would have made money obsolete. I just looked at him like I couldn't believe what he just did!

"You need to be up there!" He told me and walked away.

Completely puzzled, I shrugged my shoulders and realized I had more room to dance and yelled thanks to the guy as he was walking away. Sherry came later with someone she had met at the bar. I saw her with a guy and waved to her so she knew I acknowledged her. Later, I joined them.

"I can't believe you!" Sherry exclaimed.

"Why?" I asked.

She leaned closer to me and said, "I tell this guy I am with my friend and he asks where you are and then I look up and see you dancing on the stage! I can't believe you, man! I was almost embarrassed! Not!"

I smiled and explained what happened. The night went on and we left around one o'clock. I called my friend Aldo. His house was on our way home. He was still up. Sherry and I went over there to visit with Aldo. Soon after our arrival, Aldo's roommate got there. He had a friend with him too. We all partied a little while longer. Sherry was a little paranoid. She wanted get going. We stayed for almost two hours. It was late. I agreed and we went home. Sherry crashed on the couch and I went to my room to sleep.

When Monday came, Frank called and informed me when the meeting would take place about selling the business. I called my lawyer, Tom to tell him I needed him to be present at this meeting. I informed him of the time and he scheduled it. I also inquired about the police calling me in for questioning.

"You did call them, didn't you?" I demanded with desperation.

"Yes. Would you please stop worrying about that? Just sell this business and pay the bills with the money from that. If the insurance wants to drag this out, we'll sue for the money you paid for lawyers fees since the death," Tom reassured me.

The day for the meeting came. It went great! I made the deal. Tom had reviewed the proposal and my counter proposition. We eventually came to a mutual agreement. I settled for $9,000,000.00. A bit less than what I wanted but a little more than the original offer. I needed money now. I had to do the right thing with the money. I had a huge mortgage that was fourteen grand a month with taxes and insurance. The car payments totaled a whopping thirty four hundred. Then, I have the rest of the bills. The electric, water, food, things we need to live. I had to invest a portion of the money to try to have a monthly return for now to pay all of these bills. I would still get a salary. I had an income from working and widow's benefits, but that wasn't enough. I had the money from my small business investments, so I would receive interest and dividend checks every month. I kept some money in a savings account. But after I pay off some bills to make sure I can maintain everything, I won't have hardly anything left. I really need the insurance to pay off all of the debts Ralph owed.

I heard from Aaron later that day. He knew that today was the day of my big meeting. I told him the meeting went great. I didn't want to upset anything or other people wouldn't understand. It wasn't any of his business. I liked playing the poor struggling widow, at least until someone patronized me. Then, I would let all of my anxiety out on that poor person. Aaron invited me to eat some lobster with him. He wanted me to drive to a local pub where the owner gave him full reign of the kitchen to help cook the food.

I arrived about an hour later at the pub. It was fun going into the back kitchen of a restaurant I didn't work at. I had my choice of food. There were shrimp, lobster and fresh crab legs. It was delicious. As the time passed, we went to a friend's house of Aaron's. We arrived and Aaron introduced me to everyone. Approximately fifteen minutes later, someone walked into the house through the front door. It was Aldo! My friend Aldo! Aldo was with one of his friends. He had on a tee shirt and a pair of jeans with some sandals on. I was so surprised and glad to see a familiar face.

"Oh my God! Aldo!" I exclaimed rushing over towards his cute long- haired skinny physique. I gave him a great big hug and kiss.

"Do you two know each other?" Aaron questioned.

"For many, many years, my friend." Aldo replied.

"What are you doing here?" I asked Aldo.

"Lissa's sister lives here," he answered. Lissa is Aldo's ex-wife.

"You are kidding! What a small world we live," I

exclaimed. Everyone talked for a while. We were also engaging in a little extra curricular activity. It involved a white substance. Aaron, Aldo, Lissa's boyfriend and I went to the enclosed patio in the back to play some pool. We had a great time talking. I asked Aldo where his girlfriend was. He said he didn't know and didn't care.

"That woman is crazy!" Aldo declared with sincerity from his big brown eyes.

I remembered when Aldo came to our house in the beginning of the year and didn't know what to do about this woman. He was literally scared to break up with her. He didn't know if she would carry out her dangerous threats. Also proceeded to inform me that the girl kidnapped his beautiful German Shepherd dog!

"Unbelievable!" I shouted. "I love that dog. How could someone get that desperate?"

We all had fun. I really liked Aldo, maybe even more than a friend. He invited me to his Forth of July party at his house.

"That would be great!" I told him.

I wanted to go to that party stag. I knew that for sure. I could sense that Aaron really didn't amount to much. He was just an old concert stage roadie that wasn't working right now. He didn't have much to offer me. I wanted to experience life in a new way with my newly found freedom. But life with someone that just wanted to party and lived this long without much in life really wasn't for me. I missed my late husband, but I also liked being able to do whatever I wanted and not have to answer to anyone! Ralph was a great guy, but he was extremely possessive and controlling.

I communicated with Aldo via email and on the telephone about the party on the Forth of July. The time was passing by quickly the next few weeks. The work was good. I felt a lot less stress and hired more people for work. It was still hard for me at work, sometimes. Since the buyout, some new people were there. I had to do some training and it didn't seem the same. Everything seemed so distant. I was there to answer questions basically. That was all right, I guess. I was there and I was needed. I was actually working very hard. It was probably for the better. Working kept my mind occupied and me busy and not thinking of my real problems. The days wore on and it was close to the Forth of July. I was starting to get so excited.

The night came and I got dressed in my Tommy slacks that were white and slightly flared. The waist of the pants came just below my belly button, exposing my belly button ring. I wore a red and blue, cropped shirt showing off my flat and tone tummy. I had on my blue high-heeled sandals that were great for dancing. The bottoms would slide easily on a smooth floor.

Tim, Aldo's housemate, greeted me at the door. Tim was a younger man that would remind one of a beach bum. Tim was thin and tanned with blonde hair and blue eyes. Tim gave me a big hug.

"Aldo! It's Pam!" Tim yelled over the music. I looked around and his house was set up for this party professionally. Aldo had a D.J. spinning records with huge speakers blaring in the dining room. There were black lights everywhere and some strobe lights. I walked into the kitchen and Aldo walked up to me and hugged me then planted a wet kiss on me.

"Where is Cindy?" I asked him, hoping she wasn't there. Cindy was Aldo's girlfriend, the one that he wants to get rid of.

"She is here somewhere," he answered. We walked into the family room. I told Aldo I needed to go to the bathroom.

"Come with me," Aldo told me, taking my hand and leading me into his bedroom. He pointed to the bathroom in his room and I proceeded to do what I needed to do. I came out of the bathroom and Aldo was still there waiting for me. He walked up to me and grabbed my hands with his.

"I have always wanted to do this," he said while taking his arms and pulling me closer to him.

"Do what?" I asked innocently.

"This," he answered moving his face closer to mine. Aldo gave me a nice, wet juicy French kiss. His hands were caressing my back and a portion of my ass. I liked it too. I have always liked Aldo. I remember once, Ralph had me meet Aldo to pick up some pot. Aldo and I went for a cruise in his car and when it was time for us to part, we both had to catch each other before we did kiss. It seemed like the natural thing to do. Maybe it was just his custom and I felt guilty because I was attracted to him at that moment, but I was married. It was never mentioned. I stopped kissing Aldo before things got too hot. I had just gotten there. I followed him out to the patio where others were smoking. There was a joint being passed around. I lit a cigarette for myself. Tim leaned over to me and handed me a pill.

"Welcome to the party," he stated. I looked down at the pill.

"What is it?" I inquired.

"It's 'X'." Tim informed me.

"I have never done 'X' before." I confessed.

"Don't worry. I wouldn't give you something you wouldn't like," Tim confirmed.

I took the pill. I had done acid in high school. I started to feel the rush. My body was heating up all over. I tried not to puke. I went and got a drink of water. I looked around and noticed everyone was sucking on a lollipop. I saw Tim. He became somewhat distorted looking. I was seeing things in a different manner. The 'X' was starting to take effect. I saw Tim and walked over to him with a big smile on my face. I was so happy to see him. He had the big bag of lollipops. Tim gave me one out of the huge bag he had. It was a good thing. I walked around the house stepping to the beat of the music. Later, I saw one of the people that were at the house when I was with Aaron and Aldo stopped in. It was Aldo's ex-wife's sister's boyfriend.

"Where's Aaron?" he asked me.

"I don't know! I am just glad he is not here! You didn't invite him did you?" I responded.

"No," he assured me.

"Good." I claimed.

"Are you rolling?" he asked.

"Yes. It's my first time, too. This is really wild," I

yelled over the loud music. I had the lollipop in my mouth and wandered around the house looking at all of the lights and the pictures. The black lights throughout the house were awesome. My white pants were glowing in the darkness with the black light. I was looking at everything like I was seeing it for the first time. I danced so much that night. I showed my age later by doing the 'Moonwalk.' I did it perfectly. Tim literally fell and was rolling around on the floor laughing. He couldn't believe that I could do it so well! I had the most fun that night. It was great meeting new people and enjoying the time there with one of my best friends. I stayed the night there. I slept on the couch. No one else slept. Aldo's girlfriend was eating those beans like candy. She must have had 5 that night. I waited and drove home early in the morning. These crazy people were still up partying when I drove home. I found out later, the party continued another 3 days!

I had been talking to Aldo more and more as the weeks passed. I told him I wanted to take the kids somewhere on a vacation. I sure needed one and I know they needed one too.

Aldo called me one night and asked me if I would like some company on the trip.

"I have been thinking that I needed to get away too. Cindy is driving me crazy," he confessed. "I could drive and help with some of the expenses. It would be like my vacation too."

"That isn't a bad idea, Aldo. I can't think of anyone else that I would like to have with me, especially with the kids. They know you. They wouldn't feel funny around you. I would like a man to be with me. I am a little leery about being a single woman traveling with my children. That would be really great Aldo!" I confirmed. The plan was set. Aldo would join my kids and me to Washington D.C.

Work went on as usual for the following weeks. I had to create a strategy for the company to keep on going without me. I created training manuals, hired new people and still made sure things were being run properly. I was having some problems with a few vendors wanting to be paid and they already were paid. I was also having trouble with some fellow employees at work too. I could feel the tension and some resentment with ultimate respect as well from them. I wasn't the most popular person there, but everyone was overly nice to my face. I in return, just remained calm and returned the cynical warmth with a smile. It wasn't easy with everything else going on in my life. The following Saturday morning I was on my way to the store to get some groceries and I passed out at the wheel. Luckily, I was not going fast. I had crossed the highway and while going through a light, apparently passed out and ran over a "speed limit" sign and crashed into a fire hydrant. I remember being awakened by a paramedic. I had the doors to my Hummer locked as I always do, but had no idea what was going on. I was extremely incoherent. The Paramedics had to break my rear door window to unlock the car and retrieve my unconscious body. They lifted me up out of the Hummer and onto a gurney. I later called my sister from the hospital and she went to get my Hummer from the towing company that hauled it away. I was dismissed from the hospital later that afternoon.

The next Monday I called an old friend of my late husband's. His name is Bruce. He owns an automotive repair and body shop. He made a few calls and found a window and replaced it for me. I asked him how much I owed him and he told me not to worry about it.

"We'll work it out," he said with a smile.

I wondered what he meant by that exactly. Bruce was not married, but he has a boy and his girlfriend who is also the mother, lives with him. Bruce was always very nice and completely respectful. He was a friend of Ralph's for years. I continued working throughout the month. Bruce never asked me for anything. He did call to make sure I was doing all right.

The time came for our vacation to Washington D.C. Aldo, my kids, and I were all going to the country's capitol. Aldo was a very good friend to Ralph and me. My late husband, Ralph,

They think I Killed My Husband!

knew Aldo since he was 12 years old. Aldo had helped us with our computer system and other things. He was indeed a very good friend. We took my Hummer since it would be more comfortable for the kids. I could fold the seat and we could make a sort of bed for them to sleep through the night. Aldo didn't want to stop for a hotel. He just wanted to get there as fast as we could. It was a great trip. He also brought plenty of weed with him. After the kids went to sleep, we would smoke a little bit. We made it to D.C. early afternoon. I had made reservations at the Embassy Suites in Chevy Chase. It was connected to a mall and right across the street was Neiman Marcus. I am in heaven. We drove through the city and saw a quick tour of the sites.

We arrived to our suite. It was great. The kids were going to sleep in the front room on the fold up couch. Aldo and I would share the bedroom. When I made our reservations, I did have a choice of twin beds, or one King size bed. Our room had a King size bed in it. I couldn't imagine how that happened. It could be because I requested it. Upon our arrival I just played stupid. That was okay.

We ventured out to gather some information and see what we needed to do to better our adventure. We discovered so many things. Neither one of us had been there. We found the Metro Rail system. We unanimously decided to take the Rail everywhere. Which meant a lot of walking. We planned out our tours and made arrangements to obtain the tickets we needed to see some of the sites. Once we arrived at the Metro Rail just a block from the Embassy Suites, we were trying to locate the proper train to take. Once we figured that out, we all headed towards that terminal. The four of us had to go up the escalator. My children were old enough to know better, ran up the escalator. They were excited and my daughter lost her balance and got caught in the escalator. I rushed to help her of course.

A few minutes later, Aldo and I heard over the loud speaker, "People with small children, please take their hands and keep them close to you at all times." I was so embarrassed. Aldo had a talk with the kids and I listened and backed him up totally. It was nice to have some support with the kids. I sure was glad that Aldo came with me.

We walked around Washington D.C. It was beautiful. The time of year was a little warm, but I don't recall a cloud in the sky the entire week we were there. We arrived from the Metro Rail to the Washington Monument. I could see the Capital. The Capital Building looked almost 2 dimensional against the deep light blue color of the sky. It was magnificent. I had always wanted to see the Nation's Capital. It was wonderful. We walked over to the Lincoln Memorial. It was breathtaking. I was actually there. I have seen this place in movies, but movies give it no justice.

We made an about face and started to walk down the National Mall towards the Capital Building. Aldo told my kids to hurry up and run over towards the pool of water in front of the Capital. He said that he would take their picture. Once the kids were way ahead of us, but still within our sight, Aldo pulled out his pot pipe.

"What are you doing? Are you crazy?" I asked.

"Chill out. It's all right. They can't see us. Besides, if I am going to smoke pot, what better place to do it than the Capital Lawn? " Aldo replied.

"But, what about the Secret Service agents with all of those black sedans out in front of the capital?" I asked, demanding a reply.

"Be cool. No one will notice." Aldo said, while firing up the pipe that he held clutched in his hands.

I took a hit as well. No one noticed. It was fun. We took some pictures by the shallow pool and walked around to the Capital building. The stairs were enormous! I had no clue how big everything was! The steps must have been three floors! Just standing at the top of the steps, everyone down below seemed very small. The day seemed to whip by. We stopped at the grocery store near the hotel and bought some food.

We ventured out to so many places. We went to the National Zoo, the Arlington Cemetery, and even the outside of the Pentagon. We drove around the parking lot of the Pentagon.

They think I Killed My Husband!

We were afraid we might get shot if we tried to get in.

When the time it came to go to bed, Aldo and I slept in the same bed, but nothing physical or passionate happened. The kids were staying out in the front room of the suite in a fold out bed that came out of the couch. The third night we were there, we all got ready for bed. The kids were exhausted, so it wasn't hard for the kids to fall fast asleep. Aldo and I were in the back bedroom watching T.V. and smoking some pot. We would blow the smoke out of the window so no one would smell it. I got into the shower to clean up before bed. I exited the bathroom and walked into the bedroom with my pajamas on.

Aldo looked at me and asked, "Are the kids asleep?"

"I don't know. Let me check." I replied. My son was almost snoring and my daughter was asleep too. I returned to the bedroom where Aldo was sitting on the bed. I climbed under the covers and got into the bed. Aldo climbed under the sheets too.

"Would you like a massage? I have this stress cream that when rubbed on your temples, will help relieve stress. Pam, you have been stressed out." Aldo told me.

"All right. Who am I to turn down a temple massage?" I replied.

Aldo gave my temples a wonderful massage. He started to caress my face and twirled his fingers gently around the lines of my face. It felt so relaxing. Aldo leaned over and kissed my forehead. I could feel the sexual tension building though. I suppose it was due to feeling more comfortable and trusting with Aldo.

Aldo turned to me and said, "I have tried my best to be good while sleeping with you Pam. You are just too sexy. I don't think I can hold my self back any longer."

"Aldo! You're kidding," I said sitting up to look at him.

"Oh, no. Not at all! I want you so bad." Aldo said to me with such passion. He was leaning towards me to kiss me. I kissed him back. We started to touch each other around our torsos and Aldo was feeling my soft supple breasts. We laid back on the bed. Aldo was on top of me. We were engaged in such a passionate kiss.

Aldo asked me, "Do you want me as much as I want you?"

The only way I knew to get my message across while still engaged in a passionate kiss. I felt like grabbing his genitals. They were soft and his cock was already hard with excitement. We both excitedly started to take off the rest of our clothes. There we were. After all of these years, finally in bed totally naked with each other. Aldo began kissing and sucking my neck and chest. His masculine body on top of mine. His skin felt so smooth next to my chest. I looked into his eyes and he looked into mine. He inserted himself inside of me. He felt so good. I had to try to stay quiet. The children were in the next room! We were making love so passionately and wild! I realized we were sideways on the bed and my head was hanging off the edge. I was seeing everything upside down! It was beautiful. I hadn't made love with anyone since my late husband. Sure, I have had sex, but I don't think of that as making love.

The next day, we went back to the city and walked around. The news crews were set up outside the National Court building. Some woman was testifying against the President that day. Later that day, we all went out to eat. At a nearby table we noticed the same men earlier during the day. We thought we better go. We made it an early night back to the room. While I was in the shower, Aldo called his girlfriend. He had been trying to break up with her for quite some time. He came to Ralph and me to try to help him with his problem. He cried to my husband that he did not know what to do about this woman. She was making him miserable. So, poor Aldo has tried to get rid of this girl for eight months now. She even kidnapped his dog at one time to make him talk to her! I was a little upset hearing that he was even talking to her. He was trying to calm her down and console her for some reason. I was confused, especially after what happened the night before. So, I left and I was going to get a drink. I went to the Cheesecake Factory that was located inside the mall that adjoined the hotel we were in.

I arrived at the Cheesecake Factory. I was a little upset.

They think I Killed My Husband!

So, I drank two "Screaming Orgasm" drinks and bought a piece of cheesecake. There were some friendly gentlemen a few stools down from me at the bar. One was from Germany the other from Amsterdam. He was a tall, dark and had a kind face. The other from Amsterdam was blonde with curly hair and not too terribly handsome. They were interested in talking to me, so I let them listen a bit. The one from Germany bought me another shot, then another. I barely made it back to my room. I was a little turned around in the mall. But, I found my way. I returned to the room. My children were watching television. I told them to start taking a shower.

"Where's Aldo?" I inquired.

"He's still in the other room talking to Cindy, his girlfriend," my son replied.

"Oh! Well, get into the shower now, so we can get some sleep," I demanded. I walked into the bedroom of the suite. I found Aldo still on the phone. The shots of liquor I drank abruptly in the restaurant started to hit me like a brick wall. I suddenly felt a little sick. Then I started to feel extremely sick. I ran to the bathroom to throw up. I was so intoxicated. Aldo quickly got off of the phone and tried to help me. He gave me a trash can to hold on to and he got a washcloth with some ice and rubbed my forehead with it. I felt so embarrassed, not to mention how unattractive I felt. Aldo didn't care. He held the can and rubbed my back while I puked. He was a true friend.

The next evening, Aldo and my kids and I went to dinner. We went to Georgetown, down by the Potomac River. We ate at a nice restaurant. Later, just before sundown, we went to the Washington Monument. We forgot our cameras the day before. We were in line to go up the elevator. The sun was going down. I wanted to get some good pictures from the top of the monument at sunset. We were still waiting and the sun wasn't. I had to figure out something. We went out and sat on the grass away from the other people waiting. I saw that the people getting on had a red mark on their tickets. I had an idea. People were getting in with a ticket with a red mark on the ticket. I took my red lipstick out of my purse and marked each one of our tickets.

"I hope this works." I commented questionably. It worked like a charm. We got right in. It was so cool. I got what I wanted. I was able to get some great shots of the Nation's Capital at sunset from the great height of the top of Washington's Monument. It was wild being up in such a narrow building at that height. There were some short chains hanging inside the monument. I was standing still and if you looked at these chains closely and long enough, you could see these chains sway. But the chains were not swaying. The force of gravity was making them hang down. It was the Monument that was actually swaying. That was frightening.

Later, we went back to our hotel. Aldo wanted to go out without the kids. We had a talk with them and requested that they not answer the door for anyone. We have the key. There was no need for them to leave the room either. They said that they would be fine. My children were engaged in a good movie anyway. They wanted to rest. Aldo and I made our way to the car. We drove towards the entrance of the city. We were close to the river and parked along the park. It was a very dark night. It was a beautiful night though. The Moon was ½ full and extremely brilliant. Aldo and I walked through the park. We walked past the small chain fence, which were meant to keep people from walking on the grass. We saw the statue of the Soldier's War Memorial in the distance.

"Let's go and see the Memorial!" I requested.

"OK. Looks like its right over there." Aldo said.

We walked straight towards the statue through the grass and suddenly, the grass came to a cliff. I almost fell.

"What is this? Be careful, Aldo. I almost fell." I informed Aldo.

"Look! It slopes down!" Aldo yelled walking down to the right of the so-called "cliff" of the sloping grass. I followed him down. He was ahead of me. He walked around the front of the cliff where I almost fell.

"Oh shit, Pam! We were walking on the Wall!" Aldo yelled to me.

They think I Killed My Husband!

"What do you mean, *The Wall?*" I asked.

"The Veteran's Memorial Wall!" Aldo repeated in more detail.

"You're kidding! I feel terrible!" I said, as I was turning the corner to see the wall. It was so awesome. I was facing the wall and saw all of those names of people I didn't even now, but fought for me. They died for us! The most wonderful thing was while facing the wall, I looked to my right and just over the horizon was the Washington Monument. It was standing there in such glory. All lit up in the night. The Washington Monument is also perfectly lined up with the sidewalk I was standing. The sidewalk seemed to point to the Monument. It was so beautiful. I turned around and could see the ½ moon overhead. Aldo turned and kissed me. I kissed him back. It was such a nice moment.

"I wish we brought a camera! That would make such a great picture!" I exclaimed.

Aldo kissed me again and said, "Take a picture of it with your mind. Don't ever forget this moment. I know I won't. We are friends forever. I mean that."

"I know. I know, we will always be friends. No matter what," I responded and kissed him again.

"No matter what." Aldo told me while kissing me and holding me in his arms. I felt so secure. I could feel the love. The next day we had to get ready to end our vacation. I hated to leave. The capital was such a Yuppie Heaven. I would have loved to have been a lawyer living there. I guess that's not where I belong.

I hadn't had a chance to go to Neiman Marcus yet. It was right across the street from our room. I wanted to go before we left the city. I went with my daughter the next day. We had a fun time. The salespeople were so nice. My daughter and I went to the fur department. I was looking at the furs they had on the hangers and apparently the salespeople were bored.

"Would you like to try that on?" the salesman asked.

"Oh, it would be nice. But, I will be honest, I don't need to buy anything like that. I live in Florida. Thank you, though," I told him.

"That's okay. No one needs anything like that. Here, try this on," he said. "Would you like to try one on too?" he asked my daughter. Her face just lit up. We had a great time playing dress up in the fur department. There were pink furs and striped furs and long black furs and short white fur jackets. We tried on so many of them! We could have tried on all of them! I don't think I ever had a more enjoyable time in an upscale store. Usually the help is so stuck up they think you may steal something, no matter who you are. This was not the case at all. We made it back to the hotel. We had to gather everything and pack for the trip home the following day.

I returned to work that following Monday. I received a call from the police regarding my husband's death.

"This is Pam. May I help you?" I asked the other party on the phone.

"Pam. This is Sergeant Thomas. We need to see you for further questioning," Sergeant Thomas said.

"Didn't we get that finished the last time I was called in?" I questioned him.

"Mostly. The autopsy is showing some sort of poison in his bloodstream." Sgt. Thomas informed me.

"Poison?" I exclaimed! "How can that be? Are you sure someone didn't screw things up?" I retaliated.

"When can you come in?" Sgt. Thomas asked.

"Let me call my lawyer and I will let you know," I said and immediately hung up. "Unbelievable!" I thought.

I quickly called Tom to find out how soon he can join me at the police station.

"What has happened? I thought this was done." Tom inquired.

"I know. We were finished until the autopsy report showed up with poison in his blood." I told Tom.

"Poison? But, he died of a massive heart attack. How much poison was found? How did poison get into his system? Was it enough to kill him?" Tom asked me.

They think I Killed My Husband!

"That is what we need to find out," I answered.

"No, I am your estate attorney. You need a defense attorney. I would love to help you, Pam, but I just deal with paperwork. If I have been in a courtroom, it was to deliver documents," Tom told me.

"What am I going to do? Who am I going to call at this minute? They want me to go down there now!" I cried to Tom on the phone.

"Didn't you have some guy that worked for you that was an attorney? What was his specialty? Call him!" Tom suggested.

"Who, Jack? I don't know if he can practice. He was Disbarred. He may be able to practice after I put in a good word for him as a former employer of his. I guess I could give him a call. Thanks Tom." I said my Good-byes with Tom and called Jack to see if he could help me at the police station.

"Hello?" Jack answered the phone.

"Jack! It's Pam. I need your help. Are you able to practice law again?" I inquired.

"Yes. Since you were kind enough to write that letter for me. Thanks, that really helped. Why, what did you need?" Jack wanted to know.

"Well, the police called and want me to come downtown to the station and answer some questions. They found poison in Ralph's system." I informed him.

"What? Don't say anything unless I say you can. And that is only after I tell you what to say! Do you understand me? I will meet you there in the parking lot in twenty minutes. This is extremely crucial." Jack insisted.

The time came to go to the station. I was dressed like I was going to the office. I wore one of my most conservative suits. I met Jack in the parking lot as planned and we walked in together. Jack was there with me, by my side.

"Now, let me start off by saying that this is a preliminary stage. We are just questioning right now." Sergeant Thomas said.

"May I sit down somewhere?" I asked.

"Of course, please sit down. Any one of these chairs will be fine," Sergeant Thomas confirmed while taking a seat.

"Is Mrs. Garcia being charged with anything?" Jack questioned the officer.

"No, not yet." The sergeant replied. "But, if she cooperates, it would help."

"Yes, help convict her," Jack hastily said.

"But, I didn't do anything!" I exclaimed nervously.

"I didn't say you killed anyone. We are just trying to get the facts so we can figure out exactly what happened," the sergeant explained.

Jack leaned over and told me not to say much. "Just answer 'yes' and 'no' or one word answers."

At that moment the police detective walked into the room. "How far have you gotten, Sarge?" he asked while closing the door.

"Just started," the sergeant replied.

The detective was a tall handsome man. He stood tall with his broad shoulders that had muscles bulging out of the sides of his sleeves of his short-sleeved uniform. His skin was olive and slightly tanned. I saw his name tag. It read, "Detective Tony Perez." He had beautiful, thick black hair. His eyes were like the emeralds I wore on my hand. His face was slightly chubby with high cheekbones and a chiseled chin. Tony was the human specimen of the Michelangelo. I could see the texture of his protruding muscles covering the front of his chest. This made me wonder about his important protruding muscle. My eyes began to wonder a bit south. I saw he had quite a bulge in the front of his pants. I instantly caught myself before anyone noticed.

Tony started to discuss some issues with the Sergeant Thomas.

"Try to contain yourself, please!" Jack leaned over and quietly told me.

"What do you mean?" I whispered.

"Let's keep this professional. You're husband just died. Don't make it seem like you aren't in mourning," Jack warned,

They think I Killed My Husband!

cynically.

"I resent that! My husband died. I didn't. Don't you appreciate the form of a healthy, maintained body? I know how much time and effort it takes to be in that good of shape!" I whispered loudly in my defense.

"SSHHHHH. Shut up!" Jack whispered back to me as Sergeant Thomas and Detective Perez were finishing up their intimate discussion.

"Mrs. Garcia, I'm Detective Perez," he introduced himself. "I will be asking you some questions. These questions are standard procedure. Please don't take offense."

I looked directly into his eyes. I just wanted to dive right into those gorgeous green emeralds. His eyelashes were black mops. I could feel the chemistry and sexual tension building. I remained outwardly professional. I sat up straight, casually crossed my legs with the calf of my lower leg rested on the knee of the other. A position that I know flatters my legs.

"I will have to discuss everything with my attorney before answering," I answered with quiver in my voice.

"That'll be fine," Detective Perez confirmed while looking into my big brown eyes. He remained outwardly professional as well.

The sergeant took the list of questions and decided he would ask the first question.

"Did your husband have any enemies?" Sergeant Thomas asked looking at me as though I wasn't even there.

"No, not that they would actually kill him for whatever reason. I wouldn't think. But, that's me. I wouldn't kill anyone for any reason. I can't speak for anyone else though," I reciprocated.

"He didn't have any enemies?" Detective Perez inquired, while leaning on the desk towards me.

"Not over something that someone would want to kill him!" I concluded, shrugging my shoulders.

Jack leaned over and informed me, "But, were there some issues that could implicate someone else?"

"I guess," I softly told Jack.

"Can I ask the questions here?" Detective Perez inquired sternly.

"You can't keep me from conveying with my client. Watch it, Detective." Jack reinforced his position.

"Fine. Now, do you know of any trouble your husband may have been in? Who are some of the people he was around in the last few months?" Detective Perez asked me.

"Well, other than the fight he got into before he died, I really don't think he had and quarrels with anyone. None that I know of."

"Mrs. Garcia, were you having an affair?" Tony Perez questioned.

"No! Of course not!" I exclaimed looking back into Tony's luscious green eyes. "I never cheated on my husband."

"We are trying to narrow it down. It doesn't look good right now for you, Mrs. Garcia. The autopsy shows cyanide in his system. Your husband had no enemies and you are the beneficiary of the life insurance. This shows motive. One clue that is pointing to you." Tony informed me, with his stern, deep voice.

"This fight, Mrs. Garcia, where was it?" Sergeant Thomas wanted to know.

I told him, "It was that Gay Club downtown. My husband and I used to go there all of the time. Every Saturday night was 'Lesbo-A-Go-Go.' Nothing but a flock of girls for me to pick from." I looked over at Detective Perez. I stared into his deep green eyes. "Could I have some water?"

"Sure, I think I'll get some for myself too." Tony said, while instantly getting up and going to get some water for me.

"Don't say too much." Jack warned me.

"I won't." I assured him.

Detective Perez re-entered the room and sat down with the cup of water. He slowly handed me the water. My hand touched his as I retrieved the cup. With my head still aimed down at the floor, I looked up at his face and peered into his eyes and innocently said, "Thank you."

They think I Killed My Husband!

Tony nodded his head to acknowledge my gratuity. Tony looked at me with a puzzled and curious expression. "Why would you and your husband go out to a gay bar?"

I continued to stare at Tony. I took a sip of water and rolled my tongue across my top lip to catch any liquid that may drip. After that move, I leaned over and I answered in a shy and succumb voice, "I wanted to suck on a nice juicy pussy. Ralph loved to watch me with other girls. That night I was dancing with this gorgeous redhead. She and I were grinding on the dance floor, then her boyfriend started to dance with us. I could feel his big dick getting hard against my ass." I stiffened in the chair as though I could feel the guy's dick at that very moment. I must have appeared uncomfortable and sat up straight and added, "That's when Ralph got upset. He must have seen it." After sitting back, I looked up at Detective Tony with a slightly seductive look. Tony was just starring at me in awe. All I could do was turn my head to hide my smile and sneer just for a second.

"Did you enjoy these sexual encounters, Mrs. Garcia? Or did your husband make you do these things for his sexual pleasure? I don't know of a woman that would let herself be used as some sex object and not let it get to her. Maybe you wanted the money and your freedom from this asshole that just used you and controlled you all of your married life," Detective Perez retaliated!

"Maybe someone at the bar did it?" I defended.

"Now, why would some stranger want your husband dead?" Sergeant Thomas interrogated.

"I don't know. I am not them and I know I didn't do it," I answered with a little bit of resentment in my speech.

Jack came to my defense and asked, "Didn't the autopsy show the cause of death to be from the heart attack?"

"Yes, initially. There were some things that came out in the blood tests later. He might have died from the heart attack itself, or from the cyanide. We don't know if Ralph could have survived the heart attack. The cyanide could have been administered after the heart attack started, or if the cyanide induced the heart attack due to the lack of oxygen," Detective Tony informed us.

"Mrs. Garcia was the only one there with her husband in this duration." Sergeant Thomas added.

With the look of great fear on my face, I didn't know what to do. I looked at Jack to see if he had any ideas. Jack leaned over and told me not to panic.

"This information is strictly circumstantial." Jack said.

"Yes, it is." The Detective said looking at me with those luscious green eyes of his.

I looked up at the detective with such sadness and innocence. "Am I being placed under arrest?" I asked meekly.

"No, Ma'am." Detective Tony confirmed. "We need more evidence before we can arrest someone for murder. You wouldn't mind if we looked around your property, would you?"

"You need a search warrant for that," Jack interrupted.

"Of course," Sergeant Thomas clarified. "Detective Tony will be handling the investigation of this case. Mrs. Garcia, Jack, you will be notified by him when they will be there, the sooner the better. I do believe we will be there tomorrow morning."

"Can you be there with me, Jack?" I begged.

"I'll do some schedule rearranging for you. I'll be there. I might be a little late. What time will you all be there?" Jack insisted.

"We are drawing the search warrant for approximately 10:00 A.M." Detective Tony replied. "I may be there early to finish up some questioning, if I may."

"Oh, no. She is not going to answer any questions unless I am there. Good try, Detective." Jack confirmed.

"It's okay. You can come a bit early, but I won't answer any related questions." I confirmed to Detective Tony. I looked into his eyes with such a lust of hunger. Then I realized the expression on my face must have told the world what I was thinking. I quickly looked down and I could feel my face getting a little red.

I left the police station. I was never more scared for

my life. I am going to have to defend my innocence. I was so confused. How on Earth could there be poison in his system? Cyanide works in minutes once administered. I was trying to think of who else could have possibly done such a thing, and why? Would he have survived the heart attack? When could someone give Ralph poison? Could small doses through the night kick in later? So many questions were running through my mind. It doesn't help that the business we have is importing and exporting gold and doing gold plating. One of the ingredients in the solution is cyanide. I had to get all of that stuff that we have around the house somewhere else. Where could I keep it? Who could I trust? Aldo! I thought to myself. Jack caught up with me and told me not to worry.

"I know you didn't do it. Did you? I know how Ralph can be. I don't think you could actually kill him. They have to prove you did. They don't have anything yet. I'll call you tonight. You can call me if you prefer." Jack confided as we walked out to the parking lot.

"Jack, you know the electroplating work we do in the business?" I asked leading to more information.

"Yes?" Jack stated questionably.

"Well, the solution to harden the metal has cyanide in it. Should I take the machine and the solution somewhere?" I asked Jack confused.

"Oh, shit! You are kidding, right? If they find that stuff, that is some heavy evidence and could place you under arrest." Jack confessed. I started to cry.

"What should I do, Jack? I couldn't kill anyone! Especially the one person that was the world to me! I couldn't murder the father of my children! Ralph adored me and I adored him! How could anyone think I did this!" I said with great desperation.

"Should I hide it somewhere?" I questioned.

Jack replied, "Well, it's a matter of time before they find out about the gold plating part of the business. If you hide it somewhere it may go worse for you in the long run. But, if you want to stay out of jail, you might have it repaired somewhere for now."

"This doesn't look good for me does it, Jack?" I asked wiping the tears from my face. "What are my kids going to do if I go to jail? Don't they think I would have thought of that? I would never do anything to take me away from my kids. I wouldn't do anything to take their father away either!"

I have to get that out of my house. Maybe they won't find out about the electroplating. I worked so much with the import and export of the business that I hadn't done much with the plating system. I had to get the extra machines and the chemicals out of my house. I was in a state of panic. I was innocent. I got into my car and called Aldo on my cell phone. The phone was ringing. Aldo picked it up.

"Oh, thank God! Aldo!" I screamed quietly. "Aldo, you need to be at my house tonight! Please! I can't explain now."

"Pam, would you settle down? Now, what is going on?" Aldo pleaded.

"I can't explain over the phone. Would you please get over here? If I ever needed you before, it's life or death now!" I explained.

"Are you okay? You aren't hurt, are you?" Aldo questioned me with concern.

"I'm fine for now. I won't be if you don't get your pretty little ass over here as fast as you can!" I told him.

"I'll be there in a half an hour." Aldo blurted and raced out the door. Aldo arrived finally. I was pacing the floor and getting all of the stuff together that I wanted Aldo to take with him. I looked through the garage carefully making sure that nothing was left, not one box, or label with warnings on it.

"What is going on, Pam? You sounded so desperate on the phone. Is it that bad?" he asked me.

"Yes, it is. They found traces of cyanide in Ralph's system." I informed him.

"So? Why would you be alarmed? I am sure you didn't put it there." Aldo tried to reassure me.

"You don't understand. The other part of the business other than importing and exporting the gold, I have, is electroplating gold and the gold solution has cyanide in the chemicals to harden the metal when plating. If they find this, it's evidence enough to convict me or at least throw me in jail," I explained.

"You're kidding me, right?" he asked, unbelievably.

"No, I'm not! I need you to take this stuff right now. Rent a storage unit, or have your house mate Tim rent one. I need this electroplating stuff out of here now! The police are coming in the morning to look for some clues. I don't know whom or when cyanide could've been injected into Ralph's body, maybe the paramedics, maybe at the club with a drink? I know I didn't do it! But, I don't need to take any chances either. It would be a quick case if they found this stuff here. At least I can buy some time and the real culprit could be revealed." I explained further.

"Let me have it now and let me get going so I might not be noticed as coming here," Aldo answered.

"Oh, thank you, baby. I love you! Here is the stuff. Open your tailgate and get going," I said with great appreciation. We loaded up the equipment for about an hour to make sure it was out. Aldo left after I said good night.

The following morning Detective Tony Perez showed up at my door by 8:30. I just got out of the shower and was getting ready to start my day. I dried my hair and put on my makeup and was about to get dressed. I was in my bedroom deciding what to wear. I heard the doorbell ring. I quickly scurried about and put on my bathrobe to conceal my naked body. I opened the door and there stood a sexual fantasy. Detective Tony was standing on my porch in his tight police uniform that was unable to conceal the rippling flesh of his body. He had on some dark sunglasses. I asked him to come in. He removed his sunglasses as he stepped into my home. He looked at me with those piercing green eyes of his. I got more nervous from the sexual tension than from the real reason of why he was here.

"I apologize for arriving this early, Mrs. Garcia," the detective said.

"That's okay. Would you like some coffee?" I offered.

"That would be nice. Thank you," he said with a smile.

I walked into the kitchen and wrapped the belt around my robe a little tighter.

"Are the other officers on their way?" I asked from the kitchen.

"There should be a couple more on their way. I just wanted to be the first one here since I am heading up the investigation," Tony informed me while gazing up and down my body from the next room.

I caught a glimpse of Detective Tony checking me out from the corner of my eye. I turned towards him with a cup of coffee for him. I was carrying another cup for me in my other hand. I was making my way back to the living room with my hands pre-occupied with the coffee mugs and I failed to notice the belt to my robe was loosening with each step. By the time I entered the living room, my robe was slightly open in the front. My belt was still tied, but barely. The robe being just opened all the way down to my waist, I was unaware that with each step my thighs would flash instantaneously a hint of what was below the belt. I carefully handed Detective Tony the cup of coffee. He looked up at me and smiled and thanked me.

"You're welcome," I said smiling back shyly. Looking down with shyness, I noticed my robe had begun to disrobe! With my free hand, I tightened my robe again. I could feel my face getting red with embarrassment.

"Excuse me." I told him. "This darn thing never stays put."

"That's okay," Detective Tony stated with a smile. "I didn't mind one bit." Tony just looked at me. We both made eye contact and instantly we could feel what each other was thinking. Upon our mutual realization, we both quickly looked away uncomfortably. I quickly changed the subject.

"How is your coffee?" I asked him.

"Fine. Perfect, it couldn't be better. Thanks," Detective Tony said politely, while taking another sip.

The doorbell rang. I saw the rest of the investigative team had arrived and asked Detective Tony to answer it, while

I went and got dressed. I returned to the living room to find several officers in my home.

"Before I will allow you people to rummage through my home, I would like my attorney to be present," I demanded. "He should be here any minute."

"We need to start now, Ms. Garcia. Here is the search warrant. This allows us to search your home without you here. If your lawyer is on his way, then there shouldn't be any problems," Tony sternly informed me.

"Okay. What exactly are you looking for?" I questioned nervously. I knew they were trying to find cyanide somewhere in some sort of container. I was so glad that Aldo has my electroplating materials, I thought to myself. I hope there are no kitchen cleaners or other chemicals I didn't even realize would have cyanide in them in the house. The doorbell rang again. It was Jack. I was so happy to see he had arrived.

"What time did they get here?" Jack asked me.

"Detective Tony arrived at 8:30 and the rest of them got here around nine or so," I answered.

"Why was Detective Perez here earlier? Why didn't he arrive with the rest of them?" Jack inquired with a little sneer.

"I don't know. He said he wanted to be here a little bit earlier than the rest of them since he was in charge of the investigation," I explained. "I need to talk to you in private, now Jack."

"Lead the way," Jack acknowledged. I walked out onto the yard and towards the lake. Jack was walking beside me.

"I got my electroplating equipment out of the house. A friend of mine came over last night and picked it up," I told him.

"Pam, I need to know. Did you give Ralph the cyanide with those chemicals?" Jack actually asked me.

"No! Of course not!" I exclaimed, then started to break down in tears. My legs went weak. By the time we got to the dock by the lake, I had to sit down. I just wanted to die myself. All I could do was continue to cry.

"I know this looks really bad, but I wouldn't dream of

killing anyone! Especially not one of the people I loved most in this world," I insisted lifting my head from my hands wiping my tears from my face.

"Save it for the jury Pam. You need to keep your head straight now," Jack advised.

"I resent that! Do you actually think I could've killed him?" I questioned loudly. "I didn't do it! I don't know how or when cyanide could have entered his body! I was trying to save him, not kill him!" I adamantly stated. Jack wiped the tears from my face with his handkerchief.

"I know, I know. It's just the interrogating lawyer in me, Pam," He told me with a serene, relaxing tone.

"If we can buy some time with them not finding anything incriminating right now, but it's only a matter of time before they find out about your electroplating part of the business." Jack finished saying.

"Hopefully some other clues will emerge if they are investigating other avenues." I reassured Jack and myself.

"I hope so, for your sake. It is circumstantial. If it gets to trial, that may be enough to persuade a jury." Jack bluntly and honestly commented.

"Well, I will put my faith in God. I didn't do anything wrong and I feel sure that will come out in the end. In the mean time, you have to keep me out of jail, Jack!" I told him faithfully, yet forcefully.

I returned to work the following day. My time there was quickly coming to an end. I had approximately a couple of months there. Roberto was working like a champion. He was managing the employees while I was training the office manager and the marketing managers. They were doing fine and learning quickly.

The holidays would be upon us shortly. The air had a wonderful new crispness to it and the trees were luminous of different colors and losing some leaves. My children's birthdays were coming up soon. I decided to throw a party in spite of the recent passing of their father. Their paternal Grandparents were coming into town. They would also bring their other Granddaughter Lisa and my late husband's brother, which was Lisa's Father. I did enjoy having them in my home for the weekend. I know my children loved seeing them. Hector, a tall thin man with olive complexion, Lisa's father was always a little crazy. I enjoyed talking with him until late hours of the morning. He would bring a little bit of extracurricular mind altering drugs. We would stay up and talk all night long. We talked about Ralph, and the past good times.

Friday evening came and the in-laws were due here in a couple of hours. The house was immaculate. Rita came early afternoon and did a great job cleaning. Sherry was over with her kids by early evening. She hung out with me while I was waiting for my children's family to arrive. Sherry was waiting with me for a slight ulterior motive. Hector, my brother-in-law, would be bringing some "extra-curricula's" with him. The three of us would probably go out later.

All of the kids were playing. The boys were on the Play Station 3 and the girls were playing the X Box games in the kitchen. It was nice to see the kids having a good time. Their spirits were high with anticipation of the Grandparents coming with their cousin. The kids were keeping themselves busy while Sherry and I went into my bedroom to smoke some cigarettes.

"So, what has been going on with you lately?" Sherry asked.

"Oh, man! What a question! Where do I start?" I replied.

"Could this help you out about now?" Sherry asked me, while pulling her hand out of her pocket that held a little baggie with some white powder.

"Why did you bring that? You know Hector is coming with some." I concurred.

"I know. But, I like having my own shit. Here," Sherry told me while handing me a bag of weed. "Roll one and I'll line us up a couple."

"Okay, but you'll have to twist my arm," I said, holding

my arm towards Sherry, half-twisted.

"Oh," Sherry giggled and grabbed my wrist and gave it a little twist. "There, now you can say I twisted your arm."

"Right!" I exclaimed as I walked to the bedroom door to make sure it was locked. I sat back down and put a magazine on my lap and started to crumble up some pot. Sherry was busy crushing the little rocks into powder.

"What's been going on with me lately, you asked? Where do I begin? You can't say anything to Hector, or anyone. Do you promise not to say a word?" I made her swear to secrecy.

"I promise. You know me, Pam. I swear I won't say a word to anyone. So tell me." Sherry pleaded.

"Well, the forensic investigation found cyanide in Ralph's blood." I stated.

"So, what does that mean?" Sherry inquired seriously.

"That means evidence shows that by having cyanide in his system, he may have been murdered." I replied holding in my tears.

"Murdered!" she yelled. "How the hell did he get cyanide in him?"

"I have no idea, maybe in his drink at the club, or maybe a sick paramedic. There were 3 to start then one left in the middle of the ordeal. I still couldn't tell you who or what exactly he was or his purpose. But the insurance initiated the investigation to make sure he did die of natural causes. The first autopsy showed the heart attack as the reason for death. So, the insurance company demanded they have their own forensic scientists do an autopsy. I guess it was more thorough. Maybe they got some lab results mixed up or maybe they are saying this to get out of paying me my insurance benefits right away, if at all, if they try to pin all of this on me," I clued her in.

"On you?" Sherry blurted out with disbelief.

"Yes. I have Jack working on my side. I better get Johnny Cochran, the way this is going," I said sadly.

"Oh, don't you worry. You didn't do anything and that'll all come out in the wash. You'll see. It'll be a bitch in

They think I Killed My Husband!

the meantime. Here, you need one of these." She said handing me the tray with some powder lined up on it. I took the tray and proceeded to snort a line of coke.

Sherry said to me with a smile and jest, "You don't even have a joint rolled yet? Here, give me that. You roll like shit, anyway."

"Here, be my guest." I stated with a touch of sarcasm. I handed Sherry the tray with her share of lineage left on it. She quickly snorted them up and lit the joint she rolled.

"So, have they tried to accuse you of poisoning Ralph?" Sherry wanted to know.

"They are investigating the possibility. They searched the house already." I informed her.

"You mean they got a search warrant and everything? How awful!" She protested.

"I know. It was horrible. But, they didn't find anything.

"See!" Sherry exclaimed with a positive attitude. "They didn't find anything because there was nothing to find!" I didn't tell her about the electroplating materials and how I got that stuff out of the garage. I didn't want to even give her any slight reason to think I may have done this horrible act. People, no matter how well you know someone, you just can't be too careful. Besides, this is something that shouldn't be said to anyone and I do mean no one!

The in-laws arrived later that evening. The kids were all playing together after giving all of the family 'welcome kisses.' Hector, Sherry and I went to my bedroom to smoke a cigarette. I designated my room as the smoking room. I opened up the French doors to the veranda to allow some air circulation. Hector started gabbing about how long the drive was while opening a little baggie to do a couple of hits. He also shared with Sherry and me by handing the goods to Sherry. We all started talking about work and different things. Then as usual, Hector took control of the conversation and began telling stories of his High School Football days and the late 70's disco days. Hector could go on for hours about his experiences in the early disco days.

He told us about getting into fights at clubs and going to South America when he was younger. He tried to paint a picture of himself to us like he was some sort of drug king pen. Whatever! I knew better! Who would really want to be 'Scarface'? The guy was a little mentally off. His heart was great, but I think that too many years of doing drugs had made his mind go just a beat off.

The rest of the weekend went fine. I didn't mention the murder investigation to Ralph's family. I didn't want to upset anyone before it was necessary. The kids had a great time with their cousins. The Grandparents had a good time too. I love to see everyone together. It's such a great thing to be able to appreciate being with family and loving each other. What is even more wonderful is identifying this situation and hold on to it and cherish it. That's where acknowledgement of this appreciation touches you in such a way that all you can do is smile. Needless to say I had a great weekend too. I actually was able to get my mind off of what was going on around me in the real world.

I returned the following Monday to the "Real World." Work was going all right. Actually, work was going very smoothly. I went to my office to have some coffee and read some news on the Internet. I turned on my radio to the local upbeat station. The station announced that they were giving away tickets to a local concert. The group performing was a new, "boy-band." I saw their video on MTV and I thought they were really good. I knew my daughter and niece were "ape" over these guys. So, I used my cell phone to call and try to get the tickets. By using my cell phone, I was able to get through faster. I just kept hitting "Send" on my cell phone and I eventually got through to the station! Once I started to hear the phone ring, I had a feeling I might win the tickets! I did! I was the ninth caller! I won 4 tickets to the concert! We were going to be in the VIP section of the audience too! I walked out to tell Roberto!

"Guess what?" I asked.
"What?" he responded.

They think I Killed My Husband!

"I won 4 tickets to the concert Friday!"

"That's great, Pam! Can I go?" he asked sort of jokingly.

"I am going to take my kids and see if my niece wants to go. If she can't, you can." I told him.

I went back to my office and heard the last part of the taping of me winning. I was so excited. My life could still go on and I could still treat my kids to some special things. The next song that played on the radio was "Just the 2 of us" by Will Smith. I couldn't hold back my tears when I heard the part of the song when he says, "Daddy loves you." It was like getting a message from Ralph from the great beyond trying to tell me that same message. Some may say its coincidence, but I would like to think Ralph wanted to help and give something nice for the kids' birthdays.

I left work a little early so I could make it to the radio station and get the tickets. It turns out, since it was a radio promotion, the station gave me a letter of authorization to take with me to the concert. Good enough. I left the station and went straight home. I couldn't wait to see the look on my daughter's face. I arrived home and asked my daughter if she liked this particular Boy-band.

"Yes. Why do you ask?" Serena inquired.

"Well, I sort of won these tickets to their concert Friday. Would you like to go?"

She started screaming! "No way! NO way! Are you for real? For real?"

"Yes. I am very real. Do you want to go?" I asked again.

"Aaaauuughhhhhhhh!" she screamed while jumping up and down, pulling on my arm.

"Uh, I guess I should take that as a 'yes.'" I stated calmly. "Do you think I should ask your cousin, Jasmine?"

"Yes! Of course! Jasmine would love to go! Are you kidding?" Serena exclaimed.

I called my sister to make sure that she would allow Jasmine to go. Jasmine was still only 14 years old. She was the spitting image of my sister but with blonde hair. My sister said that would be great! She also invited us for dinner and asked me to ask Jasmine then.

"Of course! It'll be great! I know she likes this band. I can't wait to see her face." I squealed like a schoolgirl. "I'll be over later and ask her."

"If you like you may join us for dinner later. You might as well if you are going to come over." My sister invited us for her usual good cooking.

We all got ready to go over to my sister's house. I made sure my children had their baths and were good and clean. I wouldn't have to hurry to leave after dinner if the kids had their baths already. We arrived for dinner. I asked my sister to get Jasmine so I could ask her if she wanted to go to the concert with us. I knew I didn't have to really ask, I knew she would want to go.

"Jasmine, you know that new boy band that is really hot right now and is having their concert this weekend here?" I asked.

"Yeah????? What about them?" Jasmine asked back.

"Well, I have 4 tickets for V.I.P. Section of the concert. Now, there is one for me, one for Rafael, and one for Serena, so I have an extra ticket. Would you like to go?"

"You're kidding! Oh my God! Oh my God! Yes. Yes. Yes! I would love to go! Thank you! Thank you! Thank you!" Jasmine screamed while jumping up and down the entire time answering me. We discussed the arrangements and time for our departure for the night of the concert. Jasmine was so cute. She stopped jumping, but she was still bouncing on her toes while we discussed the evening. Dinner was wonderful but it was getting late, so my kids and myself went home to get some sleep and begin a new day.

The day came to go to the concert. I left work early so I could get everything done that I needed to do. I got home and told the kids to shower and put on something nice to go to the concert. I begged them to please hurry so I may do the same.

While they were getting ready, I went and picked up Jasmine. I asked her to help my kids get ready while I was showering and getting ready myself. She agreed of course. We made it back to the house and I started getting ready to go. I put on my new white Tommy Hilfiger pants with my new white crop top. I looked pretty good if I say so myself.

We took off for the show. It was about an hour drive to get to the concert. We also left early enough to beat the crowd. Jasmine had her backpack loaded with her camera and some pictures of the group, just in case she could get close enough to any of them to get an autograph. Serena had her camera too. We put in the group's CD that I had and listened to it all the way to the concert.

"I hope we can get their autograph's, or at least be able to actually touch one of them!" Jasmine exclaimed.

"Leave it up to your Aunt Pamela. I'll see what I can do too," I replied.

"Do you think you could get us backstage?" Jasmine excitedly asked.

"I don't know about that, but I'll try to think of something. Okay?" I said.

We arrived at the concert with plenty of time to get a good spot. We all went to the bathroom to relieve ourselves. I put my cell phone down on the counter to wash my hands. The restroom had several young girls in it. I turned to grab a paper towel, turned around and told the girls to hurry up. Serena and Jasmine were finishing drying their hands. Jasmine noticed some other girls walking out and giggling. The three of us all walked out together and met Rafael outside. This was nice, my kids and my niece and myself all out on a family night out. I reached down to give my sister, Jasmine's mother, a phone call.

"My cell phone!" I screamed. "I must have left it in the bathroom!" I ran back to the bathroom with the kids right behind me. It wasn't there. That's when Jasmine told me she noticed those girls leaving the bathroom giggling.

"I bet they took it," she said. "Cause you turned around, then I saw them leave quickly."

"You are probably right. I had it in my hand and put it on the counter to wash my hands." Let's go report it and call the phone company. The kids and I went to the lost and found to report it stolen and also to see if by chance anyone may have turned it in. No such luck. I called to have them turn my phone off immediately. After this fiasco was over with, we ventured back over to the concert. The V.I.P. section was still not full. We stood right in the front along the ropes. The stagehands and camera crew and managers were running around getting ready for the show. I was so disturbed about my cell phone. One of the cameramen was walking in front of us for a few minutes. I figured he would be someone to ask to announce if anyone found a cell phone to please turn it in to lost & found. It was worth a shot. As he was walking by, I got his attention.

"I lost my cell phone, or rather I think someone took it. Could it be possible to ask over the loud speaker if someone found a cell phone to please turn it in at the Lost & Found?" I quickly asked him.

"No. I can't do that," he said with a look of sympathy for me. "But, do you see that guy in the suit walking around? He may be able to help you out. His name is Bill"

"Okay. I'll ask him if he comes by. Thanks," I said with a smile. The cameraman walked over to the other side of the stage to continue with his work. Frank, the man in the business suit and clean shaven walked by me.

"Bill," I said.

He looked at me very inquisitively. Probably wondering who I was and how did I know his name.

"Yes," he answered.

I quickly told him of my dilemma, and asked if he could announce on the microphone if some found a cell phone to please turn it in.

He sadly looked at me with his small and older blue eyes and said, "I wish I could, but I can't. I am sorry."

"I understand. That's okay." I replied trying not to look so disappointed.

The cameraman walked back over to us. "Was he able

to help?" he asked.

"No. Darn it! But, he seemed to wish he could have," I told him.

"By the way, my name is Greg," The cameraman said.

"Hi, Greg. I'm Pamela," I answered. "Would it be possible for you to go backstage and get my niece's pictures autographed? Or are you too busy working?" I asked Greg.

"I am too busy working," Greg stated.

"Okay, no problem. Just thought I'd ask," I answered agreeably.

Greg walked over to the other side of the stage again. I checked the time on my watch. The concert should be starting soon. We were starting to get squished and squeezed by the other fans there. I was doing my best to stay up in the front. It was starting to get difficult though. We were in the VIP section and we had more room. The regular ticket holders were pushing and squeezing so much that there was not any more room! All of the sudden someone grabbed my forearm. Startled, I looked up and saw it was Greg.

"How may people in your group?" Greg asked me.

"Four. There are my two kids and my niece and myself," I quickly answered.

"Come with me," Greg replied.

I motioned for the kids to follow me. We held hands and went under the ropes and went up to the stage area with Greg.

"They need some fans by the stage for filming. So you and your kids can stand in front of the stage," Greg said.

"How cool! Thank you! Thank you so much!" I told Greg. He went back to doing his job.

"I can't believe we are up here by the stage!" Jasmine said excitedly. "You said to leave it up to you Aunt Pam!"

"I guess we got lucky! I guess maybe they felt bad about me having my cell phone stolen," I told Jasmine. A few more minutes went by and Greg made his way back toward us.

"You know this is going to cost you dinner with me," he whispered in my ear.

"Oh, really?" I replied.

"Yes. But, there is only one problem. I don't have your phone number to call you later," Greg stated to me. " I have to get back to work. Write it down on something and I'll do the same. I'll be back by before the show starts."

"Okay," I said without thinking. He was cute. Why not? I asked myself. So, I got out a business card to give to Greg. He swooned by me again. I gave him my card as he handed me a scratch paper with his pager number on it.

"Thanks," Greg said. "I'll call you. You are so cute." I looked down and twisted my long black locks with a smile and little look of embarrassment. "Thanks," I said, as I raised my head up and looked him in his big blue eyes.

The concert was starting. My kids and my niece were right in front of the stage. They literally had their chins resting on the stage. My niece was in hog heaven! I know we got some great pictures of the band! We were on the filming too! It was just the back of our heads, but we were on T.V.! It was a great night in spite of my cell phone getting stolen. Maybe that is what made my night such a great night! If it wasn't stolen, I wouldn't have been so adamant about speaking to someone that could help me. So, even though something bad happens, something good could actually come out of it. Maybe so, but when will something good come out of my husband's death? I haven't figured that one out yet.

They think I Killed My Husband!

Chapter 4

Life after work?

My contract was coming to an end at work. I was so happy. I would get the remainder of money owed to me and actually take some time off to let reality set in. Being at the business my husband and I started felt like he was still alive. I know in a way, the business was his life and that is carrying on what he left behind. But, my Ralph is dead. I need to realize that. I feel like he is just out in the field selling or out of town while I am still doing the business. I am still bitter and angry. I feel extremely stressed out. If the job and losing my husband weren't enough, the police have to hound me too! I have to deal with trying to convince these people that I did not kill anyone! I would be so glad when I can take some time off.

    I saw Roberto at work and we were discussing some of our fun times we each have had in the past, some together and some when we were with other people. We laughed. I told him about the cameraman, Greg. He started to tease me.

    "And have you talked to Dennis lately?" Roberto continued to tease me.

    "Yes actually, I have," I informed him.

    "So, how's he doing? I haven't talked to him for a while," Roberto told me.

    "He's doing okay. I talked to him the other day. He is moving back with his Grandmother. He said she is not doing too well." I went on and got Roberto up to date with Dennis' life. I was surprised with Dennis and Roberto as best friends, I was talking to Dennis more than he was.

However, I was still extremely happy about not having to come in to work anymore after this week. I was sitting in my office finalizing some paperwork. I started thinking. Finally, I can stop! I haven't stopped! I suddenly realized that I really haven't stopped. What will life really be like now? What will I do? I already re-programmed my new phone with all of my contacts. I would like to take a vacation, but I can't go too far for too long. Since I am still being questioned. I guess, I need to ask Jack what exactly are my rights? I would like to go and see the children's grandparents and maybe slip off and see Dennis. He is just in the next town over.

What would I tell my in-laws? Is it wrong of me to want to be with someone? I thought, maybe so, but I could hear Ralph say to me that day, "I'd marry again in a couple of months." Meaning, if I died before him, he would have no problem finding another replacement for me. In a way, I had his blessing to go out and continue my life without him. That's the only one whose blessing would really matter to me. I keep telling myself this, trying to make it easier, but why am I even worrying about it? Whom am I trying to please? I have so much on my plate anyway. Do I really need sex this badly? So many sorted things go through my mind. Then I hear the strong morality of my late husband's thoughts of what I should do to be a perfect mother. That was fine. But, while he was alive, I got laid everyday. That was okay since it was by the children's father, not that they saw or knew anything anyway, just to ease my conscience. But now, what do I do? Go without sex? Why? I wouldn't subject my children to my personal life issues. I can get a baby sitter and go somewhere else. But, I should be with the children. I should be with them as much as possible, especially now at this time in their lives. I am so confused. I would like to be able to have someone in my life, a companion, my companion. I wanted Ralph back. How I wanted that so badly. This is when I get angry. I noticed my crying rages seem to be more intense while I am menstruating. Maybe there is something to that hormonal rage syndrome. I want him back and I will never be able to have him beside me ever again. It's starting to seem so final now. I am angry. I am angry with God for taking away the father of a couple of great kids. I was angry with Ralph for not taking better care of himself and trying to act like such a macho man that night. It sometimes feels like he may still be fucking with me, even from the grave. I don't know how any substance could have gotten into his system. Maybe somebody slipped him something or Ralph did something to himself. I may be going insane too. Trying to deal with this whole situation is making me feel near crazy.

"Hey Pam!" Roberto shouted into my office as I jumped what seemed like ten feet out of my chair. "Let's go for some coffee."

"Sure," I said as I got out of my chair checking my heart beat on my chest. "What's the occasion?"

"Just that we won't be able to have our little chit chats together as much. If at all." Roberto commented.

"I'll be a phone call away. No different than if I was in the next room. You know that. I'll be looking forward to you calling me. I'll probably get so bored at times." I assured Roberto. We went to the corner convenient store to get some coffee. Roberto told about his plans with Dixie. They were to be married soon. He told me of their plans to find a house after their first year filing taxes jointly. I was trying to pay closer attention, but my mind had started to drift off to where I was when he invited me to get some coffee.

"Maybe I should see a shrink." I said to myself.

"What?" asked Roberto.

I didn't realize I said that out loud to get a genuine response from Roberto. I boldly repeated what I was thinking.

"Maybe I should see a shrink."

"Well, if you are asking that question, maybe you should. It probably wouldn't hurt considering everything you are going through." Roberto consoled. "You could get into gardening." He laughed and so did I. We both know that every plant I've received died already. I can't grow anything.

Later the following week, my life of leisure started. I

was home alone after the kids left for school. Bruce, Ralph's friend stopped by on his way to the repair shop. Bruce was extremely cute and recently broke up with his girlfriend. He was slender with dark hair and hazel eyes. I guess being a recent widow that men think the lonely widow needs some servicing. Since he had no girlfriend now, he did too. He proved that I could grow something if not a plant!

He came in my house and looked at me and asked, "Could you help me? I seem to have a problem. I helped you fix your car, now can you help me?"

"A problem?" I asked. "What kind of problem?"

Bruce pointed down towards his groin. I saw that huge cock bulging through his shorts and all I could get out of my mouth is, "How is that a problem?"

"Well, can you help me?" Bruce snickered.

"Let me see. I don't know. I have to get a hold of the situation," I said with a quiet, steamy voice as I felt his big hard cock in my hand. I stroked it up and down, feeling the velvety smoothness of the soft skin that surrounds that hard stiff male penis. I wanted to lick it so bad. So, I just started to lick Bruce's lips. He began to kiss me back. I could feel his tongue around the inside of my mouth. I loved it. I began sucking on his tongue like I would suck on his dick. Slowly sucking his tongue in and out of my lips. I was teasing Bruce making him long for that licking and sucking action to be done unto his big hard cock. My lips were going up and down on his tongue. As I sucked and massaged his tongue with my lips, I stroked his big hard cock up and down with my hand. I started to get a little rough.

"Oh yeah, baby. That's it. I like it a little rough. Oh, ohhh. Let's go into your bedroom," Bruce suggested. After hearing him suggest that, I literally pulled him into my bedroom. I immediately unbuttoned his pants. I knelt down on my knees and helped Bruce out of his shorts. Since I was on my knees, I proceeded to suck his big erect cock. I rubbed his balls and sucked his cock with my mouth sliding up and down it and my tongue doing little swirls at the same time. Bruce squirted immediately. Talk about being a little disappointed. Oh well.

They think I Killed My Husband!

"Oh, man! I am so sorry, baby. You just turn me on so much. I can't help it." Bruce tried to convince me. I was convinced all right. But, I need a little more time than that.

"I'll make it up to you. I just haven't gotten any in so long! I gotta go to the shop. Stop by and see me if you like," Bruce told me.

"Okay, Sweetie," I answered with great disappointment. He left the house after probably being there for 10 minutes. He has such a big cock I was indeed disappointed. So, I took a shower to start my day. I had several errands to run about town. It was nice to finally get some time for myself and not have to worry about the business or finances. The only thing I had to worry about was convincing the police I did not kill my husband. I couldn't believe that I was a suspect! I presume that it is obvious. I was the last one with him and he did have a healthy insurance policy.

After I ran my errands I went back home to watch my favorite soap, "All My Children." I have been watching that ever since high school with my Grandmother. She watched the show since it first started. I also had to think about what to do with my boat. I decided to trade it in and buy a new one with the money I got for the business. Just as I was thinking about this and watching my favorite soap, the phone rings.

"Hello?" I answered.

"Pamela?" I heard on the other end.

"Yes?" I replied.

"This is Detective Tony Perez. How are you doing today?"

"Fine. What do you need Tony? I do believe this is not a social call," I said.

"Unfortunately, it is not a social call. We need you to come down for further questioning," Tony demanded.

"I better call my lawyer, Jack. I want him with me of course. Have you talked to him?" I asked.

"No, not yet. I figured you could call him and let me know when you could come down to the station tomorrow," said

Detective Tony.

"Tomorrow?" I replied loudly. "You don't give a girl much time to rearrange her plans! I hope Jack will be available as well."

"Call me back and let me know please," Detective Tony told me in an extremely professional tone.

"I will. I have the number." I told him and hung up.

"This sucks!" I was thinking to myself. "I can't even watch TV without this crap to deal with."

I telephoned Jack later after my daily soap opera. I couldn't use Tom, my accounting attorney, so Jack said that he would represent me Pro Bono to get in good graces with the State for his law practicing. I couldn't afford to trust anyone else.

Jack said loudly and firmly, "Yes. I can make it tomorrow to the police station. I'm also going to set this Detective straight, that he is to call me direct first and shouldn't be talking to you. They are just trying to catch you off guard and without legal representation. I guess someone could at least give the police an "A" for effort!"

The kids arrived home later in the afternoon. I fixed some supper and then they got ready to go to Scouts. I took them both to their Scout meetings and returned home to finish up the dishes.

Later in the evening, Greg, the cameraman from the concert, called me. It was a nice surprise. He asked me if I would like to go motorcycle riding. I loved to ride on motorcycles. I agreed and we set a date and time. We chit-chatted for a bit, until I had to pick up the kids from their Scout meetings.

I am so proud of my children. They have held up like champs through this whole ordeal. I don't know how they are going to handle seeing their mother being accused of possibly killing their father. Losing him is bad enough, but to think of their Mother as creating the loss would be imaginable.

We all had to get up early the next morning. The kids got to school and I met Jack for an early breakfast. We had to have a quick meeting before the interrogation. I met Jack at the Denny's in town. I hopped into his car for a moment first. I had only one question on my mind and I needed to ask.

"What if they arrest me?" I asked Jack, worriedly.

"They don't have enough hard evidence to arrest you yet." Jack replied.

"Yet?" I exclaimed. "Like what kind of evidence? What would be considered hard evidence, Jack?"

"Like finding any kind of cyanide in your possession. Or a receipt from purchasing some," Jack responded.

"What if they didn't find anything?" I inquired.

"Well, then you got lucky," Jack said. "Should you be telling me something, Pam?"

"No, I don't believe so. Do you know if they found anything, Jack?"

"I guess we'll find out here in a few minutes." Jack announced.

Jack and I finished breakfast. I couldn't eat too much. My appetite wasn't quite up to speed. We rode together to the police station. Upon our arrival, we let the lady at the front desk know who we were and whom our appointment was with. The woman had long blonde hair and appeared to be in her mid 40's and apparently working for the money and probably not making a whole lot of it. She, being the receptionist leered up at me from the desk that if looks could kill, I'd be dead. The receptionist phoned Sergeant Thomas. Detective Perez came through the door a few minutes later. The receptionist immediately changed her attitude and called attention to herself so Detective Perez would notice. He generously smiled back to succumb to her needs. Detective Perez escorted us to another office within the station. As I walked past the receptionist she leered at me again! I could only think that this woman is definitely crazy!

"Follow me this way," Detective Tony instructed. I was more than happy to follow Detective Tony anywhere as long as he was in front of me. I could look at that ass walk in front of me all day! I had to remember why I was there. I must keep my mind straight.

"Have a seat Mrs. Garcia. Jack," Sergeant Thomas instructed. "Would you like some water before we get started?"

"Why, yes. Thank you. I would like some. How about you, Jack?" I inquired nervously.

"Sure. Thanks," Jack agreed.

Detective Perez was sent to get the water for us.

"I'll get right down to the chase," Sergeant Thomas said with a certain amount of firmness and arrogance. "We found some invoices from a few years back for some gold solution. The invoice had an extra hazardous material shipping charge. Would you know what would be in this to require it to be considered hazardous?" Sergeant Thomas asked me.

I felt like fainting. I didn't kill my husband. But, I did gold plate. The solution to make it contains cyanide. Should I tell everything I know? Does he already know the answer to this question and if I lie will he know I am lying? Or is he trying to make it easier on himself to hope I will just sing like a bird and educate them on all of this. I leaned over to look at Jack. Boy, did I need help.

"What are the dates on these invoices?" Jack requested. Sergeant Thomas was about to announce the date when Detective Tony returned with the water.

"These are dated a couple of years ago." Sgt. Thomas announced.

"Well, wouldn't you think whatever was shipped at that time would have been used up by now?" Jack retaliated.

"Not necessarily," the Sergeant replied.

"Didn't you search the house? This is all you found. I would presume that whatever was in these packages is gone. There is really nothing you can hold her with, is there Sergeant?" Jack interrogated.

"No, I suppose not. Mrs. Garcia, do you know what was shipped?" Sergeant Thomas asked.

"I can't remember. My husband could have ordered the stuff. He was always working on his cars and boats," I reminded him.

They think I Killed My Husband!

"Yes Ma'am," Sergeant Thomas said.

With that, we ended the questioning for today. Apparently the police needed some more time for digging for clues. I hope their primary concern is revealing the truth and not just trying to convict me on circumstantial evidence to close the case. What if it was something stupid like someone at the lab got labels mixed up on slides or test tubes? Maybe that's how he got cyanide in his system. It wasn't even his system. Are they investigating that possibility? I doubt it. I went home and just wanted to be alone. I had to think and clarify my mind by going about and doing things to keep me from thinking about how my life is and what I am dealing with. I have to stop and think once in a while what I am doing and the realization of my life. I am so stressed out. I miss Ralph. He would help take so much weight off of my shoulders. All I could do is sit and cry for the rest of the day until the kids came home from school.

A few days went by and I heard nothing from the police. I was fine with that! I received a call one night from Greg. I had forgotten all about our motorcycle date. He told me about his line of work leaves him with a crazy schedule. He said that he was definitely not working Friday morning.

"Would that work for you?" Greg asked.

"I was going to take my Mercedes in to get the oil changed. Why don't you follow me to the shop? I could leave my Benz there and we can go ride," I suggested.

"What time do you want me there, Doll?" Greg asked.

"Around 11:00 A.M. is fine."

"See you then. Bye, Baby Doll."

"Bye," I said back.

I put the kids to bed after I helped them with their homework. I tucked them into bed and gave them each a good night kiss. All I could think is how lucky I am to have them with me still. I would hate to think of having to live my life without them in it. I have lost the most significant people in my life. My mother and father died suddenly and recently, now my husband. I could not bear to lose my children. I started to cry.

Then, I started to think of how my children are going to grow up without their Father. It was hard for me to accept the fact that my parents were gone. My children were going to grow up without their grandparents as I did. I always wanted my children to experience the joys grandparents bring to your life throughout your life. I didn't even know my grandparents. At least my kids knew their grandparents for a few years. But, my daughter won't have her father walk her down the aisle at her wedding. He won't be there for their high school graduation either. The thought breaks my heart over and over, every time I think it. My children are being so strong. They don't understand or I would like to think that. They are truly amazing.

The next morning we all got up and I assisted the children with their preparation for school. After getting them both to school, I proceeded to shower and get ready for Greg's arrival. I pulled out my leather outfit. It was a black pair of fringed shorts and a vest. I wore a leather hat and a pair of fringed black leather boots to complete the ensemble. I asked the gardener to open the front gate so Greg could enter the property without a problem.

    Greg arrived right on time. I hate to be left waiting. I can understand 5 minutes or so, but no more. I opened the door and Greg's mouth just hung open for a minute or so it seemed until I started laughing.

    Greg shook his head a couple of times and said, "You look great! I wasn't expecting that! Nice little place you have here," he said as he looked around at the decor in the front foyer.

    "Thanks. Are you ready?" I asked.

    "Let's go. You lead the way." Greg insisted.

    "Follow me," I quickly replied. We got to the Mercedes dealer to drop off my Mercedes. I had my 5 minutes of fame as the employees of the shop admired the black leather outfit I had on. Greg and I left on his motorcycle to enjoy the beautiful day. We went riding up towards the Everglades. The weather was perfect. The temperature was 70 degrees Fahrenheit. The sun was warm where the wind was cool. The sky was at its bluest and sun was it's brightest.

I noticed that morning Greg was a little bit older than I had thought. I also had never seen him without a hat on. Today I found out why, he was completely bald! I couldn't believe it! He had pretty eyes though. He was also very nice and gentlemanly. We stopped along a dock along the river deep in the woods. We walked on a pathway that led past some trees into the woods even deeper. We were where no one could see us. It was nice, romantic even. But, I didn't feel that chemistry. We kissed on the dock. It was very quixotic. Greg caressed my cheek and swept his fingers across my face. He was very respectful to me. He stopped before things got out of hand. We headed back to the cycle and hopped back on and continued to ride.

We stopped and had lunch. Greg indeed did have a busy schedule. Being a professional cameraman, one never knows where he may be from one day to the next. He did invite my children and me to attend a taping of the Lotto show. He would be back in a week for that taping.

"I'll get some more information when it is closer. I know it is a week from Sunday," Greg told me. "So, mark that on your calendar."

"It's marked. Sounds like fun! Thanks!" I squealed. "My kids are going to love that!"

The next few days were quiet. It was nice to relax for a bit. I still had some issues to go through. The houses and cars all had life insurance. So in my eyes, the beneficiary is the creditor not me and should be paid. I have other lawyers working on that. I have also hired an investment firm to help me with the lump sum I will be receiving for the sale of my business. I still had plenty to keep my mind occupied.

Sunday came and the kids and I were on our way to the studios. They were very excited.

"Do you think we'll be on T. V., Mom?" they asked.

"We'll be in the audience. Unless they do an audience

scan, I doubt it. But you never know! Greg did say that members of the studio audience get picked to participate. It is a game show." I informed them.

"Cool," they exclaimed!

We arrived at the studios and parked the car in to closest parking lot. We rode on a tram from the parking lot to where they do the tapings. We met Greg in front of the studio he was working. We walked inside and the stage was up front with props set up and curtains in the background. We walked in and tried to find our seats. The audience sat in sections and in rows that sloped upward like at basketball arenas and auditoriums. The camera track was in front of all of the props. It looked like a metal train track, but a little smaller.

After the show, we received some token prizes and Greg escorted my kids and me through a gate, which led to the theme park. This was extremely cool and unexpected. The kids were shocked. So honest, they were concerned that someone was going to know and kick them out of the park. I assured them it was fine. The security saw us go through and waved. Greg had to return to work and said he would call me later. The kids and myself proceeded to enjoy the day.

I paged Greg later that week and thanked him for a wonderful day. We talked and I didn't hear from him for a few weeks. I did hear from Jack. It wasn't good news.

"The police have been doing some research," Jack clued up.

"What do you mean? What have they found out?" I needed to know.

"They went and interrogated some of your business contacts," Jack informed me.

"My business contacts! Oh, this is great! Now, I will never be able to do business again! What gives them the right to do that?" I demanded.

"They have the right, Pam. They did not however divulge information pertaining to the case. Detective Perez discovered you did gold plating for them. But, you haven't done work for a couple of years for them." Jack said they reported to him.

"Yes. I had to help my husband with our business," I said with frustration and attitude.

"Pam, I am just telling you the facts and what the jury is going to look at. If circumstantial evidence is strong enough, it can turn into a conviction where a jury is concerned," Jack sternly replied. "But, I will also add that the Detective told me some of them offered their opinion and thought very highly of you."

"That's good, I guess. Does it really matter?" I questioned.

"It could," said Jack.

"So, do they want to see me again?" I asked Jack.

"I don't have the exact date, but I know he said he did want another deposition," said Jack.

"It'll probably be pretty soon, won't it? What am I going to do about all of this? You have to help me Jack! You just have to!" I screamed desperately.

"Calm down, Pam. You know I will. But, you must tell me everything! I mean it, Pam. Do not leave out a single detail. If there are any loose ends or things you may have found that would put you in jeopardy, I need to know. Because, if you did put the cyanide in his system, I can help you the best I can to try to get you off. At least to be prepared if something gets found out, you can't afford surprises more than I can't afford to hear surprises. Did you finish him off? Be honest with me. It's very important," Jack demanded.

"No! I swear to you Jack, I didn't! But, we do need to figure out our plan of keeping this gold plating crap to a minimum." I replied.

"What are you suggesting, Pam?" inquired Jack.

"What I am suggesting is for you to make sure that this gold plate stuff remains simply circumstantial. I need to make sure of this though. I stopped doing gold plating when I had to help Ralph with the business. I haven't done any work in a couple of years. I didn't have the material! That's the truth!" I retaliated.

"Okay, okay!" Jack came back. "Like I said, I don't

want any surprises."

"I'll tell you everything I do. OK?"

"OK," said Jack. "Promise me you won't leave out a single detail."

I was so stressed out with everything that I had gone through and with everything I had to keep going through, I needed some release. I needed to go out and dance. I didn't have anyone to go with me. I didn't have many single friends. Dennis moved and Sherry moved. They were the only people I knew that may actually go out with me. I could go by myself. It would be like old times. When I was younger and first moved into the area, I went out by myself all of the time! I know a little bit more of being careful now that I am older. I think back and wonder how I lived through some of those nights.

I went out later that Friday night. I loved to dance. I sure do miss Ralph. He took me dancing almost every weekend. I needed to get away just for a few hours. I called a sitter for the kids and I put on a pair of black spandex Capri pants and black tank top with high heels and headed out. I took the Mercedes to be comfortable. On the way to the club I smoked a joint to get relaxed. I still feel so guilty going out without Ralph. I never went anywhere without him, it seemed. But, it did feel good to get away. It felt great, actually. I arrived at the club downtown. I parked the car in VIP valet and got out of my beautiful gold metallic Benz 500 SEL wearing my black outfit and looking good. All eyes were on me as the valet opened up my door. I handed him a twenty and told him to take care of her. I entered through the double doors and the hot blonde girl that every expensive club has at the door, smiled and said hello. I walked into the club and the lights were swirling and colorful. Lasers were spinning and the regular lights were flashing many different colors. The music was loud and upbeat. I loved dancing to the new mixes. I went to the neon lit bar and got a drink. The dance floor was a little crowded. I finished my drink and tried to make my way on to the dance floor. There were entirely too many people on the floor. I couldn't dance the way I like to dance. I decided to walk around. I went upstairs in the club and the upstairs seemed desolate. I walked around the balcony and watched the people below. Then I noticed the D.J. booth and walked towards it. I stood behind the D.J. booth and watched him mix the music with the computers he had. The light show was also being controlled entirely by the computer system too. I had more room to dance up there anyway. I started to dance behind the D.J. like no one was watching. After some time passed, a tall, young man walked by me. He was a minimum of 6' 4" with his hair cut extremely short. He had on a nice professional suit. He was fair skinned and had bulging blue eyes. As he passed and I saw him turn around and take another gander at me. He decided to approach me with a puzzled look on his face.

"Are you here alone?" he asked.

"Honestly, yes I am. I can't seem to get any room on the dance floor to dance. I came up here and thought I'd hang out. Are you here alone?" I replied.

"No. I am here with some friends. Come down stairs with me. Would you like to dance with me?" he asked.

"Sure. What's your name?" I questioned.

"John. What's yours?" he replied.

"I'm Pam. Let's go." We went to dance downstairs. He was very tall. His blonde hair was very short and stood up on its end. His eyes were like clear sky blue marbles. I could tell he was very young. We were dancing and he pulled me close. I could feel the strength of his huge strong thighs between mine. He pulled me so close I was practically sitting on his huge and rigid thigh. Then, I could also feel something else getting hard and strong. He was so tall, I felt his big cock against the bottom of my tummy. It did feel very tempting. We talked and danced for a couple of hours. He later asked me if I wanted to go somewhere else where we could be alone.

"John, what do you do?" I asked.

"I play Baseball in the minors. I am a pitcher. I just had an operation on my shoulder. I am not in the best shape right now," he told me.

"You could have fooled me," I exclaimed!

"Could you give me a ride? I came with my friends. I don't have my car here," John noted.

"Sure. What did you have in mind?" I asked coyly.

"C'mon. Let's get out of here." John insisted. So, off we went. I drove my car and decided to go to the beach. While I was driving to the beach, John unzipped my pants and started to play with my pussy. He was licking the side of my neck and nibbling on my earlobe while I was driving down the expressway. I engaged the cruise control on the car and spread my legs. John had easier access to my pussy and was playing with it with his fingers and teasing me. I was so horny. I could feel the wetness on the tops of my thighs. His fingers were tickling my clit and he held my panties back while he tasted my juices. I kept driving and had to divert his attention. I started to undo his pants too. I took one hand and slowly unzipped his pants then unbuttoned them. I wanted to play. His cock just sprang right out of his zipper. So, I grabbed his big hard cock and started to rub it up and down with my spare hand. I continued stroking his joystick while approaching a tollbooth. I didn't care. We did stop for a second and handed the attendant the money then proceeded where we left off and drove away. Within a half an hour, we arrived at the beach. We each ripped off our clothing and exited the vehicle. We strolled naked along the ocean. We found a secluded spot between the sea oats and John took me into his arms and started to kiss me. His warm, wet tongue inside my mouth felt like I was going to ooze down into his mouth like his favorite ice cream on the fourth of July. He kissed so well. I just started to melt into his arms. My body liquefied in the heat of all the passion. I wanted him so bad and right now! He lifted me up and then laid me down on the sand. I was startled!

"I thought you said your shoulder was just operated." I asked.

"It was. But, I want you so bad." John said, as he slid his tongue down my torso towards my vagina. John started to massage my sweet, erect nipples with his hands. He was making me so horny. It felt so good. He proceeded to take his soft, wet tongue back up and down my taught, tanned torso. He swirled his tongue inside my belly button and sucked my skin and gave me a love bite. I rubbed his head with my hands. His hair felt peachy smooth and was short, easy to maintain for an athlete. He made his way back down to my pussy. Pulling my legs apart and sliced my lips open with his soft and wet tongue. He flicked his tongue up and down and back and forth my clit. Then he got a really good taste of my pussy juice. He made me wild with excitement. All I could do was moan with ecstasy and delight. I almost started to cum, but then he pulled back. I sat up immediately and kneeled towards him. I leaned forward and he leaned back slightly. I immediately started to suck on that huge hard dick. He got a condom out and put it on his big love stick. He pushed me onto my back when he climbed on top of me. John took himself and rammed his cock up my hot wet pussy. He gave me quite a jolt. Even though I was wet and more than ready, his cock was indeed big and satisfying. I screamed in pain as it felt that wonderful. He kept sliding his cock in and out of my pussy and he rose to his knees. I lifted my ass up in the air to keep that big cock inside of me. John then started to play with my clit.

"Oh, my God!" I thought to myself. "Ohhh! I'm cumming! Auugh!" I screamed. I came. I began thrusting my hips back and forth uncontrollably. I could feel my eyes rolling to the back of my head. John kept himself sliding in and out of my pussy. He felt incredible. He turned me over to get me from behind.

"You have a beautiful ass." John told me. " I want some."

Before I could say anything, he stuck that huge cock up my ass! I screamed again! This time it did hurt. I wasn't used to getting it up the ass. I was so into this fuck, I didn't care. It actually felt good after he pumped me a few times. He then reached around and played with my pussy again. He stuck his thumb up my pussy and played with my clit while his cock was taking my ass! I loved it! I was oblivious to anything else in the world going on around me.

Then I heard John yell, "Go get your own show!" I looked up and realized there was some bum walking back and forth, watching us in action! Oh, man. I may have been embarrassed if I thought the guy was anyone I knew. We continued like no one was watching. I started to cum! The thought of getting caught with our pants down, literally was such a turn on! John was cumming too! I could feel his cock swell in my ass and I could feel the pulsation of his love juice squirting into my body. He was groaning with pleasure as I was squealing with ecstasy! John regained composure enough to yell at the stranger, "Hey, go find your own show."

We tried to get cleaned up. It was difficult in the sand and no towel. We just shook off our clothing the best we could. I could still feel the grit in my ass and pussy. But, I didn't care. It wouldn't be for long. I took John home and got his number and he got mine. I really didn't expect him to call. We both got what we wanted. He was ten years younger than I was. It would have never worked anyway. We were two ships that passed in the night, like the Titanic and the iceberg. What a night to remember!

I awoke the next morning and I couldn't walk very well. I was completely exhausted. I took the kids later to a movie. We had a relaxing time. I started to fall asleep in the movie.

Chapter 5

The Hell Begins

The kids woke me up when the movie ended. I almost forgot where I was. We drove home. The kids were telling me about the movie along the way.

"I can't believe you fell asleep Mom," Serena exclaimed!

"Yeah, the movie was so loud, Mom. I can't see how anyone could sleep through that," Rafael exclaimed!

"I know, I know," I replied. "I guess I really needed it. I didn't realize how tired I actually am."

"Can we stop and get something to eat?" my daughter asked.

"Absolutely not," I said sternly. "We are going home and straight to bed! All of us!"

We arrived home and went to bed.

The next morning I awoke to the sound of someone knocking at my front door. They kept pounding. I was trying to get my mind acquainted with reality. I was still in a deep sleep trying to clear my brain. I looked around and sat up in the bed for a moment. I wondered if I had forgotten to close the gate last night. The knocking was getting louder.

"Just a second!" I yelled towards the door. "Who is it?" I asked as I was walking to the front door while tying the belt of my robe.

"It's the police. Please open the door, Mrs. Garcia. This is Detective Perez," the voice proclaimed from the other side of the door.

"What is it now? Did you find out anything new, like all of this is probably some sort of mistake?" I opened the door and looked at Detective Perez with my eyebrows lifted and wanting an answer.

"May I come in? It would be better for you that I come inside, please," Detective Perez informed me.

"Oh, all right," I replied. I opened the door and Detective proceeded to enter my home. "What's going on?"

"Mrs. Pamela Garcia, we have a warrant for your arrest. You have the right to remain silent. Anything you say can and will be used against you. You have the right to an attorney. If you cannot afford an attorney, one will be appointed to you. Do you understand?" Detective Perez so professionally read me my rights.

"Yes." I humbly said. "May I call my lawyer?"

"Of course. When we get you downtown to the station. You have to come with us right now!" He was diligent.

"But, what about my children? I can't leave them alone! How terrible to do this in front of my children," I screamed! "Can't you at least let me call my sister so she may be here when they wake up?"

"We are up, Mom." My son said from the top of the stairs. I looked up and saw him standing there, trying not to cry and trying so hard to be brave. My heart just broke seeing that look of determination and bravery on his face. He has been through so much already. Will this bitter nightmare ever end? We all do what we have to do, I guess.

"Call your Aunt! Have her come and pick you up. I guess you are going to have to stay with her for a while." I instructed Rafael, Jr.

"How long are you going to be gone? You are coming back, right?" My son asked with tears streaming down his face and his lower lip partially sticking out while he tried to keep it in.

They think I Killed My Husband!

"Of course I am coming back. They are just making a mistake. I'll call Jack and he will get this all straightened out. Don't you worry, Honey. I love you and Serena. Now go do what I said."

Rafael, Jr. went back upstairs and used the phone in the toy room. I looked at Detective Perez with such hatred that he just looked away from me.

"What a prick!" I thought to myself. "To think I actually thought about him in that certain way. Unbelievable!"

"C'mon, Mrs. Garcia. We have to go now." Detective Perez calmly stated.

"May I put some clothes on?" I asked. "You woke me up and I haven't gotten dressed yet."

"I'll get one of the females officers to go into your room with you while you get dressed." Detective Perez insisted as he tapped another officer and whispered to him to retrieve the lady officer from outside. I waited in the hall until this woman came inside. She looked like a big, butch, class-A Bitch in a uniform. She looked like one of those butch-lesbians from the club Ralph and I used to go to. I quietly found some comfortable clothes and put them on. I could hear my son talking to his Aunt on the phone in the other room. I guess I will call Jack from the station.

I entered the living room and Detective Perez proceeded to direct me to the squad car. He put his hand on the back of my head to assist me into the car.

"Hey! You don't need to be so pushy!" I declared.

"Mrs. Garcia, you need not be so demanding. You are in no position to be." Detective Perez reminded me.

"Fine," I said. I sat down and did not utter another sound. We arrived at the station and I proceeded to telephone Jack.

"Jack, they arrested me!" I yelled over the phone.

"What do you mean?" Jack asked.

"What part of that don't you understand? Tu no comprende? Te quires en Espanol?" I said sarcastically. " I am in jail. I am using my one phone call to call you. Find out whatever you need to find out to get me out of here. If you need my checkbook, it is in my purse at home. Do you still have my sister's phone number?"

"Yes. I should still have it. Why? Is that where the kids are?" Jack inquired.

"I told my son to call his Aunt and to have her pick them up. Hopefully I can be home shortly. How soon can I be out of here, Jack?" I wanted to know.

"Let me find out everything first and get the bond money together and I'll tell you everything I know as soon as I know." Jack reassured.

"Thank you Jack! I'll be waiting! Like I have a choice!" I told him.

Jack went out to take care of my business for me. I hope he gets me out of here soon! I now have plenty of time to think, that's for sure. I sat in my cell thinking. Thinking about everything that I have gone through in the last year. I was feeling such anger towards Ralph. Why did he leave me? How did he get the cyanide into his system? If he had taken better care of himself, I would not be sitting here in jail right now. His children would not be without their mother. He said he would never leave me. Where are you, Ralph? Why aren't you here? You said you would take care of me, always. Is God punishing me? What did I do that was so bad? I only tried to do the best for my children and my family. It wasn't fair. How did I get into such a mess? It's bad enough to lose my husband, but to be blamed for his death is almost too much to handle. I must do what I must do, just sit here for now and wait. Wait for answers to questions that may never be answered. I sure wasn't going anywhere at the moment.

Just at that moment the guard was bringing in another prisoner. She looked like she had just gotten picked up for prostitution. The guard had a hold of her arm and flung her into the cell and quickly closed the door.

"Hey! Ow! Go easy Swiney! You are hurting me," the girl yelled out.

"No one could hurt you, girly. You're so stoned, you're

They think I Killed My Husband!

just made of stone by now." the guard said to her.

"She is still a human being," I corrected him. The guard and the girl looked at me with the same puzzled look.

"What's it to you?" the guard asked scowling.

"Nothing. I am just trying to defend another human being. Animal activists would be in a fit of rage if dogs were being treated like that in a kennel," I commented.

The guard just looked at me with a bit of resentment. His eyes were squinting and his mouth frowning.

"What? You want of piece of me? Give it your best shot! I'll have you working your piddley-ass, $20,000.00 per year salary entirely for me if you lay one hand on me, that is, if you still have a job. There is Human Rights Watch that would love to have another statistic." I warned him.

He just scowled even more and walked away. I just kept looking at him with a look of intimidation. If I learned anything from Ralph, it was how to handle some people in a situation, especially in jail. He had spent some time in prison when he was younger. I know I will have to sleep with one eye open. I also could trust absolutely no one.

"Hey, thanks!" The girl said to me. "You really know how to handle yourself in here. Have you been in here before? I haven't seen you around. What's your name?"

"Does it really matter?" I asked. "I won't be in here for very long."

"Hey, just trying to make small talk," the girl said to me.

"Well, don't." I demanded.

"Oh, well now. Aren't we a bit touchy?" The girl responded. "O.K. I'll leave you alone for now. I'll let the 'Miss Goody Too Shoos' be in her little world," the girl said as she lay down on the cot in the cell. The girl was still dressed in her evening clothes, which consisted of fishnet stockings along with black thigh high boots and a leopard print dress with a matching scarf that was a hit in the eighties. Her hair was frizzled and bleached blonde with bright red lipstick with blue eye shadow and too much eyeliner and mascara that was

125

running. Such a touch of elegance I thought to myself sarcastically. I couldn't believe I had to be sitting in here with this person. It was bad enough to be here anyway, but to have to put up with that! I think she was in need of deodorant. I am not in the best of moods either. I stretched out on the cot I was sitting on and just closed my eyes and tried to pretend that I was in a different place.

"So, what's a little 'Candy-Ass' like you doing in a place like this?" the girl asked once again.

I opened one eye and looked over at her with it. I couldn't believe she was even speaking to me, let alone calling me a 'Candy-Ass'. Who does this woman think she is? I couldn't let this go unanswered.

"You talking to me?" I asked the girl.

"You don't see no one else in here do ya, Bitch?" she replied.

"No. It's just that I cannot believe you are still talking, especially to me." I reminded her.

"I was just wondering what your name was. I'm Krystall. You seem pretty upset. What did they arrest you for? Did you get too many traffic tickets?" Krystall kept asking and started giggling.

"Why is it so important to you? What's it to you? I don't think it's any of your business." I gave her the same response with a little more attitude.

"Well, you don't look like you are in the same line of work as me." Krystall commented.

"Gee, ya think?" I replied sarcastically.

"Ha, ha," Krystall gently said. "Can't you be nice? I'm on the same side of these bars as you are."

"What are you in here for? Why did you get brought in at the time you did? I would have thought the prime hours for people in your line of work would be anywhere from 9 P.M. to 4 A.M. But, you were brought in at 10 o'clock in the morning. Why?" I retaliated.

"Why should I tell you all of that? What's it to you?" Krystall inquired.

"Exactly. Thank you. Now, maybe you understand why I am not going to answer your nosey questions. If you can't answer my questions, why should I answer yours?"

"Okay. I'll go. It's obvious what I do for a living. That is what I am here for. I was leaving the hotel this morning when they arrested me at the hotel. So, there you go. Now, you answer my questions. Starting with your name," Krystall demanded.

"I don't have to do what you say. It is better to have friends than enemies, though," I said, displaying my awareness of her. With a cynical aura I stated, "I am in for murder. The forensics found cyanide in my husband's body. I am their number one suspect. I didn't do it. They have circumstantial evidence that can put me here, so here I am!" I finished with a big sarcastic grin to go along with my arms up in the air finishing my speech.

"You still didn't tell me your name," Krystall enlightened me.

"My God. You don't give up do you?" I replied in awe.

The next morning, on Monday, I heard someone walking down the corridor, a guard came to the door. He looked at the two of us and asked for Pam Garcia. I held up my hand and said it was me. Immediately, I looked over at Krystall. She had a sneaky smile on her face. It was similar to that of the Cheshire cat. I rolled my eyes. I really didn't care. The guard opened the gate and put handcuffs on me and led me out of the cell.

"Am I getting out?" I asked with great anticipation.

"I think so, but they don't tell me much. I just keep you all in line and come get you when requested, " the guard answered.

We arrived at the end of the hallway of the jail and the guard opened the door. I entered the offices of the jail department and there stood Jack, my lawyer.

"Oh, Jack! Please tell me I am out of here now!" I desperately pleaded.

"Not quite yet. I am working on it, though. I need some signatures from you to get the money you need to make bail.

The Detective wanted to talk to you about some of Ralph's habits. I told him he could when I arrived and with myself present," Jack explained. "Where are your clothes? You look terrible in orange."

"Thanks, you look marvelous too. This ought to be fun. So, how long after you leave can you be back to get me out?" I needed to know.

"Probably two or three hours at the most. Here, just sign these papers." Jack commanded as he handed me several legal documents and a pen.

"What are all of these for?" I asked while reviewing them quickly.

"They are from an assortment of banks." Jack quickly informed me.

"What are you trying to do now, Jack? Have a helpless widow sign away her life savings to her lawyer with his famous last words being, 'Trust me,'" I asked half jokingly.

"Pam! I'm surprised at you. I'll let that one go, considering your recent environment over the last couple of days. I called your accountant and your estate attorney to have them get everything together that I would need to get you $100,000.00 for this bond. So, they went to the banks drawing up the transfer of funds and your accountant also gave me a couple of checks made out to the bank. I will go and have them make cashier's checks payable to the bondsman. Look over these carefully and know what I am saying is true," Jack quickly put me in my place. "I also had this temporary Power-of-Attorney drawn up."

"Let me look," I began. "That is so much money! This will leave me broke. I will have to put the house up for sale." I humbly stated. "What about this Power-of-Attorney?" I questioned.

"Well, this has been one hell of an ordeal, Pam. If anything should happen and you stay in jail or if you should be arrested again, I can just go and get the money for your bond myself in the future. But, only if you are incarcerated," Jack specified.

They think I Killed My Husband!

I signed the papers trusting Jack, then, we proceeded to the other room where Detective Tony Perez and Sergeant Thomas were. Jack was right there with me.

As we were entering the room, Jack whispered, "You don't have to say a word if you don't want to, remember that!"

"Shh! I know," I whispered back as we began to sit down at the table.

"Good morning, Mrs. Garcia," Sergeant Thomas said with a big smile.

"Sergeant Thomas, Detective Tony, good morning to you, both. To what do I owe this great pleasure?" I inquired.

"We need to ask you a few more questions," Detective Tony stated. "Mrs. Garcia, was your husband a good husband?"

"Of course he was. He was the best father anyone could have had." I replied.

"Was he a good husband? You stated that he was a good father, but was he a good husband? Was he good to you?" Detective Tony questioned.

"Yes, yes. He was good to me. My husband was very jealous, but would never admit to it. Other than that, he adored me," I concluded.

"Did he have any bad habits? Let me be more specific. Did he use illegal drugs of any kind?" Tony questioned again.

"Not that I am aware of! This is ridiculous! You have all of the test results! You tell me whether he did or not!" I retaliated with a vengeance. Jack caressed my hand, signaling for me to calm down. I did just that. Jack looked at me to give me an approving smile that made me feel better.

"Mrs. Garcia, were you having any trouble in your marriage?" Tony kept on.

"No. We were not having any difficulty at that time." I answered snottily.

"All right. We are just trying to get more of a feel to your situation Mrs. Garcia. The ambiance of the evening, if you will. You were at the South Comfort Club downtown. Is that correct?" Tony continued.

"Yes." I added.

"Were you two apart at any time during the evening?" Tony asked.

"Sure, I always danced on the dance floor while he sat up on the barstool and watched and drank. He would go to the bathroom, or I would, or he would go back to the bar and get a drink. I didn't pay attention. I was enjoying myself dancing. Doing my thing, if you will," I informed Tony.

"Did Ralph associate with other people at the club?" Sergeant Thomas jumped in.

"Yes, sometimes. I would return from the dance floor and find him talking to someone else quite often. There was even a couple of guys that liked him that worked there and he would be friendly back to them. We were never close or had any relationships with these people. Ralph was a likable person if he chose to be. If he didn't like you, you knew it," I enlightened them both.

"These people you would find your husband talking to, who were they?" the sergeant kept on.

"Some were girls that he would try to get me hooked up with. Some were guys that happened to be there and he may have started a conversation with them or the other person may have started a conversation. Whatever the case, he would communicate with the outside world whenever he was in it," I stated with a smirk.

"Did you notice him talking to anyone else the evening he died?" Detective Tony asked me.

"No, but I did notice he went somewhere and left our drinks on the bar as to 'hold' our stools. I was out on the dance floor dancing. Maybe someone slipped him something then! Have you thought about any of those possibilities?" I asked.

"It seems Mrs. Garcia, no one else has motive. I do know that you have financially gained from this. The big cash policy I know hasn't been awarded and won't until this case is over and you are not guilty," Sergeant Thomas explained.

"In which I must be proven guilty, Sergeant. I haven't been proven yet, and shouldn't be because I didn't do it. I needn't remind you of that," I defended.

"You are the only one with motive Mrs. Garcia," Sergeant Thomas reminded me.

"So? Do you really think I would kill the Father of my children? My children loved their father so much. You don't have a clue! I would never do anything to hurt my children in any way! Do you have any children Sergeant?" I turned around and looked at the Sergeant in his cold blue eyes.

"Yes I do, Mrs. Garcia," The sergeant answered.

"Could you ever do anything to the Mother of your children?" I asked.

"No. But, she never gave me a reason," he retaliated.

"Neither did my husband. I had a maid 5 days a week. He took me out every weekend. He sent me flowers every Valentine's Day. Ralph literally spoiled me. Now why would I hurt someone that would do all of those things? Another thing, I have only suffered financially since this ordeal. The insurance refuses to pay and with Ralph having been the company's backbone, and the mental and obvious physical situation I am now in, I had to sell the business to pay my debts," I said back.

"Money and love, Mrs. Garcia makes normal people do crazy things. Things we wouldn't think we would do or even capable of doing. Were you having an affair with anyone, Mrs. Garcia?" The detective abruptly asked me.

"No! Of course not! Neither one of us had the opportunity to do so. We were together constantly," I said.

"So, you mean to tell me you and your husband were never separated? If you had the opportunity to cheat, you would have?" Tony asked with skepticism.

"No! Yes, pretty much together. Oh, you are confusing me on purpose! We worked together, lived together, raised our children together, gone out together and after doing all of that together, there is no time for anything else," I retaliated.

"So, was he possessive, Mrs. Garcia?" Tony had to ask. "He had to be around you all of the time. Smothering you?"

"No. We just got along so great! We always had a good time together. I guess you haven't had anything like that, huh?" I questioned the Detective. He cleared his voice and straightened up and proceeded with business as usual. The Sergeant saved his colleague and started to continue the interrogation.

"Now, from the information that was gathered, your house on the lake was paid off. Your rental home was paid off. Your cars were all paid off. Your boat was paid off as well. Oh yes, and you sold the business. How much did you get for that?" Sergeant Thomas said being as much of an asshole as he possibly could.

"Does it matter what I made out of that business deal. I helped start and build that business. I earned that much. You have it all wrong anyway. I had to sell the business to pay off those debts. Now with the bond, I have practically nothing," I affirmed.

"Yea, right. Now, you are pretty much comfortable already, are you not? Your husband had a cash insurance policy with the beneficiary being you. I do believe this pay off is worth approximately ten million dollars. That is a lot of money Mrs. Garcia. I have seen people kill for $80.00 at the ATM machines. Some of the best people could have a breakdown and do anything! Are you getting the picture from where I am standing Mrs. Garcia?" Sergeant Thomas inquired leaning down in my face.

"Yes, she does!" Jack stepped in. "Now you can stop harassing my client any time, Sergeant."

"I wasn't harassing her," the Sergeant said, in his defense.

"Maybe I need to remind you that people in America are innocent until proven guilty. So if you have no further questions gentlemen, I need to get my client back to her cell so I may proceed to run some errands and have her out of here by this evening," Jack concluded firmly.

I just looked up and smiled sarcastically at the Sergeant and made a slight glimpse to Detective Tony just to see what his facial expression was. He seemed very cold. He had a wall built up. I couldn't tell what he was thinking. All I know was that he was so fine, a perfect Adonis. I wish I met him under better circumstances.

"Could I have a moment alone with my client?" Jack

asked the officers.

"You have 5 minutes." The sergeant said as they walked out of the room.

"Pam, this doesn't look very good. I'm not saying anything, but all of the evidence does point to you. Money is the strongest motive for murder, and you are getting a bundle. He wouldn't kill himself would he?" Jack announced.

"No, I wouldn't think so. Can we talk about this later? I need you to get me out of here, today, please!" I begged.

"I'm out of here. Guard? Can you make sure Mrs. Garcia gets back to her cell safely?" Jack requested with confidence.

I arrived back to my cell and 'Miss Krystall' was still there to keep me entertained. I need to get out of here and try to gather my own clues. Apparently, I feel that I must prove my innocence. I shouldn't feel this way. Aren't we taught 'Justice always prevails'?" Then, I think about how many innocent people get locked up for crimes they didn't commit. I watched the Discovery channel and they talked about some guy that was let go after spending over 20 years in prison for something he didn't do.

Interrupting my train of thought, Krystall had to open her mouth. "Back so soon? I thought you were gone for good. Oh lucky me. I guess you and I are going to spend a little more time together than we expected."

"Don't get your hopes up, Kristi. I will be gone for good in just a short while," I snarled hoping she would shut up.

"Still as touchy as ever! Sounds like they pissed you off!" Krystall kept talking.

"Am I talking to you? Did I ask for your opinion? Am I even making a sound? I am sitting here minding my own business not uttering a sound and you won't shut up! Why do you care? God. Just leave me alone!" I yelled with my every last ounce of energy I had! I had quite a bit stored up too! It felt kind of good. I sat back down feeling a bit overwhelmed after that rush of emotional energy. All I could do is sit and come to the realization that I may be spending actually quite a lot of time in here. I looked at the walls around me and then looked up at Krystall and all I could do was cry. I put my face into my hands and just cried.

"My kids. What are my kids going to do without me?" I thought to myself. My whole life started to flash before my eyes. I missed my kids. I wanted to hug them and kiss them, put them to bed at night. I miss that most. I don't know what I'll do if I can't do that every night. I can't believe this is really happening. I feel that I am going to wake up any minute from this nightmare. Ralph will be there, right beside me and the kids rushing in, waking us up to see where we would go that day. The good old days, we were a complete family then. I had my best friend to talk to and the love of our children together and watching them grow. It will never be the same again. I have no one to share my children with. It seems to kill the joy when you have lost the one you shared the joy of loving your children with. I love my kids dearly. I miss my late husband very much. I never thought I would be going through any obstacle of life such as this.

Jack came back later that day and bailed me out. We had to think or do something.

"Apparently the police are satisfied that I did it and aren't trying very hard to find out anything else about the case," I told Jack while he was whipping out of the parking lot in his BMW.

"Do you want to put a Private Investigator on it?" Jack inquired. " I know of a good one. I need to find out some things myself to back up our defense."

"Like what?" I expelled with a sigh.

"Find out how many other random poisonings there have been around here lately if any. It's like you said, 'it could be some crazy killer slipping people cyanide at random.' Highly unlikely, but I want to positively cancel it out. Then I'll go on to the next. Maybe it was just a mistake at the lab." Jack predicted.

"Then what's next? Suicide?" I humbly asked. "I don't

know what else to tell you other than I didn't do it. If there is someone out there poisoning people, he or she needs to be stopped."

"I will do everything I can, Pam. You know that. I believe you didn't kill him. Hell, the lab may have just screwed up. I'll confront that situation too. I'll make them do another blood or DNA sample." Jack said as he pulled into my driveway.

I looked up and saw a bunch of news reporters and photographers! "Holy Cow!" I exclaimed in disbelief. "Am I that much of a celebrity? I would have rather done something else to receive this attention!"

"Well, this is just an other addition to the pot of stew you are in. None of this is going to be easy. Let's face it, it's a great story for the locals," Jack confirmed.

I made it through the sea of reporters and answering 'No comment' to each one of them. This was enough to make anyone crazy. I just wanted to see my children. I had to shower and with the reporters still on my property, I didn't know what to do. I called my sister and requested she bring the kids to me. Now, what to do about these pests outside my house trying to get some sort of story? Should I call the police? They would probably just laugh and say that's what you get. It's still my right to vacate unwanted trespassers from my property. I called the police to see if they would help me remove some of these monstrosities from my lawn. The police did come and ask the reporters to leave my property. The reporters did in fact leave for the time being.

My life has gone completely upside-down. I was living a roller coaster with Ralph, now it has gone into high gear! I watched myself on the news that night. I hate the media. What they don't know, they theorize to fill in the gaps. The reporters would fill in the gaps with something really juicy of course, to create more interest and make more money with it. So what, if you sue them for 5 million or so, they made 10 times that at least.

It was getting close to the holidays. Ralph's family was planning a party. It is to be a grand family celebration! The family all want to enjoy each other while they can. We all realize that life can change in an instant. Ralph's cousin was going to have the Noche Buena fiesta at his house. His house was bigger and more centrally located. This was good for me, and then I would only have to drive about an hour. I had to make my plans. I wanted to see Dennis sometime soon. Dennis lives in the same area as Ralph's cousin Barney.

"This is going to be a nice holiday after all," I thought to myself. The night of the Christmas Party arrived. I wanted to wear something festive but conservative since it was at a family home. I decided to wear my white 'Tommy' slacks with my red turtleneck sweater. The pants and sweater fit very well, yet I am totally covered.

"Perfect." I said looking in the mirror getting ready to go. I have the kids already ready. "Come on you guys! Let's go! Now! I don't want to be too late!" I yelled trotting down the stairs.

We arrived at the party fashionably late. The music was playing on the back patio. Barney had a table full of liquor and mixers and a bar outside by the pool. The D.J. was spinning Latin mixes that you couldn't help but dance to. More and more of the family came as the time wore on. I was dancing whenever any of the other girls or guys were dancing. I didn't want to be the only one dancing even if I wanted to dance. A couple of girls in the family started to dance together. I joined in. We were having a great time dancing. Ralph's mother kept trying to get my attention. Finally, Maria, Ralph's sister came over to me and pulled me from the dance area. She leaned over and told me that Mami doesn't want me to dance with those girls.

"Why doesn't she want me to dance?" I asked Maria.

"It's not that she doesn't want you to dance. She doesn't want you to dance with those girls," Maria corrected me.

"Why?" I wondered and asked. "Aren't they family?"

"Yes, one is and the other girl is her girlfriend. Like boyfriend-girlfriend. Get it?" Maria explained.

"Are you kidding me? If I dance with those girls and have fun innocently, that will put the question mark if I am gay?" I asked in disbelief.

"Yeah. Come with me and let's get something to drink." Maria invited.

We mingled with some of the family members I have already known for years. Then we went and she introduced me to some of the family members I haven't met yet.

"Pam, this is Juan and Pablo. They are Barney's nephews. Juan is going to save me a couple of dance's aren't you?" Maria introduced me to them.

Juan and Pablo were both in there twenties. Their exact ages, I wasn't sure of. Both men were tall and handsome. Maria went off with Juan and started to dance with him. They looked and danced great! Juan had Maria spinning and dipping and dancing all around the back patio. The music was so loud! I excused myself from Pablo and went inside to use the bathroom. Once I entered the house, I heard my cell phone ringing. It was Dennis calling.

"Hello." I answered the call.

"Hey! It's Dennis. Where are you? Sounds like the fuckin' circus!"

"No, not exactly. But close!" I laughed. "I am at the family Christmas party. I am having an OK time. I am going to try to get out of here soon to come by and see you. I don't know exactly, maybe within the hour or so. I'll call just before I leave. OK? Bye!"

"Bye," Dennis hung up.

I went to the bathroom. I pulled out my little baggie and did a couple of hits. I walked back out to the party. As I was walking out of the sliding doors towards the back patio, Juan walked up to me and grabbed my hands.

"Come and dance with me." Juan said leading me out to the patio to dance. "I have been wanting to dance with you all night." Juan confessed.

"Really? I was watching you dance with Maria. You dance great by they way. I was hoping to dance with you too,"

I confessed back. Juan and I danced to about 3 or 4 songs. I know I was starting to sweat a little.

"I have a new SUV." Juan told me. "It's a Land Rover. Do you want to see it?"

"Sure, why not? Where is it?" I replied, courteously.

"It's just out in the front. Come on." Juan said grabbing my hand and pulling me through the house and out the front door. There were some other members of the family out front smoking cigarettes and talking where it is a little quieter. We said hello to everyone and walked out to his new Land Rover. Some of the extra family members came out to the new truck to see it too. Juan was very proud of it. Everyone told him how nice it was, including myself.

"Oh, man. I just remembered. I need to get some more soda for Barney. They are almost out. I told Barney I'd get some since my car is the furthest out. Come on. We'll be right back." Juan assured me.

"Cool. Why not? I haven't ridden in a Land Rover before." I agreed and proceeded into the Land Rover. Besides, what could happen? He is family. We drove through a lot of residential streets. I was wondering where he was going.

"You are so hot," Juan said to me with lust in his voice. "I was watching you dance earlier. You are so hot. I want you so bad."

"What do you mean? We are almost family." I retaliated. Juan pulled into a construction area then to a lot with a house that was half built. He stopped the vehicle.

"Uhh, this does not look like the 7-Eleven." I nervously told Juan.

"I know. I want you to do something though." Juan told me as he put the car in park. The night was so dark. I could only see Juan's shadow.

"What is it you want me to do?" I asked keeping my guard up.

"I want you to make this hard." Juan said to me in a deep, seductive voice. I looked over and could see him holding his cock upright with his hand. I was confused.

All I could think of to say was, "That isn't hard?" It was so big, and if that was soft, oh man, how big did it get? What to do? No one would know anything. Juan was such a strong and handsome and in shape man. "No!" I thought to myself. He is family, not really, but sort of.

Then I told him, "No, Juan. You are my little cousin. Even though you are not exactly little!"

"No! I want you! I want you now!" Juan exclaimed as he got out of the truck. I didn't know where he was going.

"What are you doing?" I yelled out the door.

"I am peeing. I'll get back in the car in just a second," Juan said.

I am still trying to get a grip on what just happened here. I would leave, but had no idea how to get back to Barney's house. I guess he made a reality check and we should be on our way after he pees. Then, I see Juan open the back seat door and gets in the back seat without his pants on.

"What are you doing?" I questioned.

"I want you, I want you now," Juan protested as he grabbed my wrist. Juan tried to pull me, but I kept my arms bent and my wrists were clenched to my chest. Juan kept pulling me by my wrists and my whole body finally got pulled between the bucket seats over the center console and into the back seat. I kept my body tight and stiff. It almost seemed easier for him. My arms stiff against my torso had made my physique a single unit more easily maneuvered. Juan managed to pull me through. I am now in the back seat with him. Now, I am a little scared. He wasn't taking 'no' for an answer.

"Juan, no. We need to get back. Please, Juan." I begged. Juan just opened up his car door and stood outside and grabbed my ankles. He pulled me towards him until my knees were at the edge of the seat and my feet were dangling just out of the door. Juan spread my legs apart and stood between them.

"Just a taste, please?" Juan asked as he unzipped my pants and pulled them off of my legs.

"Oh, my God! What are you doing? Don't I get a say on this?" I frantically asked Juan.

"Oh, come on. You want some. Just let me have three strokes." Juan begged as he started to play with my pussy with his hands. My pussy was wet. Juan leaned over and started to taste my pussy juice. It did feel sort of nice. But, this is not of my choice either! Juan was very strong. I didn't want to piss him off either. I didn't know what he was capable of. He was going to take me, apparently, whether I like it or not. What would he do if I were to try to physically fight him to get away? Would he hit me? Possibly beat me? I just lied there and let him do whatever he wanted to do. Juan sucked on my clit and swirled his big wet tongue all around my pussy lips. Slipping his tongue in and out of my hole and sliding it up to my clit and teasing me. He climbed onto the car seat, and lied on top of me. He kissed me a long, seductive French kiss. While kissing me, he took his big hard cock and rammed it into my pussy.

"OOWWW!" I screamed. His big hard cock was a little shocking when inserted and rammed inside. Am I a sick pervert? Juan stroked me again. I could feel his cock rub the wall of my vagina and tap the top.

" I wasn't enjoying this." I thought to myself. Juan stroked me for a third time. I looked up and told him, "Okay, you had your three strokes. Now we have to get back to the party." I stated.

To my surprise, Juan response was, "Yes. You're right. Let's go." Juan said as he got off of me and out of the car. Juan picked up my clothes and gave them to me. I didn't know quite what to say. I got back into the front seat and finished zipping up my slacks. I told him I needed to get back as soon as possible. "I'll take you back now. But I still need to get some soda at the store." Juan informed me from the other side of the vehicle putting on his clothes.

"Drop me off about a block away." I told him. I don't know why. I guess it was the guilty feeling I had. I felt ashamed. I didn't want to be seen getting back to the house with him. Maybe no one will know I was with him all of this time. Everyone was wondering where I had gone. I just said I was out front having a cigarette and went for a short walk. The weather was warm and dry and nice. The night was black as ink. I don't know if anyone believed me or not. I don't know what was said while I was gone. I left shortly thereafter. I made an excuse and left. Maria reluctantly agreed to watch my kids while I was gone for a couple of hours. I called Dennis and told him I was on my way. After driving through traffic for about an hour, I pulled into the driveway. Everything was so serene and secluded. Dennis had a lot of trees on his property. I could hear all of the birds and the sounds of every animal. He would always take care of his trees by fertilizing and feed the squirrels and had bird feeders in the trees. Dennis came out to meet me at my car and help me with anything I may need help with. He was a sight for sore eyes. His gorgeous tan body and perfectly shaven legs. He is so hot. I love to look into those baby blue eyes.

"Hey!" Dennis said, giving me a hug. "Are you alright? You are shaking."

"I don't want to talk about it. It's nothing anyway. Just hold me. Please?" I meekly said.

"Of course, Baby. Anything you want," Dennis assured me while taking me into his strong, pumped arms. His arms felt so good around me. Dennis looked down and took his hand and touched my chin and gently pulled it up, raising my face to lock my eyes with his. Then leaned toward me softly pressing his luscious lips onto mine. I was on the verge of simply melting.

Dennis pulled away just enough to be able to look at me in my eyes at short arms length, "You feel so tense. Sit down on the floor and I'll give you a massage." Dennis had a mattress on the floor in front of the television. He liked to be comfortable. He still had normal furniture everywhere else. I sat down on the mattress and Dennis kneeled down beside me.

"Lay down." Dennis commanded. " I want to give you a massage. I'll start with your neck and scalp then work my way to the shoulders. How does that sound?"

"Sounds pretty good," I said as I lied on my stomach.

Dennis started rubbing my temples with his fingers and the base of my head with his thumbs. He then slowly moved his hands down to the base of my neck. He began massaging my neck and the tops of my shoulders. I felt his lips on the skin of my neck. It felt so good, it gave me goose bumps. I clenched one shoulder up and then Dennis slid his hands down my arms and crossed his hands in front of me and grabbed my shirt and swiftly whisked it off over my head! I turned to look at him and he rotated me around from my stomach to my back. I looked up and suddenly found myself looking up into his beautiful blue iris. I put my arms around his neck and he lowered his naked skin onto my flesh. Dennis kissed so well. I loved to kiss. Especially when the other person is a good kisser too. Whether they are a good kisser or not determines whether they are good in bed or not, usually. We continued to kiss for a while. His skin felt so good rubbing against my skin. His hands were caressing my hair and my ass. I was totally enveloped in the moment. I was getting so hot. I wanted Dennis! I loved feeling his tight, muscular chest on top of my chest. Dennis stood up on his knees again. He bent over and unzipped my slacks and insisted he was going to give me a body massage.

"So now I am going to massage your legs. I will start with the feet though and work my way up." He informed me.

"Who am I to argue with that?" I asked sarcastically. Dennis placed one of my feet on his thigh. I was lying on my back, he started to massage the base of my foot. His fingers working down to the toes, made it feel like stress was being squeezed out of my body like toothpaste from a tube. He took his time and massaged each one of my toes and every muscle in my legs. His hands were massaging my thighs and he placed my smooth toned legs into a position to where they were slightly bent at the knee feet on the floor and approximately 8 inches apart. He kneeled with his knees between my feet. His hands were on each side of me massaging my outer thighs and glutes. Dennis slowly started working his thumbs around my inner thighs and pussy lips. He started massaging the inner lips with his thumbs. He eventually made his way into the labia folds and stuck one thumb up my now wet pussy, just teasing me. He slid his arms around to the other side of my legs massaging my outer thighs. Dennis then proceeded to bow down closer towards my vagina. He got on his hands and knees and licked my pussy apart. He opened my lips with his fingertips exposing my soft, pink clit. He stuck his tongue way out of his mouth and made it come to a point. He used only the very tip of his long tongue to tickle my clit and wet my pussy. He swirled just the tip and flicked it back and forth on my engorged clitoris. I was in another world at this time. He made me feel so wonderful. He kept flicking his tongue on my clit! I was going to cum!

"Uhhh. AHHHHHHHHH!" I sang out in unspeakable pleasure. I came so quickly!

Dennis climbed up to me and kissed me on my lips so I could taste myself. He slipped his swollen dick into my soaking wet hole. Dennis was moving in and out of my hot and wet pussy. I looked down my taught torso and at his six-pack abs and could see his dick going in and out of my pussy. Our skins slapping, stomachs smacking, the cock slurping, made for pure animal lovemaking. I felt Dennis' sensitivity. Dennis was about to reach climax! I could feel his dick swell up and he stopped pumping his body into me. Then, I could feel the thrust of the sperm as he ejaculated. It was wonderful. I was in total oblivion. Dennis dropped himself onto me out of pure exhaustion. I put my arms around him and kissed the side of his neck. Dennis' neck was soaked in hot, clammy sweat. It tasted sweet. Dennis was breathing very hard right into my ear as he lay on top of me. We just stayed there in total exhaustion until we fell asleep.

I talked with Maria the next day after I picked up the kids and she told me that after I left, her cousins, Juan and Pablo went out clubbing and Juan got into a huge fight with some guy and the other guy broke Juan's nose! Juan was in the hospital! I guess there is poetic justice after all!

The children and I drove home from the family ordeal. It was good to be home. Thank goodness the holidays are almost over. Now, all I need to endure is New Year's Eve at home alone.

I had no time to waste though. I called Jack on the phone to tell him I hired a private detective.

"I would like to meet and review the investigator's credentials." Jack informed me.

"Of course! I have called one of the best in the city. His name is Martin Powers. Aldo recommended him to me," I said. " I have a meeting scheduled with him the first day after the holidays at 10:00 A.M. Will you be there?"

"Yes. I will be there. How much of a retainer did he ask you for?" Jack kept inquiring.

I replied, "Well, to start with, I know his price starts at $10,000.00. Then as his expenses go beyond that, he will bill more."

"I hope he provides receipts. Is he good? What cases has he solved?" Jack kept asking.

"Ask him tomorrow at the meeting, Jack. OK?" I stopped him cold. " I have to go. I have a lot of things to get done. I'll see you tomorrow."

"See you then," Jack said. "Bye."

"Bye," I closed and hung up. All I could do right now was sit at home with my children and wait for tomorrow.

We all played Monopoly that evening. We had some quiet, quality time. I needed some time with my kids. It was a long time coming, it seemed. My son tried to ask me some questions about that morning when the police came. I told him it was a huge mistake on the cops' part and he shouldn't worry about it. The truth will eventually be revealed. I also informed my children that I will be hiring a private investigator to find out who or what really happened. If he can't find out exactly what happened, then I must find a way to show that I didn't do anything to harm their father.

New Year's Eve has arrived. I have never been so bummed out on a New Year's Eve in my life. Of course, I had no date. Dennis lived out of town and I know he has other girl friends. We had not reached that serious point. We both knew it wouldn't get there because of the distance. I am far from ready for a relationship with anyone! So, because of this frame of mind I am in, I have no date. Oh well, that's life. So, I stayed home with my children and bought some sparkling grape juice for them and some champagne for me. We watched the ball drop in New York City on the television. At midnight, my children and I held our glasses high and made a toast to Daddy.

"We all miss you very much. No dollar amount in this world could ever replace the love you have shown us. We love you and to a new joyful year!" We clicked our glasses together and sipped our drinks. We watched a little more of the television live celebrations from New York City. I told the children to get to bed. It was getting much too late. I didn't feel much like celebrating too much anyway. The kids went to brush their teeth and get ready for sleep. I followed upstairs to make sure things were getting done. I peeked through their doors. They each were in bed and almost asleep. I could not believe it. But then again, they were tired. I went to my bedroom suite to get ready to retire. I got undressed and went into the adjoining bathroom to clean up. I stood naked in front of the mirror over the sink in the bathroom. My face looked tired. My body looked very taught and toned. I started the water in the shower. I held my hand out under the water to feel if the temperature is where I want it to be. I entered the shower and turned around to get my entire head wet. The water enveloped my scalp like warm ooze trickling my hair, my body slowly coated with this warm smooth liquid. I felt so lonely in this big house with no one but my two sleeping children and me. It was too quiet. The quietness made me feel that much more alone. I washed my hair and my body and began to shave my legs. I shaved my bikini area. I remembered the time Ralph shaved all of my pussy hair. That was such an awesome fuck fest in the shower. I got horny thinking about it. I shaved my pussy hair bald. I soaped my vagina all up again. I started to play with my clit. I took my other hand and placed my index finger on my side of my pussy lips and my middle finger on the other side. I pulled up with that hand ever so gently until the lips were spread exposing the inner pussy lips and clitoris. I could feel with the other hand's index finger the amount of exposure the swollen clitoris was getting. I took my index finger and swirled all around the clitoris and making my way in and out of my wet pussy hole. My newly shaven pussy felt so soft and smooth like a little baby butt. I played with my clit. I started to think about that time when Ralph shaved my pussy for me while we both took a shower at the same time. Ralph sat on the floor of the shower so he could be eye level with my pussy to enable him to shave it more closely. The water rolling down my skin and tickling through the lips of my vagina, felt like it did when Ralph was caressing his tongue across my clit that day. I was playing with my clit some more and getting so hot. I remembered Ralph sitting in the shower with his hands placed on the back of my ass. As he sat facing me on the floor of the shower, pulling my pussy into his mouth, I could almost feel his tongue on my clit. My bald, virgin like pussy went into his soft shaven mouth. The lips of his mouth kissed my pussy lips and he proceeded to French kiss my pussy. He took his long tongue and swirled it around my clit. The feeling was so much more intense with my pussy shaven. I could feel every movement of his tongue and lips and even his nose movements were intense. I started to think of that in my mind and continued to play with myself. I started to come almost immediately. I had the most intense orgasm, almost as good as the ones I had with Ralph. Only Ralph would hold my hands and control my body so I could do nothing but stand there and keep having orgasms! But after a while, one tends to get tired and frankly my muscles cannot take being so tight for such a time. After a while it just starts to tickle and I can do nothing but laugh like a mad person. I imagined all of this while I was still cumming like a mad woman, my hips thrusting in and out uncontrollably.

    I was screaming, "Fuck me! Stop! Oh my God! This is why I married you! Auughhh!" I had to stop. I was out of breath and energy. I finished my shower and rinsed off. I turned the water off and walked out of the shower and grabbed a towel. I stood there thinking about the wonderful orgasm I had. I also thought that it was so wonderful because

They think I Killed My Husband!

I was thinking of Ralph. I really must have loved him. I started to think of him and became immediately satisfied. It was wonderful to think of Ralph and experience pure love filled ecstasy again. But the truth still remained, Ralph was not really here, I missed him so much. I laughed with the remembrance of being totally in love and cried because he would never physically be with me again. My heart was literally torn apart. Happy New Year.

Chapter 6

New Year
New Discoveries

The holidays were over and it was time for everyone to get back to work. I wanted introduce Jack to a Private Investigator that came recommended. My appointment with him was scheduled for 10:00 A.M. I awakened early that morning to give myself some extra time. I had to get the kids off to school too. They were used to sleeping in and it was going to be difficult the first day after Christmas vacation. I had gotten them to school and I had some things to discuss with Jack before meeting with the detective. I had to know the variety of outcomes of what my future could be.

Jack and I were to meet at Denny's after I dropped the kids off at school. I arrived before Jack. The middle-aged, graying brunette Hostess seated me in a booth.

"Would you like something to drink while you are waiting? Coffee? Orange juice?" The slightly heavy, scowl faced young waitress asked me as she placed the menus on the table.

"Yes, please. Coffee would be great. Thank you," I answered looking over the menu.

Just as the waitress went to get my coffee, Jack arrived. I waved my arm in the air over the menu so Jack could spot me a bit easier.

"Good morning," Jack said to me as he was scrunching into the booth seat. Jack's suit looked like the surface of the deep sea, shimmering like an expensive set of navy silk sheets.

"Nice suit," I told him.

"Thanks. It's Armani," he replied as he started to look over the menu.

"Now, I see where my money is going," I stated. The waitress came back with my coffee.

"Can I get you something to drink?" The skanky, middle aged waitress that smelled of cigarettes asked, looking at Jack.

"Yes. I think I am ready to order too," Jack answered her, closing the menu and placing it on the table. "I'll have the 'Steak and eggs, toast and orange juice."

"I'll have the bacon and eggs and some O.J." I told her. She gathered the menus abruptly and left the table.

"Do you have any ideas or leads of who might have wanted your husband dead?" Jack asked looking up at me with his eyebrows raised.

"Well, I have been doing some thinking," I replied.

"Okay, let's hear it," Jack said leaning back and folding his arms for the moment.

"I would like to see a second blood test result, with a lab I hire." I stated staring into his eyes with confidence. "I think that would eliminate the possibility that the results were mixed or confirm it."

"It will take a process of elimination of every possibility." Jack confirmed. "This detective will be here at 10? Is this okay to have the meeting here, Pam?" Jack asked.

"Of course." I responded as the waitress arrived with a tray of breakfast and juice for us to eat. I quickly got quiet and sat back in the booth to make room for the waitress to place the plates down.

"Can I get you anything else?" she asked before she left us alone to eat our breakfast and finish our conversation.

As there was a notion of objection from him, Jack shook his head, no.

"Enjoy," the waitress said as she walked away from the table.

"So, what is your next step if the test results come back

from the lab the same as the first results?" Jack interrogated me to prepare me for all options.

"Well, that's where Martin Powers will come in. A very good friend of mine recommended him to me. He's getting paid enough, so he should at least earn his pay," I responded back to Jack while taking a sip of coffee. "We need to go through everything. Maybe Ralph was involved in something I didn't know about. I don't know how. We were together 85% of the time."

Jack didn't have much to say after that. He was more than likely trying to think if he remembered Ralph talking to someone or about something unusual. Jack just sat eating his breakfast with a bewildered look on his face.

We finished our breakfast and tried to think of anything that made sense. Was Ralph a victim of a random crime? Was he doing something wrong? What could be so terribly wrong that someone would want him dead? Would I be convicted because of circumstantial evidence? I hoped this Martin Powers could find the answers to these questions.

The waitress came to refill my coffee and she picked up the plates we finished. Just as she left the table area, a seemingly young and very handsome man walked into the restaurant. He had short, dark, jet black hair with the eyes that looked like I was staring into lovely delicious dark chocolate mousse pie. He was tall with a medium build. He wasn't too overly muscular which told me that he wasn't a narcissist. He wore a nice suit, but not too extravagant. He started to walk towards our table. I couldn't help to stare. His confidence and charisma captivated my entire being. I must have been staring very intensely. His eyes finally met mine. I still couldn't stop looking into his eyes. We maintained eye contact for a few seconds until he arrived to Jack's and my table.

"Pam?" this incredibly handsome man asked as he stopped and turned to me. I looked down with almost embarrassment. I am hiring this guy to investigate everything about my life.

"I wish he would investigate everything of mine." I

thought to myself. I had to control myself. I am going to have to keep this on a professional level.

Jack stood up to shake this man's hand. "I am Jack, her lawyer. I am sure Pam has told you I would be here this morning."

I remained sitting and looked up at Martin Powers.

"Pleased to meet you Mr. Powers," I stated trying not to drown in those deliciously wet black eyes that were encircled with the longest lashes I have ever seen on a man. We only talked on the phone. We haven't actually met yet.

"Likewise," Mr. Powers replied. "You may call me Marty." Martin stated while smiling and gazing back into my eyes.

"Okay, Marty. So, how good are you?" I asked with a slight smirk on my face. Marty looked up at me with a surprised look on his face. We both felt the attraction for each other and that question could have taken in more than one meaning.

"Investigating, I mean." I corrected out loud.

"Marty, how many cases have you solved and who do you work for?" Jack interrogated.

"Oh, I have been involved with many cases where I had to go under cover. These were difficult cases and some I had to do some sub-contracting work for the F.B.I. I speak 7 different languages, including German, Arabic, Latin, Japanese, Spanish, English, and French. I can pick up Italian somewhat, but am not totally fluent in that language. But, I am working on it," Marty told me with a touch of arrogance.

"Well, people that work at Disney can speak 2-4 languages. I don't want to cut you down, but I need a bit more reassurance than languages and working for the F.B.I. Have you been involved in any murder cases? Was there a client of yours that was falsely accused because of circumstantial evidence? Did you help them?" I asked for more information.

"I have had a couple of cases like that, but those cases don't happen too often. I am glad for that, too. I wouldn't want anyone to go through all of that and be innocent. I would tell you more about the work I did for the Federal Bureau of Investigation and the C.I.A. but then I would have to kill you. I sure wouldn't want to do that." Marty stated staring compassionately into my eyes. All I could do was look down and blush a bit nervously.

"All right, people. Let's keep this strictly at a business level, shall we?" Jack spoke out abruptly while waving his hands between us.

"Of course, Jack. I only do work professionally," Marty defended himself. "My only concern is to find out the truth. If Mrs. Garcia is speaking the truth and she is in fact innocent, I will do everything in my power to prove that she did not kill her husband. Maybe even find out the truth of who the real murderer is."

"Good," I said with a nod. "Then, what do we need to do to get started? My trial date is in 6 months. We better work fast. What do you need from me?" I asked Mr. Powers.

"Well, for starters, I need to ask you a lot of questions. Could I go through some of the bills and receipts of the business, you know, bank statements, stuff like that? I need to gather intelligence, as much as possible. Mrs. Garcia, is there anyone you know of that would like to see your husband dead?" Marty inquired as reached over the table and held my hand as a friend would.

Jack told Marty before I had a chance to even think. "I am sure there could be a number of people that would like to see him shot, maybe even dead. If he didn't like someone, they knew it. Ralph didn't make this kind of money being nice to people," I just looked at Jack very surprised.

"I have to agree with Jack. I loved Ralph with all of my heart and he loved me, but he could be 'Class -A - Son of a Bitch' when he wanted to. He did a lot of importing and exporting. That was our business. I did my little business when he started in it," I confirmed.

"And what was that?" Marty wanted to know.

"I have a couple of gold plate machines. One has big dipping vats and the other is a brush on technique." I plated jewelry, automotive parts, wheels, motorcycle parts, belt buckles, tea sets, wires, you name it."

"Did your husband know how to use these machines?" Marty needed to know for some reason.

"I really don't know. He has watched me work before, but I don't know how much attention he paid. I had to stop doing it to help him with the importing and exporting. His business started to grow so quickly and he caught one person stealing almost immediately. So, I felt almost obligated to help out especially when it was concerning the money. I started working as the office manager within months." I informed Marty with a little bit of history.

"So, what happened to the person that he caught stealing?" Marty returned verbally.

"Yeah, Pam, I didn't know about this. Did Ralph go ballistic or what?" Jack wanted to know.

"Oh, he just fired the guy as soon as he found out. The guy was turning in receipts for personal items as well as business and claiming them all for business. He would go out to dinner every night on the company credit cards and when he would ask to be reimbursed, he would go to the petty cash and reimburse himself and take a little extra. Later, the accountant found that he turned in receipts for cash that he charged on the company credit cards. He asked for an extra receipt from the restaurants. All of this and we paid him a $50,000.00 annual salary plus commission. So this guy was grossing approximately $120,000.00 per year plus all of these expenses paid, company car, gas & insurance. The only thing he had to pay for himself was mortgage and utilities. So, of course Ralph was extremely upset. I don't live that carefree. I know we took the proof and had him convicted of theft. I don't know if he's out or not. I really do not care."

"Oh, but that's where you are wrong, Pam. You must find out! This could be the guy that killed your husband and wanted to frame you so you couldn't enjoy the rest of your life either. What he did was a white-collar crime. Even though he was convicted, he may be sentenced to 5-10 years and out in two. You did say this all went down a couple of years ago right?" Marty interrogated further.

"Well, five or seven years ago. I guess if you put it like that, he could very well be out by now or before Ralph was killed."

"Hmmmm, I need to look at all of the files at your office. I need to go through everything from as far back as 7 years until now." Marty suggested.

Before I could answer, the waitress came by our table to give us our check. "Oh, I am sorry I didn't realize you had another person joining you. Could I get you all anything else? Would you like some juice or coffee sir?"

Marty looked up at the waitress and agreed to a cup of coffee. The waitress proceeded with her work and left to retrieve the coffee.

I replied to Marty and Jack, "I have sold the business. I don't know if I can get the accessibility to the records that easily."

Jack answered, "Of course you can. I can call up the new owner and ask him and if he refuses, all I have to do is subpoena the records. That is not hard to do at all."

The waitress came back with Marty's coffee and another pot of coffee to give Jack and myself refills too.

"Aren't you the woman that is accused of poisoning her husband here in town? I read all about it in the paper. I told the girls in the kitchen it was you, but they wouldn't believe me."

"Well, I am sorry you are mistaken." I softly and casually answered her question.

"Oh. I'm sorry. I didn't mean anything by that," the waitress replied.

"Could we have the check?" Jack asked coldly.

Almost embarrassed, the waitress answered, "I'll get it right now, sir." She quickly turned and went to get the check.

"Oh, how I hate that. Well, there goes her tip!" I stated raising my hand to my eyebrow and rested my elbow on the table hiding my face. "How the press ever found out about all of this I will never know. I couldn't believe all of them at my house when I got out of jail. Remember, Jack?" I continued saying and laying my arm down to the table.

"Yeah, I remember." Jack stated. " I think it is public record and those vultures get the news by any means possible. Anything for a story, the juicier, the better, the more people will love and buy it."

We all finished with our coffee and took care of the tab and left. Jack said the first thing that he would do is request the records from the banks, the accountant and from the company. He and Martin Powers would be working closely together. I offered my assistance whenever they needed. I also informed them that whatever they found, I wanted to know immediately.

I returned home to look for something. I didn't know what I was looking for, but I had to try to find something, anything that I may have overlooked. The kids arrived home from their first day back after vacation. They said it was good to be back in school with all of their friends again. I was glad to hear they were doing so well considering everything they have had to go through. Every time I looked at my daughter, it was like seeing Ralph's face again. She looks so much like him. I don't know what I would do without my children.

Chapter 7

The Investigation Begins

Jack and Martin have been doing an extensive amount of information gathering from the business over the next few weeks. They piled up the information at Jack's office in boxes and files. After gathering everything they could think of for now, they asked me to help them look for anything out of the ordinary. After all, I knew best of what could be peculiar in the records. We looked through the accounting ledgers and the bank statements. We sat for hours in Jack's firm's conference room going through all of the papers and memos. We compared them to each other and most everything matched. There were some miscellaneous transactions that really didn't matter. But, then there were some checks that were $1000.00 to $5000.00 written to the warehouse manager for cash. I looked at the back to see who cashed them. The checks written to cash were signed by Ralph and one signed by the shipping manager.

"Now, why would the shipping manager be getting extra money from Ralph?" this got my curiosity going.

"What? Did you find something?" Marty asked me while putting down his pile of papers he was going through.

"Maybe. It could be nothing. There are some checks made to cash that Ralph signed. They are small amounts though. The question I have is why did our shipping manager get a couple of them? I know Ralph would get cash all of the time. I guess I need to ask the shipping manager Enrique, why he signed checks for cash or even received checks that weren't payroll checks. I checked the payroll and Enrique received his paychecks. I had no clue he was getting more than his payroll checks. But what on earth could these checks be for?" I informed Marty.

"Well, I guess that is something I need to find out Mrs. Garcia. That is why you hired me," Martin replied. "Is this Enrique fellow still working with the company? Even after you sold it? I need to know more about this person that was caught stealing when you first started working."

" I really don't know. I guess you need to go and find out. Earn your money," I told Marty.

Marty took the information about the checks and the information with him. He told me he would study it all tonight and make a list of things he will need to investigate for the next few days. Later that evening, Sherry called to find out what was happening lately. We talked for a while and I updated her on the case and what Mr. Powers was planning on doing. We didn't have too much to say. However, we did make some plans to go out this weekend.

The next day, I continued to look through the files of the business. I also made some copies of 'Bill of Ladings' from the warehouse and more checks that I found made to cash and to Enrique Gonzalez. I could not figure that out. Ralph had made out the checks. It wasn't like Enrique was stealing. Why would Ralph give him so much money? What did he have over Ralph? Was he blackmailing him for some reason? If so, what was the reason? I knew everything Ralph did, or so I thought. What was going on? This is getting too weird.

"Where else did Ralph have stuff?" I thought to myself. "The safety deposit box! I don't want to tell him about the stuff I found, yet. I forgot all about it, actually."

Ralph and I have a joint box at the bank. I had put the things I found in Ralph's own box into the old joint box we had. I went down to the bank later that day. I walked into the bank. I approached the young brunette with warm brown eyes in the banker's suit with her hair resting on her shoulders. I told the attractive teller that I needed to get into my safety deposit box. We have it mostly to keep kids' Government bonds and my jewelry in. He really didn't have anything he wanted to keep in it. It had the usual stuff in it. It didn't have anything missing and I couldn't seem to find anything more.

I continued looking through the box. I dumped everything out onto the table. There was an envelope that fell out I hadn't seen before. I opened it up and it had airline tickets and a fake passport to match. Then I saw something sort of sticking up and taped on the roof of the box. I turned it towards the light so I may see it better. Using my hand, I grabbed the item and pulled it from the tape. It was a key. It appeared to be another safety deposit box key. Perhaps a duplicate key. It had the numbers 524 on it. I am figuring that this is the box number. "But, where?" I asked myself. "Is the bank even in this country?"

The key looked pretty uniform as any other safety deposit key. I kept the key and put everything else back into the box and closed the lid. I opened the door and the teller that escorted me in, came to my aid to help me back into the vault and lock up the box.

So many questions raced through my mind. "Why was my beloved husband hiding things from me? I thought I knew him better than that." I thought to myself. I couldn't even begin to know where that key came from. Maybe it was in Egypt and that is the reason for the currency.

I turned to the young bank teller as I wrote my time out in the log sheet of the Safety Deposit boxes, "Did Ralph have another lock box here?" I asked.

"No, I don't believe he did, but I can check the computer to make sure," the teller answered.

"Please do," I commanded. As she went over to sit down at the computer to find out if Ralph had another lock box. All I could think about is finding what this is all about. I have to recheck everything with a fine tooth-comb. The credit card statements and where were those checks for cash cashed?

The teller looked up to me and answered, "No, Mrs. Garcia. Ralph did not have another lock box here at this bank. Have you tried any other banks you do business with?"

"I guess I will have to," I replied.

After leaving the bank, I took the key out of my pocket and looked at it. "This must be the key to all of the answers. I better not even tell anyone about it yet." I thought to myself.

Later that day, I received a phone call from Martin Powers. He informed me of some rather interesting news.

"Hey Pam. I found out something very interesting," Marty told me over the phone.

"Yea? What might that be?" I wanted to know.

"Well, you know your shipping manager for the import-export business?" Marty inquired.

"What about him?" I demanded.

"I went to ask him about those checks we found. I figured that could eliminate a lot of questions if he were willing to answer them. So, I went down to the company shipping dock and I was informed that he disappeared just after you left the company," Marty continued.

"What do you mean, he disappeared? You mean, no one knows where he is? You mean that no one from the business has heard from him," I retaliated?

"No. I mean he has disappeared. Some of the coworkers were his friends and one guy I talked to, said Enrique left his wife and kids. They don't know where he is," Marty confirmed.

"Oh, my! How awful! Unless she really does know or knows he'll be back for her. I bet she may know where he is. Have you spoken to her yet? I think we need to go right now!" I demanded. "What's the address?"

"1861 Liberty Street. See you there in 30 minutes." Marty instigated.

"Cool. I'll see you there!" I said, then hung up the cell

phone.

I immediately turned around to go to the house. We both arrived at the same time. Marty and I walked up to the front door together and knocked. A very nice Hispanic woman opened the door. She looked at me and asked Marty and me to come in. We followed her lead for now.

"Do you know the whereabouts of your husband, Mrs. Gonzalez?" Marty abruptly asked the wife of Enrique.

"No, I do not. Do you think I would tell you even if I did?" Mrs. Gonzalez asked us.

"Well, we were hoping you might. Mrs. Gonzalez, did you know that your husband took large amounts of money from my husband that weren't payroll checks?" I asked Mrs. Gonzalez.

"What do you mean? The only money I ever saw were his paychecks," she told me.

"Well, Mrs. Gonzalez, your husband took thousands of dollars from my husband in the form of cash, checks for cash and who knows how else. Do you know why my husband would give him this money? Was he buying something from Enrique? If so, what?" I bombarded her with questions.

"Yo no se! Por favor!" Mrs. Gonzalez screamed!

I could see she was a bit overwhelmed. I believe she didn't know about the extra money. Now, where would Enrique go with thousands of dollars in hand? "Where did he go?" I screamed back!

"He told me not to tell! Why should I say anything to you anyway?" Mrs. Gonzalez answered.

"What aren't you supposed to tell, Mrs. Gonzalez?" Marty interrogated. "Did he take a plane, a train, a bus, what?"

"No! He just left one night. He got a small bag with some things and said he had to leave for a while. Then he walked out of the door and I looked out the window and he just kept walking down the street to the corner. Then I don't know where he went from there." Mrs. Gonzalez stated.

"Do you know if he is coming back?" Marty asked.

"He said he was, but now I don't know if I should believe that. I didn't know about the extra money or how he got it. He had been going out sometimes in the middle of the week and wouldn't tell me where he would be, exactly. He just said he would be out with the boys. Now, I wonder where he really was." Mrs. Gonzalez added.

"Who were some of the 'boys' he said he was with? Maybe they may know where he is or we might find something out." I hunched. "Do you know if he knew Jerry Smith? He worked for me about 4 or 5 years ago. I had to fire and convict him of embezzling money from the company."

"No. I never heard him speak of a Jerry Smith." Mrs. Gonzalez confirmed.

"Maybe he used another name, Pam." Martin stated.

"What do you mean?" I asked.

"Well, 'Jerry Smith' is such a common name. How long did he work for you? Did you thoroughly check him out when you hired him," Martin questioned me?

"Mrs. Gonzalez, we will be in touch. Thank you so much." I started shaking her hand. I looked at Martin and shook my head towards the door. Martin got the hint and thanked Mrs. Gonzalez as well, and shook her hand. We left the house and started talking about 'Jerry Smith'.

"Follow me to my office, Mrs. Garcia. We need to get some information about this guy. I need my computer to do so. Do you have any records of his on file?" Martin requested.

"I can get a copy of his file from the office. I'll call right now and we can swing by there before going to your office." I persuaded.

"Sounds like a plan. Let's go." Martin said as he got into his car. I followed in my car and while driving I called the office and the secretary was more than happy to oblige. We picked up the copies at the office then proceeded to Marty's office. We arrived to Marty's small office downtown and he immediately hopped onto the computer and got online to obtain current information about this guy using the records we had available. The secretary at my former company gave me copies of his driver's license and social security card that Marty would need to gain access of information needed. He has access to the police files and court files and DMV files since he is a private investigator. He put in the information on all of the online services that he could and retrieved information about this 'Jerry Smith'. It turns out that this 'Jerry Smith' had alias's a page long. He had some Hispanic names, Middle-Eastern names, and Italian names.

"I remember he had dark olive colored skin with jet black hair. I just figured him for Hispanic. Enrique recommended him. I trusted Enrique. But, when this Jerry Smith character starting stealing from the company, I had to report it and press charges." I told Marty in his office.

"Would this guy seem the type that would come back and take revenge on you or your husband?" Marty inquired.

"Well, possibly. But, I didn't see him that night. The night he died. How could we go about finding this guy?" I wanted to know.

"Well, you leave that to me. I will find him and question him." Marty reassured me.

"Can we meet up tomorrow? I need to get with my lawyer. Maybe you could make me a copy of this 'Jerry Smith's' profile." I requested from Marty so I could take it to my lawyer.

"Sure. Why don't we make arrangements to go there together?" Marty suggested.

"Okay. I guess if you insist. I don't see, why not. I just thought you might have something else you may have to take care of." I replied.

"Well, when is your trial?" Marty asked me.

"It's not for a few months. You know the courts are so full and they need time for information gathering." I answered instantly.

"I do have some other things to do. I am going to call your former company and request the information on Enrique Gonzalez also. I'll just have them fax it to me. I need to run some reports on him too. Especially since you said that he recommended this Jerry Smith character." Marty stated.

They think I Killed My Husband!

"That makes sense. So, you will let me know in the morning? I'll call Jack in the mean time. I need to let him know when I will be there or when he will be available." I said as I started to walk out the door of Marty's office.

Then Marty yelled and said he would take care of this for me and not to worry.

I stopped and looked at him and said, "I'm counting on it."

I went home to be with my children that night. They were already home from school. Rita was still there cleaning the house. I spoke to her briefly. I didn't want to divulge too much information to the petite blonde hair woman. Even though she posed as no threat, people talk. One never knows whom another will talk to. She was finishing up for the day and asked if I would like to chill out with her for a while.

"Let me buy you a drink." I told her since she had been working so hard at cleaning my house and taking care of my children. The children were upstairs in their rooms doing their homework and I escorted Rita to the bar and game room in my house. I closed and shut the doors and opened up a window. I poured us each a drink of 'Black Label' whiskey from the crystal carafe and made a toast to life and living it to its fullest! I also retrieved a joint from my purse. I walked across the room and sat down in a recliner. I had just opened a window next to the recliner. Rita followed. She sat down on the barstool nearest to the recliner. We both smoked and drank the drink. I was so relaxed. I forgot the world and all of my problems for the time being. Rita was telling me about her insignificant problems. These were huge problems to her, but to me, I felt like she had it lucky to some point. I wasn't really listening to her rambling. My mind was elsewhere. She continued talking about her kids and her husband and I just sat back looking inept of the attention from her. All I could think about was where this 'Jerry Smith' person is and was Enrique Gonzalez with him somewhere? Were they the ones that killed Ralph and for what reason? Where was the safety deposit box located that I had the key for? Should I tell Marty the Private Investigator? Should I

163

just go and try to find it myself. But, whom could I really trust? I needed to get busy tomorrow and find out where this box is and what was in it.

"Hey! Hello? Earth to Pam! Are you there?" Rita said to me snapping her fingers to my face bringing me back to reality.

"I guess that was sort of kicking in." I said, as I shook my head looking at the joint and the drink, regaining my composure. "Everything was going through my head at once. I guess that happens, doesn't it?"

Chapter 8

Following the Signs

Waking up the next morning, I knew I could really trust no one. I did know I needed to find the box that I had a key for. I called several local banks. Not one of the banks in town had his name on the list of having a safety deposit box.

"Where could it be?" I thought to myself. How on earth could I find this needle in a haystack? I started to think. I looked in the safe in our closet to find any clues. I opened the safe and found some airline tickets stubs. The ones you save to accumulate your frequent flyer miles.

"How strange," I thought. If Ralph would save any stubs from going anywhere, he would have had me call them in. Where are these from? I looked at the stubs. These were flights to Egypt! When in the Hell did he go to Egypt, and for what purpose? We never went to Egypt nor did we ever talk about his journey to the country for any reason. That explains the money in the safety deposit box at the bank. This is getting a little interesting now. What was Ralph in to? Maybe his safety deposit box was there?

I got on the computer, on the Internet to be exact, to lookup banks in Egypt. I needed some information about what may be over there. Would he even have the box in his name? Would they even honor a death certificate and allow me into the box with the key? Is the box in fact over there? What was his business there? Was it another woman? Now I am absolutely insane. I found some telephone numbers off of the

Internet of some banks in Egypt. I began making some phone calls. It was very difficult. Most of the employees did not speak English. I had to wait until they could find someone that could help me. Finally, I was able to get someone on the phone at one bank. No one had any account or a box in Ralph's name. I tried at least a half a dozen banks in Egypt. Then one lady said, there is a box in his name. I asked when was the last time he had been in that box. She told me about six months ago. It matched the dates of the airline tickets that I had! She also added there was some trouble with his box about a week ago, however.

"Trouble? What kind of trouble?" I asked.

"There was a man, that looked similar to Mr. Garcia that wanted into the box. He claimed to be Mr. Garcia and had lost his key. But, we asked him to sign his name and give his fingerprint. Apparently, he did not realize we kept fingerprints on file. He had proper identification and his signature nearly fooled one new girl. But, a manager that personally knew Mr. Garcia stopped this man from getting into the box and he fled before the proper authorities could arrive," the woman informed me over the phone.

"Did you see this man? Was this man caught on any type of surveillance film?" I inquired.

"No, I did not personally see this man. I am sure we did get him on surveillance, though. I would have to know exactly who you are and see some sort of identification from you Ma'am," the woman said.

"I am in the states. I was his wife," I replied.

"Was?" she asked.

"Yes, someone murdered my husband and I must find out who and why," I told her. "What is your name?"

"My name is Layla. I work in the main section of the bank," she answered.

"Thank you so much for all of your help," I told her. "I will be arriving there within the next two days."

"Just so you know Mrs. Garcia, Mr. Garcia put your name on the box too. You should have no trouble if you have the key. We just don't have your signature on file. It is a fairly new box that Mr. Garcia said that he would have a duplicate card for you to sign and would send it to us." Layla informed me.

"That is very strange. He never spoke to me about it. How old is the box?" I asked.

"Oh, it is just less than a year or so. How long has Mr. Garcia been gone?" Layla inquired.

"Quite a few months now. I just found this key recently. I need to find out some answers." I told her.

"Well, we will be here when you are ready," she told me.

"Thank you so much again for all of your help." I thanked her and said good bye.

"This is strange," I said to myself. " I guess this must be the key to that box. Now, maybe I better put it in a very safe place. Apparently, it must be valuable." I tried to think of a place to put the key in case of a burglary or the police or should I even tell my P. I., Marty about my newly found information? I can't go anywhere. My trial will be coming up and with my bond posted, I literally can't go anywhere. I will have to wait. But, what is in the box? What is in there may prove my innocence. Maybe I should tell Marty. I don't know. I better sleep on it.

Later that week, I was to attend a fundraiser at the Mercedes store. The charity was for Canine Companions and they also had an art show and a famous pianist and singer for entertainment. It was a wonderful social event. I brought a cute doll for a present. There was lots of networking done and good food and wine devoured. I had on my designer dress and pumps. Simple black and white attire, simple yet very classy and chic. The event was great to meet some people that were in need of the beautiful Golden Retrievers that were exceptionally trained doing helpful jobs. What awesome animals and well behaved! These dogs were to these people what a seeing-eye dog is to a blind person. If someone is incapable of retrieving something or if these dogs can do what this person can not and enable a state of independence for this person, otherwise wouldn't be able to be independent, what a wonderful gift these animals are! So, to say the least this night was a truly enlightening evening. I went home that night a little more humbled. I didn't feel quite so bad about being me. I felt even more guilty and ashamed of how selfish I have been. Always wondering, "Why me?" I was always thinking that I had gone through the worst stuff that a human being could possible go through. No one could possibly have it as bad as this. What could be worse? How awful of me to be so self absorbed! I have so much to be thankful for! I have my health, my children, money, my home and so far my freedom. How awful it would be to be confined in a wheelchair for the rest of your life. I know one would just have to eventually accept and deal with it. Yea, like I am dealing with the loss of my husband, but still, even worse than that, would be your physical body loss. I would think, somewhere between that, would be losing your kids and losing your spouse.

    I asked the valet for my car, so I could retire for the evening. He most courteously obliged. I stood waiting in my high heels and my dress for my Benz. He pulled it around and I gave him a tip and I slid behind the wheel and drove home.

    I arrived at the gate of my house. The gate wouldn't open up for some reason. I kept pressing the button, but it wouldn't open. I used the intercom to call the kids and the baby sitter, but it was around 11:30 at night and they were asleep. I never even showed the baby sitter where the button was, let alone how to use it. I opened the car door and stepped out of the car. As I stood up, I felt a hand grab my waist and another arm around my chest with a blade to my neck!

    "I want that key!" he whispered in my ear with his bad breath.

    "Oh shit." I thought to myself as I almost shit on myself. What am I going to do now? Before I could think, it was dark so I took my spike heel and jammed it into his foot. Then, I spun and turned around with my heel still engaged with his foot, took a step back with my other foot and kneed him in his groin. After he bent down from that incident, I held my hands together like I had a hold of a pole or something, and I gave him a double fisted upward hammer move right into his face. That put him right on his ass with a bloody nose! I then started to take my stiletto shoe and continually kicked him in his balls with the pointy toe. When he could do nothing, I went and pressed the alarm button on the gate control panel and got my cell phone out of my car and started calling the police. I sat down inside my car with the doors locked and the windows up while doing so. I was so scared. I didn't know what to do. I wanted to drive away. Should I tell the police what the guy said to me? I didn't even know if I should tell Marty! Oh, man what am I going to do? Is that guy still out there? Why won't my gate open? Should I just drive away? Will this guy get up and try to bash my windows in if I stay here? When are the cops going to arrive? I was shaking so terribly. My heart was pounding so hard I thought it was going to come out of my chest! Right then, I heard a loud knock on my window! I looked over.

"AAAUUUGGH!" I screamed. "Oh, my God! Thank God, it's you! Fuck! You scared the shit out of me!" It was a local policeman that had arrived in response to my call.

"Are you all right, Ma'am?" The officer asked in a southern, hickish voice.

"Yes. Did you see anyone lying on the driveway out there?" I asked him before getting out of the car.

"Uh, no ma'am. I don't see anyone out here. My partner and I both looked around and neither of us saw anything. I flashed the flashlight around, there is a little bit of blood spots, but that's about it." The officer reassured me.

"Are you sure? Check again, in the bushes and look around some more. I want to be sure that whoever it was, is gone." I told him from the inside of my car screaming through the crack of the window I made by rolling it down a mere half inch.

"All right. I'll look again. But, I didn't see or hear anything," he muttered as he turned around and flashed his flashlight around on the ground some more. This officer was kind of cute. He was short and pudgy with a round face. I couldn't help but crack a smile in this dramatic situation. He looked like I was interrupting his donuts and coffee break.

I sat in the car waiting for him to return. Upon his arrival, he reassured me that there was no one else here.

He asked me, "Are ya sure there was someone here?"

"Of course I'm sure. Do you think I am crazy or something? I was attacked," I yelled as I climbed out my car! "There was a guy here and he attacked me! He grabbed me from behind and threatened me with a knife!" I continued with the slamming of my car door.

"Now, calm down. I didn't mean anything by what I said," the officer stated back to me in a semi state of panic. "Well, where did he go? And why aren't you anymore hurt than you are?"

"I know how to defend myself, thank you very much," I told him proudly. "I used to take Karate. I know how to make someone hurt. I guess he had enough and got out before you guys got here. I guess he must have taken off."

"Would you like to write up a statement Ma'am? We could go down to the station tonight or you could wait until morning and I could keep extra surveillance on the house this evening. It's up to you.

"Oh, I don't know. I'm awfully scared. I don't want to wake my kids up to go down to the station. I don't want to leave them with the baby sitter either. What if he is still out here somewhere just waiting for you to leave? Can't you guys stay here until morning?" I pleaded with the officer.

"Ma'am, I can't do that. We have rounds to make," he told me.

"You mean you have rounds to eat," I snapped back at him sarcastically. He looked at me astonished and wide-eyed. I felt so awful and so presumptuous and selfish after saying that and seeing the look on his face. "I'm sorry. I am just a little out of sorts right now. I don't even know what I am saying. Please forgive me." I begged him. I knew if I was to get any kind of cooperation from the police I needed to be as sweet as I could possibly be.

They think I Killed My Husband!

"Ma'am, that's okay. Do you have someone you can call to stay with you this evening? Or is there somewhere you and your children can go and stay the rest of the night tonight." The officer suggested since he apparently was not going to stay here of course.

"Sure. What was I thinking? Of course you can't stay here. I guess I could call that Private Investigator I hired, Marty. Maybe he can come," I said out loud while I was thinking about it.

"See there, try him. I'm sure you'll even get a bill for it. So, he'll be sure to be right over," the officer reassured me.

"Yes, I'm sure you are right. But, could you stay here until he arrives? I couldn't get my gate open either. I am going to have to try to manually open the gate," I informed the cop as I walked towards my gate. I tried to open it so I could get into my house. I started to push the gate open. It wouldn't budge. It was electric and it seemed that the electricity was not working. "There must be some way to open this thing without electricity," I grunted out loud trying to open it still.

The cop realized what I was trying to do, came over to investigate the situation and asked, "Are you having trouble with that?"

I looked over and up at him and asked, "Ya think?" I looked back down at the ground and let up on the gate. I stood up and looked at the officer and asked him if he had any kind of knowledge of these things.

"No, not really," he replied.

I told him, "They are just like garage door openers. What would you do if there were no electricity to a garage door, except it's a gate? Any ideas?"

"Oh, on a garage door, there is something to release the gears of the chain or cable. Is there something like that on that?" He was talking and peering with his flashlight at the same time. His partner got out of the squad car and started to help. He must have finished writing the report. In the meantime, I had called Marty. He was on his way. There was no way I was going to stay home alone tonight. No way in hell! Maybe

I better tell Marty about the key. One question did enter my mind though, why didn't the gate have power? Were the kids okay?

"Can't you get the gate open?" I pleaded with them. "I have to see if my kids are okay. There could have been more than one guy!"

"We are trying, Ma'am. It doesn't seem do be cooperating though. But, we did find that the wires were cut at the base of the control panel," the officer told me.

"You're kidding!" I exclaimed. "Well, that shouldn't effect the electricity to the gate, should it? Why won't the gate open up?" I kept questioning sarcastically.

Right then, Marty pulled up. He parked his car and got out. He walked up to all of us and asked, "What is going on?"

"Oh, thank God you made it. I am going crazy here. I have to get in and the gate won't open. The wires are cut to the control panel. I have just been attacked with a knife. My kids are in the house and I need to make sure they are okay," I exclaimed dramatically.

"Calm down. Let me look around. Maybe I can help," Marty calmly said to me while grabbing my upper arms so I could focus on him for a moment. I did too. I looked straight into his deep dark eyes and suddenly realized I was going to be all right. Marty let go of my arms and turned to the officers and asked them, "Have you found anything?"

"We have looked everywhere and have been pushing on this gate. It ain't going to open unless we break it. It is so dark out here too, which ain't helpin'." One officer reported.

Marty started to help them look around. It was obvious that by pushing on the gate it was not going anywhere. My next move was to do a human tower with these men and climb over the wall. The three men looked more like the three stooges wandering around in the middle of the night with their flashlights bobbing about. They were even bumping into each other at certain times and scaring one another. I almost forgot how scared I was just moments prior. After computing in my head the information I just assessed, I had to take control of these morons that serve me privately and publicly and tell them what to do.

"All right, you guys! I want you guys over here right now. That's enough. Now, I need to get into my house and I need to do that now! So, what I want you guys to do is to have two of you make like a human ladder out of yourselves and I will climb up and one of you will help me while I climb. I can get to the top of the wall and jump over and down. Then, I can at least get in the house and look for whatever it is we are looking for in the morning. Marty, could you climb up both of the officers too, so I don't have to do this alone? Who knows if there is an accomplice in the house with my children! I am so scared for them right now," I demanded!

"All right, you heard the lady. C'mon guys get into a stance. Well, where would you like us?" one officer questioned.

"Thank you. Now, if you would, stand over here by the wall and the gate. That way I can grab the gate for stability while I climb up. Oh, sir," as I looked over at the other officer, "could you stand next to your partner facing the wall? That's right. Now, I need you both to stand with your feet at shoulder width apart." I commanded while taking my feet and spreading their feet with mine. "Now, bend at the knees a little. Good. Now, I can climb onto your thigh, then grab my hand and I'll climb onto his shoulder, then up onto the wall. Get it?" I reassured myself.

"What?" the one officer asked me.

Marty got a little impatient with the officers as I was too. He immediately repeated what I had said, but also gave a physical demonstration to the officers. They just stood there with their mouths open and looked at him with blank, disturbing looks on their faces. "Do you think you could do that?" Marty blatantly asked them.

"All we could do is try," the officer retaliated. So they got into their positions and I walked over to the officers. They stood there just like the girls from my cheerleading days. I took off my shoes and I put my foot on one man's thigh and stepped up and put the other on the other man's shoulder all the while holding on to the fence and they held my torso to help me as well. Marty came from behind and pushed my behind!

"I don't think that is necessary!" I stated at first, then turned into a scream as the momentum from the push caused me to loose me control. I went up and over the fence before I knew what happened! I fell down on the other side of the fence on my hands and my side of my body and hip and shoulder. I tried rolling a bit, but it was too late. I landed so abruptly, I thought I might have broken my arm. I was set for climbing over myself. I was perfectly capable. I guess Marty just thought he would just push me over, and with my strength added to it, I went flying! "Fuck!" I screamed in pain after coming down with a thud.

"Pam, are you all right?" Marty screamed over the fence.

"Fuck! I don't know. Wait a minute while I check my arm," I moaned in agony from behind the wall while rolling off my arm slowly. I began to wiggle my fingers and move my wrist. My elbow was even able to move a little bit and my shoulder too. It was very painful though, but I don't think I broke anything. "I'm okay! But, I bet my dress is ruined!" I reassured them. "Marty are you going to climb over now?" I asked.

Marty kept trying to climb up the officers the same as I did. The officers couldn't support Marty's weight as easily as they did mine. As soon as Marty tried to put his other foot on to the other officer's shoulder, they would all fall down. They tried once again and the same thing happened. Once again, picture the three stooges. Then, Marty started to look around again.

"What are you guys doing over there? What is taking you so long, Marty? The killer could be hiding over here on this side of the wall you know, ready to pounce on me at any given second!" I exclaimed. Right then, I looked over towards a noise by the gate. The gate was opening just a little. I looked over in fear and suspense. Marty came squeezing through. When I saw him just walk through, I was so mad.

"What the fuck? How did you get through the gate when no one could even budge it open?" I asked him, angrily after being catapulted over the wall and landing in the grass almost breaking my neck.

"Oh, I looked around a little more since the human ladder trick didn't work for me as well as it did for you," he stated.

"Apparently," I replied with a smart-ass attitude as I was still in pain. "Well, how the hell did you get the gate to move?"

"Oh, I went and looked by the gears of the gate and saw within the gears, there was a rock jamming the gears causing them to lock up. So, I removed the rock. The gate still won't move much, but I managed to squeeze through." Marty told me after barely making it through the gate without ripping any clothes he had on.

"How convenient for you. That would have been nice if you could have found that before you catapulted me over the fence and nearly killed me," I scolded him.

"Well, you were too impatient. I had just barely gotten here. I hadn't had a chance to really look at the mechanism of your gate. When I realized I wasn't going to get over the same way you did, I had to find another way. So, I looked at the mechanism of the motor of your gate. That's when I noticed that there was something in the gears lodged so the gate couldn't open," he told me as he bent down to make sure I was okay and to help me up.

I sat up with the help of Marty's strong hand. I looked at him and noticed that my shoulder really hurt and my skirt was torn and my pantyhose had some major runs in them. "Do you think you could get one of the officers to hand my shoes to you through the gate? They are my good Fendi stilettos and don't want to leave them out here over night," I informed him with a demanding attitude. It was bad enough I ruined my outfit, but I was not about to ruin my shoes too. They held up pretty good kicking that guy's ass, so I would like to hang on to them and maybe register them as lethal weapons. Some turn around, I beat up my attacker and my hired private investigator comes and throws me over a wall. Now, I feel like I have been beaten up! How ironic.

"Yea, sure Pam." Marty reassured me. "Anything you want. Hey guys! Could you hand me Pam's shoes through the gate, please?" he asked them. Marty walked over and retrieved my shoes and walked back over to me and helped me up. The officers left and said they would order heightened surveillance through the night and return first thing in the morning. Marty and I walked back to the house together. I felt so scared. I had been so shaken up. The night was so long. I was exhausted.

We made it to the house and Marty opened the front door. He had his gun out and was ready for action. He walked in peering around every corner and checking every room and every closet. We made it to the kids' rooms. They were fine. There wasn't anyone in the house apparently. That was good. I still felt uneasy though. Maybe it was because I was so tired. I went upstairs to get ready for bed. I showed Marty one of the spare bedrooms but he insisted on sleeping on the couch downstairs. So, I gave him some blankets and a pillow and told him thanks and good night.

The next day when I awoke, the baby sitter was already gone and Marty had already fixed the gate before I got up. My kids were still asleep and coffee was already done.

"Good morning," Marty said to me as I walked down the stairs.

"Good morning," I automatically said back, still very tired and sore. "I smelled the coffee and that woke me up. Then I tried to get up and couldn't very easily. I am in so much pain. I feel like I have been run over by a Mack truck!"

Marty looked over at me with my robe on and the early morning pink sun shining in through the window from behind me casting me as a silhouette. As I slowly made my way towards him, my face became more visible. "Wow, you have some scrapes on your cheek. I heard you fall. It sounded like it hurt, did it?" Marty asked me with a little guilt and concern in his voice.

"Yea, it did. I do?" I said, as I reached for my face to confirm the scrapes on my cheek. I felt the pain, but hadn't looked at myself yet. "Someone gave me a push that made me go way over the wall and I landed hard on the ground. I think I landed on my shoulder and face."

"Oh, sorry," Marty stated apologetically.

"Oh, were you the one that gave me the help?" I asked.

"Yes, it was me," Marty confirmed. "I was just trying to help."

I blared back to him. "You almost killed me! I could have broken my neck! I am surprised I didn't! Why did you do that? It wasn't that far. I am perfectly capable, you know."

"Sorry. It was an accident. I got your gate working, by the way. You're welcome. Is there anything you would like to tell me, Pam?" Marty asked moving closer to me. "Why was there someone with a knife at your throat when you are the one being tried for murder?" Marty questioned me as if I was on the witness stand and I hadn't even had my cup of coffee yet!

I stopped and just looked at him with the most-blank expression on my face and told him, "I don't know anything until I've had my coffee." If he didn't buy the dumb act then he knows I am being a smart-ass and I will tell him when I am ready. If he did buy the dumb act, then he is not that bright and he must think I am stupid then I can use that to my advantage to maintain control. I'll find out in a few minutes which. Marty followed me into the kitchen where I poured myself up some coffee.

"I made that, too. You're welcome," Marty announced arrogantly. "How is it? I hope it is not too strong."

"No, it's fine. Thank you." I told him pleasantly. I didn't want to be pushed for further questioning. He pissed me off though and he knows it. But, he did stay the night after all and I will pay him. He did make coffee and fix the gate. "The cops. What about the cops? Aren't the cops coming over this morning to take a statement from me?"

"They should be here sometime," Marty reassured me.

"But, take advantage that they aren't here yet. Drink

your coffee and sit down and relax. I'm sure you could use it." So, I sat down wondering if I should tell Marty about the key or not. I had already mentioned the attacker. Should I talk about the words he said to me about the key? That would mean I would have to talk about the key. Something told me I better not for now. Something else told me that I better call Jack and have him here when the police question me or take my statement for their report.

Later, the police arrived. I told them I wasn't going to do any business until my attorney arrived. They got a little pissed, but so what? They are going to have to wait a few minutes. I offered them coffee while I filled out my story of the report. If they wanted it formally, they were going to wait for my attorney to proofread it and make sure it's okay, just as a precaution.

The kids came downstairs and saw my face. "Mommy, mommy! What happened? Your face is all scratched up! Are you okay? Why are the police here?" They both said at different times so it sounded like a chaotic mess of words that only added to the pain already going on inside of my head. They both ran and gave me a hug. I hugged them both. I assured them I was fine and everything was going to be okay.

Everything was fine for a while. I continued to investigate this Enrique Gonzalez and Jerry Smith characters. Where were they? Could one of them have been my attacker? Why did they want the key and how does someone know about it and the fact that I have it? All of these questions I have to find the answers to. I have to do it alone. I can't trust anyone, not even Marty. He thinks I am too stupid to have premeditated any plan to kill anyone. Just on that note, he thinks I am innocent. However, he believes of my innocence, I really don't care. I am just glad that he realizes I am no killer.

I had to go to Egypt to investigate this safety deposit box further. I didn't want to go alone and I couldn't take the kids with me either. I tried to think of someone that I could take with me for company and someone I could trust. Maybe Dennis would like to come with me. He has been laying low through all of this and no one really knows of his relationship with me. I could take him with me. I would love to enjoy his cute blue eyes and his tanned well built physique on vacation with me. That would be scrumpdillyiscious! I decided to call Dennis to see what he had been up to lately. I hadn't heard from him.

"Dennis! This is Pam. How are you?" I asked.

"Oh, Pam! Great! I am so glad you called. I wanted to call you. I didn't know when would be a good time. I saw you did some time in jail and your trial coming up and all," Dennis informed me.

"Yea, I know. Well, all is well. I want to know if you might be free some time in the future?" I questioned.

"Well, the reason I needed to get in touch with you is to let you know that I am moving." Dennis told me.

"Moving?" I replied.

"Yes," stated Dennis. "I'm moving to California. I am getting married to a girl I have known for years and she is an attorney and I am moving."

"Oh, congratulations!" I told him as my stomach flipped up into my heart and my heart went into my throat. "I am glad I called so you could tell me."

"Yes, me too. So what have you been up to? Have things settled down yet?" Dennis asked.

"Not really. I have a lot on my plate. I need to do so much. But, I guess you do too! So, you're getting married! Wow! I am so glad I called you. I would not have ever known! Well, you have a great life, Dennis. I better let you go," I said to Dennis over the phone.

Dennis answered, "Okay, Bye."

"Men!" I thought to myself after I hung up the phone. "What assholes they all are! I would never have known he got married!"

The next day, my house got broken into. It got ransacked! I was out one day running some errands and doing some shopping and while the kids were at school, the house got completely torn apart! What is going to happen next? I felt like vomiting. Another report was filed with the police. I don't know who it could be or what they want. That is what I told the police. I also mentioned that maybe whoever killed Ralph also would like to see me dead too. I started to get threatening phone calls as well. This was getting scary. I did a *57 on my phone though. The police told me to do that and the phone calls could be traced even if they are blocked. The calls were all made from a pay phone. That is no help. I told Marty that he should go and try to find Enrique Gonzalez or that Jerry Smith.

I asked him at his office one day, "Did you find out any more information on Enrique or Mr. Smith? I think one of them is making those horrible prank phone calls."

"I will go over and ask Mrs. Gonzalez some questions this afternoon," he informed me. "I also have surveillance around those pay phones where the calls were made from."

"Good. How much is that going to cost me?" I asked. "I hope not too much. Did you think of buying cameras or are you actually paying several different people to watch each pay phone?"

"Not too much," he stated. Later, I found out that he did hire several people for the surveillance. It was after I suggested cameras. He later bought cameras and mounted them and had only one person to make the rounds to man the cameras. So he lied to me.

"Mrs. Garcia, Pam, how well did you and your husband know Enrique and his wife?" Mr. Martin Powers asked me in a very formal manner.

"He was just an employee, a very good and loyal employee, in my opinion. Why?" I replied

"Well, it turns out that your late husband and Enrique grew up together. They went to the same school, the same neighborhood and well, hell, even some of the same teachers throughout the years," Marty told me right up front. I didn't know if he wanted to see if I was shocked or what. But, I sure was! Hell, I didn't know Enrique like that and sure didn't know Ralph did either!

Marty and I went to the Gonzalez's home later that day. It looked the same as the day we were there before. We approached the front door. It seemed a little different today. I couldn't quite place the difference. We knocked on the front door. There was no answer. We knocked again, still no answer. I jiggled the front door knob. It was locked. The door was solid, so I couldn't see inside. The curtains were drawn too. There was no car in the drive either.

"Where could they be?" I questioned out loud.

"Maybe she's at the store," Marty evaluated. "Let's look around." Marty started to walk around the house to see if he could see anything through the windows. He couldn't see anything until he made it around back. "Holy shit!" he exclaimed after looking through the back sliding windows.

"What is it?" I asked. I ran to him to see what he found. It was awful. It was horrid. Mrs. Gonzalez was mangled and beaten and her son was lying face down. There was blood everywhere or so it seemed. "It seems I am not the only one getting threatened. Oh, Marty! I am so scared!" I screamed as I jumped on him and hugged him and held him and just rammed my face into his shoulder so I wouldn't have to see the horrible view of what could possibly be my fate. Marty just held me as I cried and held on to him as tight as I could for a while. He let me go and said we have to go in and see how bad it really is.

I looked up at him with tears in my eyes and said, "You mean, to see if they are alive or not? Oh, Marty, I don't know if I can."

"I will then, and you can stay here." Marty said sternly as he went to try to slide the door open. The door was locked, just like the front. Nothing looked jarred. The killer must have been a known assailant. "I'll have to call the police and the ambulance. I don't know how long they have been there nor if they are even alive." We just stood there looking helplessly at the mother and son lying in the living room of their house. It looked like a small scuffle had occurred and there was a lot of blood everywhere. What an awful and horrible way to die. Who could have done this?

The police arrived and started their investigation. They opened the doors to the house and got in. The stench was unbearable. Apparently the bodies had been there for a few days. Rigor mortis had already set into their bodies. It was terrible. I wanted to leave. I knew the police were going to question me and I don't have a clue as to why the two victims are dead. Martin Powers knows more about them than I do. All I know is I have been getting life threatening calls and now their lives are gone.

I asked Marty, "Do you think Mrs. Gonzalez was receiving any frightening or threatening phone calls like I was?"

"I don't know, let me find out. You just keep quiet. You don't know anything, all right? You are under enough stress. Would you let me do what you pay me to do? Let Jack help with this too. Have you called him yet?" Marty wanted to know.

"No, not yet. I will do that right now. Good idea. I don't know why I can't think. One would think that he would be the first person I would think of at a time like this." I told Marty.

"I figured so much, that's why I called him already. You're welcome." Marty graciously informed me. "He is going to meet us down at the police station. That is where they will want to question the both of us."

"Do I have to go too? I thought you said you were going to take care of it and I could go home," I whined to Marty.

"Yeah, you're right. Let me see what I can do. Technically, you were just along for the ride. I was going to be here investigating by myself but you insisted on coming along. You don't know anymore than I do. Let me explain that to the police and maybe they'll let me take you home and I'll go down to the station after that and Jack and I can be your representatives." Marty calmly reassured me and left to talk to the police to tell them of his plans. Oddly enough, they agreed and Marty drove me back home.

So many things were going through my mind. Why was Mrs. Gonzalez killed? Did someone want information from her? Did they think she had the same key I did? Were they the same people calling me? Was it just a random killing? Where is Enrique? Did he do it? If so, did he kill Ralph too? My head was spinning and aching. I didn't know what to do. I needed to be home where I could rest. I arrived at home and did what I needed to do, rest. I drew up a nice hot bath in my Jacuzzi tub. By that time, my kids and I had eaten dinner and I had my sister pick them up to stay at her house. I had the whole house to myself. I was a little scared. Marty said that he and Jack would stop by later or call to make sure I was all right and to tell me about the scene we stumbled upon today. I tried to forget about it. I lit some candles and put them around the border of the tub. I put some music on too. I also put some aroma therapy bubbles into the bathtub water. It started to smell so wonderful and relaxing with the scent of the candles and the bubbles going. The soft light and soft music was creating a soothing ambiance in the bathroom. What a shame that had to happen to that woman and her son. What a horrible death that must have been for that woman. I hope I am not next. I do feel so scared. I have my gun out just in case someone tries to break in. That, I must admit is not really soothing, yet in a way it is. I put the gun down on the bathroom counter. I have a 380, semi automatic that was chrome, but I gold plated to make it look cool. It did. I got naked and climbed into the Jacuzzi tub that was bubbling and at a perfect temperature. The water was a little warmer than I was. The tiny air bubbles oozed over my pussy lips like champagne bubbling over a flute and tickling your mouth lips. The water wasn't scorching or anything, just nice and tingling and took some getting used to. I settled into the tub and relaxed a bit. The aroma was very soothing and relaxing. The pulsating water felt great against my neck and my thighs. I rinsed off my face with the water in my hands by splashing the water on my face and smoothing my hands over my face. I continued and splashed some water over my shoulders and just sat in the tub enjoying the sensation of the jet sprayers. They felt so good and soothing and relaxing. I looked up at the frosted glass window just over the tub and I saw some shadows of what looked like someone move by. I screamed and kept looking, trying to figure out what it was. The wind started to blow and the branches started to sway in the breeze and their shadows on the window moved and I jumped what seemed ten feet! After realizing the shadow moving across my window just outside my bath was just a tree in the wind, I sat back down in the tub and tried to relax. My chest was pounding like someone was being held captive inside of me and wanted desperately to escape. I thought my heart was going to leap right out of my chest! I put my hand to my chest to try to keep my heart inside my chest cavity. I found my hand slowly making its way over the smooth roundness of my big firm bosom. I gave myself a gentle squeeze. My tit felt so good and my hand felt even better squeezing my tit. I slid my nipple between my fingers and trilled the end of my nipple with my fingertips until it got hard. When it was hard, I splashed some water over it and started to blow on it and made it even harder. It looked so cute. I did the same thing to my other breast. I lightly stroked my fingers over both erect nipples and watched my nipples flitter back and forth. I stopped and pinched my nipples both at the same time with my fingertips. I continued and gave both of my huge breasts a squeeze and rubbed them and stroked my belly up and down. I turned my ass towards a jet sprayer and I could feel the pulsation pulsating against my clit. Oh, that felt so wonderful. I imagined Dennis' tongue sucking away and eating my wet and juicy pussy. I came in no time. It must have been all of the pent up stress from everything lately. That Asshole! I am going to miss him too. Men, if they don't die, they will leave you anyway. I am just better off without one. But, it sure would have been nice to have one around right now. I leaned back in the tub and continued with my relaxing bath. I shut my eyes and relaxed and listened to the music. All of the sudden the music went off and I looked up and noticed that my clock wasn't on. The candles were burning, so I had the same amount of light in the room, but I think my power went out. I wonder what could have happened? It was time to get out of the tub anyway. I slowly got out of the tub and dried myself off. I put on my cotton robe. I called Marty to let him know what had happened and to see if he could get here, or to just talk to him for now until the lights turn on. I had the phone to my ear and

I picked up my gun with the other. My gun was already cocked and ready to shoot. Marty answered his phone.

"Hello," I heard Marty say through the little box I held to my ear.

"Marty, It's me, Pam. I am so freaked out. My power just went out in the middle of my bath. I have my gun, but I am so freaked out! I don't want to do anything I might regret." I told him shakily but trying to remain in control. "I don't want to leave the bathroom, I have candles already lit in here. Besides the door is locked and I'm the only one in the house." I continued to tell him while leaning against the door to try to hear something on the other side.

"Just stay down low and don't leave the bathroom. I'll be right over. I will remain on the phone with you until I get there. Have you called the police?" Marty said to me over the cell phone.

"There is really no need to yet. I mean the power went out. They will tell me to call the electric company, not them!" I said quietly into the phone. All of the sudden the alarm started to go off! I nearly jumped out of my skin! That scared me a hundred times worse than the stupid tree branch!

"Oh shit! Fuck! That scared me!" I screamed into the phone.

"Hey! What's going on over there? Is everything all right? Pam, are you okay?" Marty was asking questions frantically and non-stop through the cell phone until I answered.

"The house alarm went off! I forgot it has a battery back-up. The policed will be here any minute now. That will be good. If the alarm went off, that means someone tried to break in!" I explained to Marty.

"Or he is still there." Marty said quickly.

"If you are trying to make me feel better, it's not working." I informed him sternly. "Wouldn't you think the alarm would have scared whomever away? I wouldn't stick around if someone's alarm was going off and I was the one that made it go off." I said to Marty in a loud whisper over the blaring alarm to try to convince both him and me.

"Maybe," he said. "Just stay where you are though. I am in my car right now on my way over." While Marty was driving over I felt sure that whoever it was had left. I couldn't stand the alarm going off any longer. I knew the cops would be over any second and I had to get some clothes on. I crawled to the bathroom door on my hands and knees with the gun in one hand. I stopped and opened the door just a hair and peered through the crack to make sure the coast was clear. I didn't hear anything except the alarm. I made it into my room, while still on my hands and knees and opened up my drawers and found some clothes and got dressed on the floor in the dark. I sat on the floor of my bedroom with my gun and waited until the police arrived. I was terrified. All I could picture was Mrs. Gonzalez and her son this afternoon. It still gives me chills up and down my spine. Now, they may be after me! Whoever 'they' may be. I needed to try to find a flashlight. I think I kept one under the kitchen sink, downstairs.

"Great! I am upstairs in my bedroom and I need to get downstairs where killer may possibly be. God, will this alarm ever stop?" I asked myself as I made my way to the control panel that was in my bedroom closet. After the noise was down to a silence, I listened. I listened for anything I could possibly hear that could let me know where someone else may be in this house with me. I stayed as quiet as a church mouse. I didn't want to let whomever know my whereabouts. I sat and waited very patiently for the police to arrive. Shortly, I heard the doorbell. I had to carefully crawl down the stairs. I still didn't want to be seen by anyone that may still be in the house. I also couldn't see very well in the dark and by crawling kept me from falling or tripping over something and making even more noise. I still had my gun so I had to be careful with that too. On my way down, I heard a noise come from the kitchen. I jumped up and turned to look. I stopped and didn't breathe. I listened again, nothing. The doorbell rang again. I tried to breathe again. I crawled down a few more steps. I heard the noise again from the kitchen. I stopped to hear what exactly it could be. It sounded exactly the same as before. I am frightened right now, but also closer to the door. I must get the door. I am sure the police are here and can arrest whoever the perpetrator is. I opened my front door to let in the police.

"Good evening Ma'am. We are here in response to your alarm. Is everything all right?" The middle-aged officer with a very sweet smile asked me.

"Yes. I am all right, for now. Could you please check out my kitchen? I heard some funny noises in there just now. My electricity is also out. I don't know why." I informed the officers. They left me alone for now to check out the kitchen and to see why the power went out. One cop said he was going to go outside and check the master switch. The other cop that checked out the kitchen said that he did not see anything. He did hear what was making that funny noise, though. It was just the ice settling inside the fridge. Since there was no power, the ice was melting just a tad. Just then, the lights came back on. It was strange to see everyone look up at the lights when they came on. It was nice to see the lights were on though. Then the officer that went out to the main box had just returned into the kitchen where we were all standing.

"What did you do?" I asked him. "I mean to get the lights back on."

"Oh, your main switch outside was turned off. The box where the power comes in off the pole outside to the box outside your house, the main switch was off. You really should put a lock on that. Anyone can turn off your power from your main box outside if you don't have a lock on your box." The officer told me.

"Oh well, that's good to know. I'll get right on that. Do I need an electrician to do that?" I asked them.

"No, but it might be better if you did call an electrician. I also didn't see anyone out there either. We can dust for some fingerprints around the box to see if we can find out anything. Did you see anyone at all?" he continued asking me questions.

I told them everything I saw that night which wasn't much. "All I saw was a lot of darkness and tree-branch shadows. Apparently whoever was here is gone now. The alarm must have frightened them away. What triggered the alarm? The windows weren't broken and the doors were all still in tact. I don't get it." The cops had to dust for some fingerprints. They found some grass impressions and scuff marks outside the kitchen window. The police found some fingerprints on the windowsill where the scuff-marks were. The police were still doing some of their investigating.

Marty arrived later. He walked in, looked around and saw me and asked, "Are you okay? I got over here as soon as I could."

"Yes, I'm fine. I had my gun with me, but I didn't have to use it." I reported to Marty while sitting on the couch sipping some tea.

"Who are you?" the police asked Marty. Marty showed them his identification and then began to converse with the officers. After gathering information he went back out to his car to retrieve his laptop so he could log his newly found data. He brought it in and started to show me a little more about his new computer. It was government issued, made by Panasonic. He could throw it into a swimming pool and it wouldn't be affected! It weighed a lot, but apparently indestructible. It was even bullet proof. The monitor was a touch screen monitor and it had a built in mouse too. It was an awesome tool to have. Marty always had all of the toys. I guess one would need all of those fun business tools when you are a Private Detective. I had so many police officers in my home right now that I could hardly walk through the family room. My hair was a mess because I hadn't had time to do anything with it. Marty was here. My head was overwhelmed with all of the excitement. I didn't have time for all of this going on right now. I had no choice either, with the killing of the Gonzalez lady and her son earlier and my husband murdered to make it look like a heart attack. This is some really spooky shit. I got checked back into reality when the police officers were getting loud and one walked over towards Marty and me.

"You mean to tell me that, that there computer is waterproof?" One officer asked Marty. "We don't have any fancy computers like that and I don't believe that any such computer exists. I think you're pretty full of it, fella."

"Well, I guess that is your opinion." Marty observed. "Everyone has one."

"Yea? Well, let's see if this here computer can withstand water." The officer took the computer and walked into my bathroom. There he proceeded to drop it into my bathtub that was still full of my bath water! Unbelievable! We followed this officer into the bathroom and Marty bent over and retrieved his computer out of the tub.

"What was the point to that?" Marty asked the officer.

"I just wanted to see if you were for real. You said that it would be unaffected if it were thrown into a swimming pool. That's about all I could take, so I called you on it. Looks like you're all wet, detective," the officer said thinking he was so smart.

"For your information, after the water gets done dripping out of it, I will continue to use it. If you notice, it is still booting up. Did you have to be such a moron about it?" Marty countered as he took a towel to dry it off.

"I'm sorry, Marty," I stated.

"Oh, it's not your fault. Besides, nothing is wrong with the computer. Like I said, nothing can hurt this thing. I think it's actually bullet proof too. You can't help what these morons do." Marty assured me as he finished drying the laptop off. We went to the living room and sat down and waited for the police to finish looking around and filling out their reports. Marty typed in the information in his laptop.

The officer that threw his computer into the tub came in and stated, "Well, I'll be. I can't believe it. Your computer really is working. I don't think anyone can do that to one of those yellow cell phones and keep them working. Where did you get that computer? We don't have anything that fancy down at the station neither."

"Don't worry about it. They only give these to people with higher cerebral clearance." Marty reassured the officer looking up at him slightly.

"Oh! Well, that's something I don't have is cerebral clearance. That must be something they install for some other agencies. Like those upper federal agencies," the officer spoke with a southern accent.

"That's right, my man," Marty replied wittingly trying to remain sincere.

"Ma'am, there is no need for us to be here anymore. We have gathered everything we can possibly gather. We can finish our reports downtown. If you see or hear anything suspicious, do not, I repeat, do not hesitate to call. We will be back down here as fast as we can. We will keep a car close by for you the next few weeks. I have ordered extra patrol watch as well. Apparently we will be leaving you in good hands," the chief investigating officer explained to me as the group left.

Marty needed to know some answers. "So, Pam tell me why would someone be turning off your main power switch outside your house? What was going to happen next?" Marty started the interrogation.

"How the hell should I know?" I retaliated. "I am scared to death! I hope what happened to Mrs. Gonzalez doesn't happen to me!"

Marty concernly replied, "That's what worries me. I wonder if I could get you out of the country or get your trial date moved up or both. Could you speak to Jack about that?"

"Why me? Why can't you? You're the one that is all concerned. Besides, he'll think I'm being a flighty, scared woman!" I exclaimed with an attitude in my voice. However, I did not yell.

"All right. I can see Jack treating you like an overzealous female. I'll talk to him. Would you like to leave the country for a while?" Marty asked.

"Do I get to pick the country? Because if I don't get to pick where I can go to, then I just don't think there would be a point of going anywhere. If there is no point of going anywhere, then what is the point of going?" I asked Marty in a playful and repetitious tone of voice.

"Huh? Yea, I don't know 'why not.' You may pick any

place you like, I guess. Did you have some place in mind, already?" Marty continued.

"No, not really, I hadn't thought about it. I would like to go to Egypt to see the pyramids. One of my goals in life is to see the Seven Wonders of the World. Are the pyramids one of them? The pyramids have always fascinated me. I want to go as soon as I can. I am scared to stay here. Do you think I can get a disguise and an alias of some kind?" I kept asking Marty like a nervous and excited as a child.

Marty stayed around until he finished looking up some information online and I wasn't scared anymore.

I called Jack later on the phone and told him about the power being shut off and the scare I had. I inquired about leaving the country. He reminded me that I was awaiting trial for murder.

"You can't leave the country. Oh my God, Pam! They'll nail you as soon as you try to step foot onto any airplane. You are out on bail. If you don't show up for trial, you will lose your bail. And that was a lot of bail money, Pam!" Jack reminded me like I really cared.

"So you are telling me that I can pretty much do what ever I want as long as I am back for the trial?" I reassured myself.

"Well, you are not supposed to leave the state without permission. Why? Why do you want to leave the country, for crying out loud?" Jack kept asking me.

"I think I'll be safer for now. Oh, Jack! What am I going to do? I need to be safe. My kids are safe with my sister for now. But, I can send them with their Grandparents for a little while." I rambled on to Jack with a quiver of fear in my voice.

"That sounds like a great idea, Pam. You do that. I don't think you need to leave the state. Why don't you just go out of town for a while? After you take the kids to their Grandparents, go the other way and take a vacation for a while." Jack insisted.

"I'll have to think that over, Jack. Could you make sure all of this is documented on my file? Not about me leaving, just the electric being out and the scary stuff like that. You know what I mean. Well anyway Jack, I will have to let you go for now. I will keep you posted. Bye." I told him that to get off the phone so I could call Marty. I wonder if I had a fake identification and a disguise on, if I could get out of the country. I could make it back in time for my trial. No one would even know I was gone. I need to investigate that safety deposit box and who tried to get into it and for what? I had to find out.

    I went the next day to the next town to buy a wig. I had to get a short-haired wig of a different color than my own. I had to look as different as possible. I went to the mall on the other side of town to look for a wig. I hoped to try to find one there. I would not think anyone would recognize me over on that side of town. But, then again, maybe I better be more careful than that. If I am going to try to get out of the country on the sly, I had better plan it out. I looked on the Internet for a wig and ordered under the name of my housekeeper, Rita. I had it sent C.O.D. and sent to her post office box. I'll just ask Rita to look for a package from Toppers and that it belonged to me and I would give her the money. The wig was a short, straight-haired and bright red in color, the color of Lucille Ball's hair, but more reddish instead of orange. It was almost shoulder length, just above the shoulders and below the jaw line. The cut was an inverted Pageboy. It was very cute and different from what I had. I was excited about ordering it and I couldn't wait to get it! I put a rush on the shipping so I could have it within a couple of days. Next I had to get some different style of clothes. Just a little bit different, to fit the wig and look so I would not be recognized. I continued looking on the Internet for some clothing. I found some great stuff and had the orders rushed. I wanted my look to be as an inconspicuous, average middle class woman. I ordered some second hand stuff from the Internet to help fit the bill. I wanted to look like just an economical American woman.

    A few days later, everything had arrived. Rita brought everything to me, with no questions. She just figured the less she knew the better off she was. I tried on my wig. It looked so different. I looked so different. I looked completely different. Like no one I had ever seen before. My hair was gone. It had been replaced by this mass of red hairs woven together on a piece of mesh, which is now mounted on top of my head. I liked my long hair better. This color is flashy, though. It is almost kind of cheap. It shouldn't be after the money I paid for the darn wig. That's all right. It will be better for effect, a bad dye job. I wanted to try it out around here though. But, someone may recognize me. Then my cover would be blown when I tried to leave the country for real. I had to plan a weekend trip nearby where I might be recognized from tabloids but not personally. That shouldn't be too hard. I can just go a couple of cities over and have a real good time. I made reservations for Friday and Saturday nights and prepared for the weekend.

I arrived at the hotel. It was on the water with a great view of the ocean. The lobby was made with coral marble tile. It had indoor palm trees and plants and a fountain in the middle of the lobby. I had an oceanfront room. The bellhop helped me with my luggage to my room. I was on the fourth level with a great balcony. I ran and opened the veranda doors as the bellhop unloaded the luggage. I could hear the roar of the ocean as the waves came rushing in. The sun was still high up in the sky. It was still mid-afternoon when I arrived. I stood out on the veranda looking at the ocean feeling the wonderful breeze and smelling the fresh ocean air. The drive was nice. I drove the Corvette convertible. I kept the top up since driving on the freeway is so noisy if the top is down. It sure will be nice to have around the beach this weekend! Reality suddenly set in and I turned around and noticed the bellhop still standing waiting for his tip.

"Oh! How silly of me! Please forgive me!" I told the man as I walked into the room and gave him his tip. "What is your name?" I asked.

"My name is Lee," he informed me. "Thank you, Ma'am."

"Yes, you're welcome." I told him as he left the room. The door shut and I fell onto the bed. "Wow, this is awesome!" I thought to myself. I must try to enjoy this a little. The suite was equipped with a kitchenette and a living area and a separate bedroom. It was like an apartment overlooking the ocean and the beach. I wanted to relax, but I was too excited. I was getting away from everything, from the trial, the murderers, and Jack and Marty and everything! The sun was out and the weather was hot and the ocean inviting. I began to brush out my hair and put it up in a hat. I put on my swimming suit and went to the beach for just a little while. I walked past the pool area of the hotel. It is a nice place. The pool area has acrylic shields to stop the wind and sand from blowing on the swimmers and sunbathers by the pool. I walked to the decking and down the steps to the beach. I unrolled my towel and lay down on the sand. The sand was warm and conforming to my body. I could hear the waves and the birds chirping overhead. The sound of the wind blowing across my ears made a lot of noise too. That noise blurred the others sounds together, the birds chirping and their wings flapping, the ocean waves breaking, the children laughing and running in the sand. It was peaceful. No one was bothering me and everything around me had such good vibes. The heat from the sun was really getting to me. I could feel my skin heating up where the sun was more directly hitting me. The wind would then blow across my body to cool me off just a little. I needed to get into the water to cool down. I was just a little too warm. I stood up to go into the water. I started to walk towards to ocean and noticed someone with a cooler. I walked over to the man. He was a short, middle-aged balding man with a beer belly at the beach with his kids because it is probably his weekend to have them. His children were building a sand castle just a few feet away. I proceeded to this man.

"Excuse me." I said to the man as he sat up to my attention.

"Yes?" he asked.

"Could I have a piece of ice from your cooler? I am really thirsty and terribly hot. I am going swimming, but I just really need a piece of ice to quench my thirst for now. Could I please?" I continued asking with a cute and almost irritating way about myself.

"Why sure! Take all of the ice you want! I can get plenty more! We're about to head out anyway. What ever you want, it's yours," the nice bald man said to me while he stood up and put his hands on either side of his huge stomach.

I reached into the cooler and pulled out an ice cube and held it in my hands and put it to my lips and rubbed the ice along the outline of my lips. Then I took my tongue and caressed the ice in a circular motion with my tongue around the perimeter of the ice. Then I slurped the water drippings using the tip of my tongue to tickle the ice cube a little while puckering my lips. I took the cube down my neck to cool off my skin. It instantly started to melt and drip water down my chest and right through my cleavage.

"MMMMMMMM. Oh! That feels so good!" Intoxicated with the hot-cold extremities, I uttered my feelings with utmost passion. I felt so relieved to have a cooling sensation and my thirst quenched, I could not help to release a total sigh of relief while I continued rubbing the ice cube down the front of my chest, just above my breasts. The middle-aged man's jaw was on the floor by the time my ice cube had melted. I looked over at the man and he was just looking at me with absolutely nothing to say. He sure could have caught some flies with his mouth hanging open like that. He wasn't moving. He wasn't even blinking. It was kind of cute.

"May I have another ice cube, please?" I asked. I held out my hands to show him the ice had melted. I looked into his eyes. I looked a little harder into his eyes. I started to wave my hands in front of his eyes to catch his attention.

"Huh? What? Oh, yea. Oh, another piece of ice? Oh, yea sure!" The man with the beer belly and short tension span told me.

"Thanks," I replied.

So I grabbed another piece and crunched it up in my mouth and went into the water to cool down. It felt great. I went for a swim and went back up to my room. I wanted to go out to a club, but I didn't know which club to go to. I was in a town I have never been before. I took a shower a started to get ready. I bought some cheesy outfits to wear. They were less expensive knock off brands that looked kind of cheap. However, they still looked okay. I put on my makeup heavier than I normally do. I used a lot of eyeliner to try to make my eyes look different. The wig, being red in color should be a lot of fun! I just had to spray on some perfume and I was ready to head out on the town.

  I locked the door and took the elevator down to the lobby. I requested my car not be in valet. I didn't want the hotel staff noticing the change in my appearance when getting my car. I walked to my car and got in. I unhooked the latches so I could put the top down. I put the top down and got back into the car. The wig was fun but at the same time very uncomfortable. It was also very different and weird. I kept seeing this different woman in the mirror. I wanted to go out dancing. I had no idea where to go. I wanted to buy some food for the weekend for the room plus I am thirsty again. I pulled over into a grocery store. I bought some food and a local newspaper. I found some ads in the paper of some nightclubs and bars in town. I figured I could check some out. The first one I went to played country music. I did not like country music, so I left as soon as I could, which was immediately. The next place I went, I found out it was a titty bar. I didn't even make it out of the car. I just made a U-turn and left. I pulled into another bar that seemed to be jamming! The parking lot was packed and the music sounded spectacular! I parked the car and put the top up and locked it up and went inside. The lights were flashing and the music was loud! The smoke filled air hovered like flying ghosts in the low glow of the lights. The strobe lights made time seem to move slower. I felt like I was in a dream. The rush of senses into my ears of people talking and the music playing with the smells of cigarettes and perfumes and liquor were intoxicating. I wanted a drink. I went up to the bar.

  "Hey Red! What can I get for you?" the bartender asked me with a smile on her face.

  "Oh, I'll have a Cosmopolitan with raspberry vodka," I

informed the girl. "Thanks," I added.

"Sure. My pleasure," she informed me as she made my drink and gave me a wink.

"Oh my," I thought to myself. "Why did she wink at me? Oh, it is probably nothing. She is just one of those friendly types and that is how she gets better tips. Yes, that is probably it."

"Here you are!" The bartender said while she handed me the drink. "Should I start a tab?"

"No, I will pay you cash as I go," I instructed. I gave her a twenty and she gave me some change in which I left a nice tip. I walked around a bit. I noticed there were a lot of women there. There weren't a lot of men to choose from. I walked around and finished my drink rather quickly. The music was really good to dance to. I could feel the rhythm move through my body. I went out to the dance floor and started to get my groove on. I spun, I danced and I got jiggy with it. I needed to get aired out. My wig was making my head really sweat and I had to pat my forehead down in the bathroom. There were so many girls! A lot of really pretty girls and some hard core, black leather looking types too. I reached the bathroom and as I stood in line for the bathroom, one girl looked at me like she saw someone she hasn't seen in years. She was beautiful. She had short black hair with red lipstick and a lip ring. She was about 5'9" tall and slender with a short mini skirt on and a cropped T-shirt on. She put her hands under my chin and stood in front of me.

"I saw you dancing. I think you are the most wonderful dancer I have seen," she told me. "You are so beautiful. I love your lips. May I kiss your lips?" she asked me.

"What? You want to kiss me?" I inquired in disbelief.

"Yes. Is there something wrong with that?" She wanted to know.

"No, I guess-," I couldn't get it all out before the girl whose name I didn't even know started to kiss my lips. It felt nice. Her lips were soft and full and thick. She started to stick her tongue in my mouth. She kissed so well, I didn't object. I kissed her back. We started to make out in the girls' bathroom. I felt like a kid again.

"What is your name?" I asked her.

"Chelsea," she told me. "What's yours?"

"Anna," I informed her. "Do you want a drink?"

"Sure." Chelsea announced looking into my eyes with her big brown eyes. She had cute short hair with an adorable pug nose with just a few freckles running across it. She grabbed her drink with her long, skinny fingers and smiled at me with her red and juicy lips. She looked at me like she was thirsty for me more than the drink. I just smiled very sweetly back at her and raised my glass to make a toast. We finished our drinks and proceeded out to the dance floor. Chelsea was a wonderful dancer. She held my hand and escorted me back to the bar and bought me a drink. A man kept looking at us. We were leaning at the bar sipping our drinks with our shoulders touching each other's.

She just yelled back at him while smoothing her hand over my chest, "Don't you wish you were me? Isn't she beautiful? But too bad, she's all mine!" I just looked at her with my eyes wide open and astonished! She simply leaned over and gave me another big, wet lip lock. My head was her melon she held dear in her hands bestowing upon her lips. I kissed her right back. She was such a good kisser. Women are so much more delicious than men. Women know what women want more than some men do. She stopped kissing me and stepped back and looked into my eyes like she couldn't bear the thought of never seeing me again. The night grew shorter and Chelsea and I had to say our good-byes.

"But why?" Chelsea wanted to know. "I can stay with you tonight. You don't know what you have done to me." she told me as we walked in the bathroom before we were going to leave. We arrived in the bathroom and had to wait in a small line. She leaned closer to me and nuzzled up to my face with her cute little pug nose that was so adorable. She must have known how cute her nose was and how luscious her lips were. It was her turn for a stall in the bathroom and she took my hand

and pulled me into the stall with her. She pulled me close and hugged my waist and started to kiss me. She kissed me hard and with her tongue. She wanted me. Chelsea began to give me little love bites along the sides of my neck and her tongue would caress my skin with each little nibble. My skin began to tingle with goose bumps all over. My nipples were getting hard and erect. I was so hot for her. I wanted her as much as she wanted me by this time. She positioned me so my back was to the back of the stall. My legs were spread apart and straddling the toilet seat. I leaned back and sat slightly on the tank of the commode.

She whispered to me, "I want you. I want you now. I want to taste you. Please, just let me taste you." Chelsea said to me as she pulled my dress up and my panties down. Her lips were so soft when she pressed them against my lips. Her tongue felt like a moist sponge drowning in my love juices. I felt so helpless. All I could do was succumb to her seduction. She felt so wonderful. I was captivated by her gentleness. I indulged in her deviousness. My mind went to another world. All I could think about was how great her mouth felt on my pussy. I didn't even think about the fact that we were in a bathroom stall. Suddenly someone started to pound on the stall door.

"Hey! Take it to a room! Some people here just need to use the bathroom!" I heard from the other side of the wall. Chelsea stood up and looked at me. She kissed me with my cum all over her face and lips and tongue. I tasted pretty good. I continued to kiss her back. I swirled my tongue in side her mouth so I could taste all of myself that I possibly could. She stopped and smiled at me.

"Let's get out of here." I told Chelsea while biting half of my lower lip and smiling. I put my panties back on and pulled my dress down and we left the stall. We then left the club.

"We can go back to my place," Chelsea said.

"I have a room on the ocean. We can go there. Then we can have room service in the morning. How would that be?" I asked Chelsea.

"Oh, wow! Awesome! Let's go!" Chelsea exclaimed and smiled while giving me a huge hug and kiss. The short drive to the hotel, Chelsea couldn't keep her hands off of me. She was just as bad as any guy. She had a sweeter way about her though. She was more sincere or gentle or something, just different. We arrived at the hotel. We left the car in the regular parking lot and walked up to my room. I still had on my wig. I don't know how she will take it if she finds out about my wig. I haven't been in this predicament before. What am I going to do about breakfast? I am going to go crazy with this wig on. I guess I better get used to it if I am going to use it when I travel abroad. Chelsea and I made up to my room.

"Nice little place, great patio over the ocean. Come here. I want you now. I want to taste you and make you cum so hard. I have my little toy with me." Chelsea enlightened me as she pulled out a tiny vibrator out of her purse. She pulled me close and began to kiss me. Chelsea also started to take off my dress. She unzipped my dress and tried to pull it over my head. I stopped her and told her I could do that for her. I had to be careful so my wig would not come off. So, as I pulled my dress off, she pulled down my underwear and began licking my pussy lips and pressed her vibrator on my clit. Her vibrator felt so good. My legs instantly became stiff and tight. I couldn't do anything except enjoy the warming and tingling sensation that was coming from my vagina. My heart started to pound with excitement. I felt like I was another person completely. The wig gave me a feeling of power and being able to be less inhibited. I was someone else, another entity entirely. I told her my name was Anna as I grabbed Chelsea's head and pulled it up even with mine. I began to kiss her. I kissed her hard and long. She still had her vibrator on my clitoris. I motioned her towards the bed. I began to strip off Chelsea's clothes. Chelsea was naked in no time at all. We fell on to the top of the bed while we were still kissing. My lips began to make their way to her torso. Her torso was muscular for a girl. She was a girl, though. I worked my way down to her pussy. I wanted to taste her like she tasted me. She moved my leg over her head. I was straddling her face now and licking her pussy. She started to lick my pussy and massage my clitoris with her vibrator. I was trying not to cum, but the more I held back, the easier it was for me to start to cum. I started to orgasm! I began screaming and moaning! My hips began to thrust back and forth uncontrollably and that is when Chelsea rammed her vibrator into my vaginal canal. I came with so much juice flowing everywhere! Chelsea's face became completely soaked! I turned around and began to kiss her mouth so I could taste myself. I took the vibrator away from her and started to massage her clit with it. I sucked on her mocha nipples atop her milky white mounds of her chest. She arched her back in ecstasy. With my legs between her knees, I spread her legs open. I put my hands under her buttocks and began to kiss her belly button and her tummy. I slowly made my way down to her clit with my slurping tongue. I kissed her pussy with my lips and sliced her vagina open with my tongue. I continued to make love to Chelsea for hours. We woke up next to each other the next morning with the sound of the ocean waves hitting the beach and the seagulls flying around in the wind. The sun was peaking through the veneers of the blinds on the windows that were on the doors to the veranda. I got out of bed and opened the doors to let the outside in. Chelsea and I ordered room service for breakfast. We had a wonderful breakfast together. She had fruit and a cheese omelet with toast and I had a cantaloupe with cottage cheese with coffee. She told me she had some work to finish up and she gave me her phone number and left. I took off my wig and showered and had a relaxing weekend at the beach. Jack tried to call me to find out what I was up to. I didn't answer my phone. I listened to my phone messages though. I called back whomever I wanted to call back and I went to the beach and relaxed and collected my thoughts the rest of the afternoon. I had to plan out what I needed to do in order to try to sneak out of the country before my trial started. I needed to find some friends of mine that would help me out as 'Anna' and make me a couple of identification cards. I might be able to get out of here with an identification card and a passport. I don't see why I shouldn't be able to exit the country if I have the proper papers. The sun and the sand were really soothing and mind clearing. I had no trouble thinking at all about how to leave the states. I could keep the kids just where they are. I wonder if I could get all of this done right away! Holy shit! An epiphany came to me! If I can get this done right now, here in this town where I don't know anyone, I might be able to pull it off. I went up to my room instantly. I found the phone book and looked up the local pawn shops. The pawn shops are usually in a part of town where people may be in the need of identification and extra money. I left my hotel room and went to the area where the shops were located. I found a local diner. I sat down at a booth and acted timid and like I was scared to death. I wore my wig and had on a pair of jeans. I ordered some coffee and hoped no one saw me. The waitress asked me if I was okay.

"Yes," I replied with my head barely lifted up to look at her. "I'm okay. Thank you. I may need to know something, if you can help," I added.

"Oh, sure honey. You name it. If you need to know anything around here, I can find out for ya. I know everybody. My name is Lola. This place around here, there ain't nothin' that don't get by me," the older waitress told me with an attitude. She was an older woman with long curly hair. These weren't loose curls. These were those tight spiral curls that hung by the thousands from the top of her head. She had big brown eyes and dark hair. Her waist thickened with the years she carried and her face still cute with the extra pudge in her cheeks and crows feet around her eyes showed her age.

"Are you sure I can't get you anything?" Lola asked, as a good waitress should.

"Well, maybe you could start by bringing me a glass of water," I insisted. Lola proceeded to bring me a glass of water while I sat there and contemplated of how I was going to bring up the subject of getting an identification card and passport.

"I know! I will tell her I am an abused housewife trying to escape from her husband. I just go by that movie with that red haired movie star," I thought to myself. "I can just try to convince them that I am trying to leave him and I need them." Lola returned with my water and set it on the table. I pulled it closer to me and put the straw into the glass and began drinking from the glass while it was still sitting on the table.

"Are you sure you are all right, honey," Lola continued to ask?

"Well, since you really want to know, I am trying to stay incognito," I informed Lola with great confidence. Lola's mouth fell open and I could actually see where her tonsils used to be.

"No!" Lola exclaimed in a loud whisper. "Why don't you want no one to know who you are? I bet no one would know who you are anyway. I ain't never seen you around here before," she completed her thoughts as should stood more erect and confident looking down at me from the aisle.

"Good. Now maybe you can keep your voice down so no one else sees me in here before and again anywhere else!" I instructed Lola sternly with a harsh whisper. I pulled her down closer to me and told her that I needed some identification cards, one a state certified looking and a passport. "I need to get away from my husband," I begged her. "Please! If you can help me, I wish you would." By now I was to the brink of tears. I had played the part so intensely and worked myself up so much that I was desperate enough to start crying a little while my forehead touched the side of her head so I could whisper into her ear. Lola stood up and looked at my face. I had sunglasses on and a couple of tears were starting to roll down the sides of my face. She couldn't see them until after a drop of time had passed then the tear gravitated out from under the sunglasses' lenses to validate my sincerity.

"There is a guy down the street. I go on break in ten minutes. I'll give him a call and take you down there when I go on break," Lola told me in a hard and cold, business voice. She looked around the restaurant quickly scanning to see if anyone was really paying attention. Lola held up her pad and pen and pretended to be taking my order. She was writing something down on her waitress pad. I wasn't telling her anything, however.

"Lola, I will have some tuna on a tomato. Is the tomato fresh? The tomato has to be fresh and the tuna needs to be white," I instructed her to bring me that order for lunch. Lola proceeded to go to the kitchen and I waited at the booth. I turned off my phone. I needed to buy a pre-paid cell phone. After I get those new identification cards, I can open up a separate bank account under the alias' name. Then I can put some of this money that I have now in there and come back later and put more into it if I sell my house or if the insurance pays me. I have to make sure I can set myself up for any kind of get away. The jury may find me guilty of murder. Then I have been getting attacked by whomever jumped me at my house! There is always someone that wants something from me. I have to be careful. I can get this bank account started and if necessary, I can transfer funds to Egypt or where ever I may end up. I wonder how the Cayman Islands are this time of year? I need to go to the Cayman Islands! I can get there quick and be back before anyone knew it. I am not far from there right now. Lola brought my tomato and tuna and it was very fresh and the tuna was white.

Lola told me about the guy down the street that could help me out with the identification cards and passports. She called him Luiz. She said that Luiz was an old friend of hers and that I could trust him. She trusts him with her life. He wouldn't tell anyone about me. I went to the location Lola told me.

Luiz was standing in the shadows of a palm tree. He walked over to me and whispered, "Anna?"

"Yes," I replied turning around to get a good look at the person saying my name. He was a short and stocky Asian man. He appeared Asian to me. It doesn't matter where he came from or where his parents came from as long as he is here and can help me get some I. D. cards and a passport. His hair was straight and spiked up and he wore a big football jersey that hung to his thighs. Thank goodness for that, because his shorts hung just below his butt. He had big, silver chains hanging around his neck and he even smelled good. Luiz motioned me to follow him through the gate of the fence into the courtyard of the apartments. I continued to follow him past the apartments and to a house on the other side of the street. We both entered the little house. The house was a nice little house. It was a nice average middle class home. The living room had a couch, table, chair and a television. We walked down the hall and into one of the bedrooms that was set up like a printing press lab. It had a computer and a couple of printers and laminators and an actual printing press. The walls were stacked with reams of paper and boxes of blank credit cards. The place was incredible. I couldn't believe he actually brought me there and showed me all of that.

"I have to take your picture," Luiz sternly informed me looking at me while smiling a little. "Is that what you want to wear? I mean is that how you want to look for the picture? Lola told me why you needed the papers. I wouldn't help if she didn't tell me. I am so sorry. No man should treat any woman bad. A woman is the greatest gift God put on the Earth. Okay, stand over here on the 'X'."

"I would like to freshen up a little," I mentioned to Luiz as I moved over towards the 'X'. Luiz agreed and I just put a little powder on my face and some dark cherry lipstick on my lips.

"Say cheese!" Luiz exclaimed as he took my picture. "What name do you want on these," Luiz asked me after he took my picture out of the processor.

"Anna Nelson is the name. That should work all right." I instructed Luiz to use that name. It was the first thing that popped into my head. For some reason I was thinking of Ricky Nelson right now. I got my I. D. cards and my passport and I had Luiz make me one credit card while he was at it. I wasn't going to use it, but at least I had it as another identification verification. I went back to my hotel later that evening after I bought my stuff from Luiz.

I couldn't believe it! Now, I could extend my hotel stay by a few days. Or better yet, I need to leave first thing in the morning and check in somewhere else as 'Anna Nelson'. I left the present hotel and went to a lesser expensive hotel. I put on the wig and stayed in disguise so I was in my Anna Nelson persona when I checked into the new hotel. I settled in for a couple more days and headed out for the bank. I went to a larger chain where I wouldn't be as noticeable or too scrutinizing either. I opened up an account and kept some cash on me. My next move would be to go to the airport and go to the Cayman Islands and open up another bank account where I could transfer some funds in to it. I need to transfer cash over no more than $2,000.00 a day. I know that if anyone deposits or transfers or makes any kind of cash or check transaction of ten thousand dollars or more in one day, the bank employees are required to report the transaction to the federal reserve government. Then the government would get involved. It may be beneficial for me to open up a business account in the Islands as well. Then I could pay the company a check, like I was purchasing something. I could stash some cash that way too. I needed to get down there and back rather quickly though.

I went to the airport to try to purchase a ticket to the islands. I actually had no problems whatsoever. I was certainly pleased with Luiz's work. No one questioned the I. D. cards. I got onto the plane with my Egyptian cash inside my money belt and some American in my purse. While I was at the bank, I bought some travelers cheques and pre-paid Visa cards in Anna Nelson's name. This was such an adventure. My adrenaline was pouring out of my adrenaline glands. I was so nervous and excited at the same time. I made it on the plane that I shouldn't have been on in the first place. Jack was going to kill me! Well, maybe not literally, but I bet the panic stricken man will just have to take a tranquilizer if he ever hears about this.

I made to the Cayman Islands. The weather was damp and rainy. Everywhere I stepped seemed like mud. I am glad I had on my older sandals that weren't an expensive label. My wig was getting soaked. Now it was *really* weird to be wearing that thing on top of my head. It was extremely heavy and uncomfortable. I should have worn a hat. I didn't even have a raincoat with me. The airport wasn't much to talk about either. I had to find a hotel to stay in, then the bank.

After checking into the hotel, I took off my wig and set it on top of a bedpost. The rooms were quaint and old with a musty and damp, beachy smell. I had a room on the bottom floor so I could walk down to the beach if I wanted to. The hotel was up on a hill, so the beach was a little further out than I would have liked. The view was great! It would have been better if the weather was nicer. I brushed out the wig while it hung out to dry on the bedpost. Then I carried it into the plush bathroom with its old fashioned tub with bird claw feet and the toilets with tanks that were four feet above the bowl. I took my blow dryer and plugged it in and started to dry my wig. I am glad now that I paid extra for real hair instead of synthetic hair in my wig. There is no telling what would have happened to it if it got wet or heated with a dryer. I still better be careful with it though. I did pay a lot for it and don't want the hair to start coming out in clumps. It actually didn't take that long for it to dry. That was a very good thing. Now, I could go to the bank and open an account with my new identity.

I had the desk clerk call me a taxi so I didn't have to walk in the rain. Even though I didn't walk, I needed to find a hat or an umbrella somewhere, too. Just getting in and out of the car and the time going to and from the bank has left me wet again. I am not as wet, but if I keep this up, I will be soaked. I bought a hat from a sidewalk vendor after I left the bank. I just gave some money to the cabby and made him get out and get it. I did not want to get wet anymore. I couldn't believe it was raining like this. I arrived at the most popular bank on the island according to a local that worked at the desk of the hotel. I went to that one he suggested. It was just a few blocks away. I opened up an account with the Egyptian currency I found in the safety deposit box. The lady exchanged the currency and opened up a money market account for me. I thanked her and got her telephone number and all of the in formation needed to make any kind of transfer. I had no idea there was such a large amount of money in my possession. I didn't know the value of Egyptian money at all. I made it back to my hotel room. The rain kept coming down. I couldn't believe how bad it was. I turned on the television to watch the weather. The weather channel showed a hurricane coming in the southeast Atlantic Ocean heading northwest! The rain that was falling was the outer bands of the hurricane that was heading straight for the islands!

"Oh, great!" I thought to myself. What am I going to do now? Jack really will kill me. At least my hotel is at a higher altitude. To get to the beach from my room I had to walk down the steps and then to the sand. That was a good thing. I called the airport to see if I could get a flight out of here. The lines were busy. I kept trying until I finally got through just to find out all of the flights have been booked until after the hurricane.

"Is there a 'stand by' option?" I inquired over the telephone. The lady told me there is always someone that cancels or doesn't show up. I instantly began packing my things to get ready to leave as soon as I could. I took a cab to the airport. The woman at the ticket counter informed me that any ticket to leave had been sold. I went to the information desk to inquire about possibly chartering a flight. The person wasn't the most brilliant person, but he was able to help me. He introduced me to a young pilot that had one of the nicest small jets on the islands. He was a handsome young man of about twenty-five years of age. His eyes were blue Topaz set in white almonds and his teeth were perfect beautiful pearls placed to God's blessing of human perfection framed with luscious and moist lips that opened to a crescent shaped smile. All of this beauty was encompassed by beautiful tanned skin topped with bleached blonde spiked hair. His name was Warren. Warren's father is a real estate tycoon. Warren is here taking care of some business for his father. He has his jet and is getting ready to head back to the states.

"I will pay you. Please, I need to get back to the states before this thing hits. I have my kids I need to get to and that is just part of it!" I let Warren know with a desperate tone in my voice, as I looked at him with my puppy dog eyes and lip

They think I Killed My Husband!

out a little bit. He looked at me and smiled right back at me with his perfectly wonderful smile to let me know everything would all right.

"As soon as I get clearance for 'Take-off' you are more than welcome to ride along with me. Since the hurricane is coming, I won't charge you very much. I may bring along other people if necessary. I won't leave anyone stranded if I feel they would be better off to leave, which I do." Warren informed me.

"Great! Thank you," I told Warren. "When will you have clearance?"

"Oh, that," he replied. "I don't know. Maybe never, maybe in a few minutes, so you better stick around and stay on your toes."

"Oh," I answered him back all wide eyed and sort of worried now. I began pacing the short area had to stay around so I wouldn't miss my flight. I could also see the television monitor. The weather was getting worse. It kept raining, but the storm hasn't quite reached us yet. It was still about a day away. I wanted to get out before the hurricane's eye was right over me though.

"Do you have clearance yet," I asked Warren about fifteen minutes later.

"No, not yet. But, let me check. If I keep bugging the control tower, maybe they will let me out." He encouraged me a little with a boyish giggle that I couldn't interpret as nervousness or just kind of hyper. He left me standing there and ran up to the lady that could check it out for him. He skipped back through the airport to let me know that he could take off in two hours and forty-five minutes.

"Awesome! I'll just sit over here and wait until we have to leave. Is there a bar close by where I can get something to drink? I think I could use a stiff one right about now," I told Warren. Warren looked at me rather strangely. I just looked at him with a weird look on my face like I did not know why he looked at me so strangely.

"I might be able to help you with the stiff one, but I think they sell liquor over at that counter where the bar stools are." Warren pointed with his long, skinny but muscular arm over towards the bar.

"Ha, ha, very funny. You know what I mean. Would you care to join me? We both have to wait," I suggested to Warren.

"Yes, but I have to pilot the jet. I think it is best that I don't have anything to drink. I will join you in some conversation though," Warren stated.

The weather started to get a little worse. The wind was howling louder and stronger. The young man brought over a young newlywed couple that needed a flight off of the island too. Warren agreed to let them join us as soon as we were able to take off. The young girl couldn't have been over twenty-one years old and her husband was probably almost thirty. Their names were Maggie and Todd Presley. Maggie had straight long blonde hair and was very petite. Todd was short and skinny and petite for a man. His hair was red and his face was covered with a lot of freckles. They seemed like an average typical American couple. Warren told the Presley's where he planned on landing in the states. I was listening and drinking my Margarita until it was time to leave. We all sat and talked and got a bit more acquainted at the bar. Warren then abruptly interrupted and said he had to go and prep the jet. We should go with him and load up our stuff. We all settled into the jet with the luggage in the cargo area and the passenger conditions left nothing to be desired. It was lavish and if the people traveling First Class on a commercial flight saw these accommodations, they would be jealous!

"How lucky can a girl get?" I asked myself. "Warren, this is fantastic! How can I ever thank you?" I had to tell Warren.

Warren teasingly told me that he could offer me that stiff one I wanted. I told him to just fly the plane and to pay attention to which joystick he was holding on to. Maggie started to laugh and while Todd just stood there not really amused. Warren was in the cockpit and there was another man in there with him. I didn't realize there was someone else on the plane with us. Warren introduced his personal pilot.

"You didn't really think I was in total charge of the plane," Warren questioned me?

"Well, I don't know. You said you were a pilot. I figured you were going to fly the plane." I replied in my defense to Warren.

Warren teased and smiled back at me saying, "I am a pilot. I can fly the jet if I have to. But, I don't want to if I don't have to. Our family has a full time pilot for the jet. I have to help him out sometimes. The jet does need two people to fly it. I am the copilot today."

Maggie started to squeal, "Hey! When are we going to take off? I need to go home before this storm comes!"

I wanted to tape her mouth shut. I think we all wanted to go before the storm came.

"Sit down and fasten your seat belt right now!" Warren instructed Maggie sternly.

"May I go to the bathroom first?" Maggie asked Warren one more question.

"Yes, of course. But, you need to hurry." Warren told her with a little less stress.

"Um, where is it?" Maggie asked with her cute, little petite voice and innocent face.

"It's to the back and on the right." Warren told her quickly. Warren leaned over towards me and said, "Is there anyway I could get away with using duct tape on her mouth?"

I just giggled and told him I was thinking the same thing. The rain was slamming down on the roof of the jet more forcefully than ever. Now that we were in the jet, I could feel the wind swaying the massive cylinder we were in. I wasn't feeling too much at ease right now. I sat down and fastened my seat belt and looked at Warren and asked him if we were going to take off soon.

"Yes, as soon as Maggie gets back into her seat. We will be heading for the runway. We need to get out of here before the weather gets really bad. Right now, we just might make it." Warren informed me seriously.

"What do you mean, 'just might make it?'" I asked him

with fear and concern.

"Oh, I didn't mean it like it sounded," Warren stated. "I mean that we need to leave now." Warren walked his cute tight behind up to the cockpit and Maggie sat down next to Todd and fastened her seat belt. The jet began to roll down the runway and I could hear the roar of the jet engines under the wings. The eggshell leather recliners in the jet were extremely comfortable. The pilot announced over the intercom to leave the chairs in an upright position and to fasten our seat belts until after we take off. I was a little tired after the Margarita and sat with my eyes shut in the chair. The rain kept coming down. The jet took off with a little trouble, but considering the circumstances, Warren did a pretty good job. The storm was awful. The plane shook in the wind and Maggie started to scream. I just wanted her to be quiet. She began to cry.

"We are all going to die!" Maggie screamed, while clenching the arms of the chairs. The plane took a heavy dive down. I thought we might just crash. All of the sudden the jet made a vertical sweeping motion upward. My stomach felt like it was going to come out of my mouth. Maggie let out a scream as if she were on a roller coaster and I just tried to keep down the drink I just had. We passed through the clouds and reached above the bad weather. We were up and flying. I was so lucky to have found this guy. I wonder if I could use him for another time I wanted to leave the country?

Maggie and Todd fell asleep together on the recliners. I couldn't sleep. I had to think about what my next move would be. I needed to figure out how to avoid the person trying to get my key. He was probably the person that killed Mrs. Gonzalez and her son. I didn't want that to happen to me. That is another reason why I bought the wig, or really the main reason.

I arrived at home, and no one was the wiser. I did it! I left the country and Jack didn't even try to call me. Marty had left me a couple of messages, but nothing urgent. I called and checked up on the children. They were both fine and having fun with their grandparents and cousins and the rest of the family. I put my wig up in the shelf in my closet and started to make out some checks for deposit for Anna Nelson. I had to start putting some money aside for later. I was afraid if the system failed I could make a getaway or if whomever it is trying to get my key to that safety deposit box tries to come after me again, I can make another quick getaway. I have Warren's number and he said that he travels constantly. He would help me if he could. However, that hurricane really put a damper on my plans. I wanted to go to Egypt to find that safety deposit box. But, I came back home instead. I returned Marty's phone messages. He wanted to know why I hadn't called him until now.

"I had a little bit of trouble with my phone. My service wasn't working for some reason, or maybe my phone. I don't know. It is working fine now. What is the big news?" I asked him on the cell phone that I pretended wasn't working for a few days.

"The police found some new evidence at the Gonzalez's home. There were at least two people that killed Mrs. Gonzalez and her son. They believe the perpetrators were looking for something. They are uncertain if they found what they were looking for. So, if they are still looking for something, then the killers may think you have it." Marty warned me over the phone.

"I know! Don't you think I am scared? You mean to tell me these Einsteins are just now figuring all of this out?" I asked him with sarcasm and concern.

"What do you mean, Pam? You know? What do you know? Do you know what the perpetrators are looking for? Because you need to tell me everything you know." Marty demanded again over the phone.

"There is nothing to tell. You need to tell me everything you know. That is what I pay you for is for information. You don't pay me, I pay you, remember? So, why don't you tell me what you have found so I feel like I have gotten my money's worth," I asked Marty with some sarcasm and sternness.

"I just told you what I know. You are the one that is acting like you know everything. I thought you might want to share everything you know." Marty was still trying to pump information out of me, for what, I have no idea. I wasn't going to tell him anything. I didn't want him to know too much yet. Marty told me he needed to go over some of the details with me in person. The police had some very interesting evidence. He said that some of the neighbors were questioned and said that the description of one of the men was similar to the description I gave of the man that attacked me at the gate of my house. Now, I have a better suspicion that it is a certain group of people or just a select few that want the key. Now, I really need to know what secrets the key holds. It must be extremely important for whomever to feel others had to die. Whatever it is, must be very valuable.

Marty had some things he had to take care of and he would be over in the morning. I just went upstairs and went to bed. I was glad to be home. I watched the television and saw the islands were just missed by the hurricane. However, they did not escape some of the wrath. The islands suffered a lot of heavy winds and rain. The roof was blown off the hotel I was staying in among others! I was sure lucky to find Warren. He is such a cutie. Too bad I am not ten years younger. I was lying in bed trying to get some sleep thinking about my whole adventure. I wonder if Warren would be able to take me to Europe or Egypt if I could pay him enough money. He said he would, so why am I worrying about it? So, I just rolled over and went to sleep.

Marty came by and we had a talk and he told me the details of what the cops had found out. One of the details were that one of the men over at the Gonzalez's home the day she and her son were killed was identified as Jerry Smith. The man that Ralph had put in jail for theft. He embezzled a lot of money from our company.

"But wasn't he good friends with Enrique Gonzalez and his family," I asked Marty?

"That is what I had found out. They grew up together and are the same age. The same as your late husband," Marty replied back to me.

They think I Killed My Husband!

"So, why would someone's friend kill his wife and son?" I wanted to try to rationalize the situation.

"Well, I could see having your best friend kill your wife, but not your son," Marty commented with a smirk on his face.

"Hey! That is not funny!" I retaliated. I sat and thought for a moment. "Do you think something went wrong? Maybe that is what was supposed to happen and his son was there by mistake!" I uttered with excitement.

"Or maybe the stakes are so high, it doesn't matter and something happened where she had to die. Maybe Enrique did something wrong or was going to do something that someone didn't want him to do and they killed his family so he wouldn't do it." Marty suggested out of thin air. "But, what could be so great? If they killed this guy's wife and kid, and maybe even your husband, and now they are coming after you too, what is it these people are after?"

"I don't know Marty," I lied. I knew some of the reason must be because of the key. What I didn't know is what was locked up inside the box the key could unlock. It must be really important. I didn't know if I should ever tell Marty. I probably would sometime, but not just yet.

Sherry called me and wondered what was happening. She had stopped by while in town over the weekend when I was in the Cayman Islands and no one was home. She said she was getting worried about me. I told her everything was fine and the kids were away with family, so they should be okay and safe. She told me if she could help in any way, just to let her know and she would be there to help out. I thanked her and told her that she would be the first person I call.

Things were quiet for the next couple of weeks. I kept mailing small deposits down to the Cayman Islands. I had to try to get to Egypt and to check out that safety deposit box. I had to get in touch with Warren. I hope he can help me when I need help. I wonder if Aldo could be able to come with me. I would feel better going with someone I know I could trust. I could trust Aldo. He would never say anything to anyone.

No one really knows how good of friends we are. I don't even think he has been called in for any type of questioning from the police. But first, I had to call Warren.

"May I speak to Warren, please?" I inquired over the telephone. I waited on hold while the woman that answered retrieved Warren. Warren came to the phone.

"Hello," he answered the phone.

"Warren? This is Anna, Anna Nelson. We met down at the Cayman Islands," I identified myself and reminded him.

"Anna! Of course I remember you! How could I forget such a vision of loveliness in the midst of all of that mess down there? How are you?" Warren said to me very warmly.

"I am fine Warren, thank you. Are you doing okay," I asked him.

"Oh, sure. I'm okay. My dad's fine too. I told him about you. He said to be careful. Women were nothing but trouble he warned." Warren informed me.

"Why would your Dad say such a thing," I asked? "You didn't tell him awful things about me to him did you?"

"No. He just knows how some women are. He has had his fill. Anna, did you need something," Warren went straight to the point. He is pretty quick for such a young man.

"Well, now that you mention it, yes. I can pay you. I was wondering if you were going to be going to Egypt or Switzerland anytime in the near future," I needed to know?

"I gather you are," Warren answered back over the phone.

"Well, I need to meet you somewhere. I don't want to talk about it over the phone," I quickly cut him off. You must meet me in front of the food court at the mall. I will pick you up in my car. Be there in three hours, exactly," I ordered.

I drove over to the next town and went to the mall and picked up Warren. I had to talk to him about when he might be able to make the trip to take me, and hopefully Aldo to Egypt.

"Hey Warren," I said as I picked him up. I had on my wig and met Warren in front of the mall by the food-court. We drove around town a little while and talked about our arrangements.

"It has to be done within a week's time. No one can be the wiser that I left the country." I told him just because I said I was trying to get out of town to rest before the business executives realized I was gone. He said he could get the jet for a week when his father gets back from South America. He should be back in a couple of days. But Warren said that his father is known for taking a few extra days. He would call me as soon as his father arrived. I gave him the cell phone number I had under Anna Nelson's name, which he still had that number from a few weeks earlier. I drove back home and called Aldo. I asked Aldo if he could meet me somewhere.

"Yea, sure Pam. Where do you want to meet?" he asked me over the cell phone.

"Where are you now?" I asked him.

"I am at the house right now," he told me.

"Did you ever get rid of that crazy girlfriend?" I needed to know. I couldn't have him trying to explain his whereabouts to this psycho woman again. I may have to rethink this plan.

"Oh, yea. She is history." Aldo reassured me. "She is gone! Thank God!"

"When was the last time you heard from her?" I asked him.

"It's been over a month. She hasn't been here or even tried to call," he reassured me again.

"Fine. I'll be there in about an hour." I told him to be ready as I was driving back from the next town from talking with Warren. I pulled up to Aldo's house and honked the horn of my Corvette. I had the top up so no one could see me inside with the windows tinted. He ran down his front walk and opened up the door and hopped into the car.

"What on earth did you do to your hair? It looks good. I just wasn't expecting it." Aldo told me after getting into the car and reluctant about giving me a kiss.

"It's a wig. I need to ask you something and you must be quiet. You can not tell a single soul! I mean it, not anyone! Do you understand? I am trusting you with my life here. Can

I trust you?" I made Aldo swear that he would not tell a single soul about what I was about to tell him.

"Yes, Pam, I swear. Now, what is it? Why do you have on that silly wig and what is so secretive? Did you do it? Did you kill Ralph? Is that why you had me take that gold plating stuff? So, you wouldn't get caught? Now you are trying to get away by wearing that stupid disguise? I can't believe you! I would have never have guessed it!" Aldo went on before I could tell him what was really going on.

"No! Of course not! But, I discovered some things that I need to get to the bottom of. But I can't leave the country because I am out on bail. I did leave the country a few weeks ago though." I informed him quietly while I was driving.

"What? How on Earth did you get out of the country without getting arrested or anyone knowing?" Aldo had to know.

"That isn't important. What is important is that I need you to come with me to Egypt. I have a way via private jet to get there. I have to check out a safety deposit box that is in a bank in Egypt." I told him quickly and to the point.

"Why do you need me?" he wanted to know.

"I may need someone to help me. Besides, a female doesn't travel all alone often. I would be less conspicuous if you came along with me. We would look like a husband and wife team. Besides, you are the only one I can really trust." I told him as I grabbed his hand.

"You didn't answer me. What's with the wig, Pam?" Aldo asked me again.

"The name is 'Anna' while I am wearing this wig in public. 'Anna Nelson' is my name while we are traveling. You do have your Passport, don't you?" I needed to know from Aldo.

"What the hell are you talking about? What are you doing? What do you need to get to the bottom of that you have to wear a disguise if you didn't kill Ralph? Why are you trying to ditch the country if you aren't guilty?" Aldo was still accusing.

"Would you shut up and listen to me! I did not kill

anyone! I was attacked at my house and Enrique Gonzalez's wife and son were killed in his home. Now Enrique is missing and this former employee that stole from us could have been one of the men at the Gonzalez's home that day. His name is Jerry Smith. I found this out from the private detective I hired, Martin Powers. I have the police detective Tony Perez snooping around my life and he has been pretty sneaky about it, too. He thinks I did it. I don't know why, but he does. I didn't kill anyone, Aldo! You have to believe me!" I shouted softly to him in the small compartment of the car.

"So, what has this private detective you hired done for you? Has he been trying to figure out what has been going on with this mess?" Aldo was trying to analyze the situation. It seemed that everyone really knew how to ask questions of what had already happened, but didn't know how to solve the 'how' thing. Except for just concluding I did it to get all of the money.

"Oh, Marty? He has done some helpful things for me," I informed him. "He stayed over after some guy jumped me at my gate house one night. The guy was waiting right outside of my manor by the lake and waited for me to get out of the car by the gate."

"Why would you get out of your car? Didn't you just go right through the gate and up to the house?" Aldo interrogated.

"That's just it! The asshole broke my gate, so it wouldn't open and I had to get out of my car to try to open the gate manually. I tried to contact the baby sitter through the intercom. The intercom's wiring was ripped out and there was a rock stuck in the gears of the gate, so it wouldn't even open up manually. The jerk cut the electric to the gate house so nothing worked. The surveillance cameras and the intercom and the electric gate were not working. When the electric is out, the gate is installed so a person can open it, but since the rock was stuck in the gears, well, I couldn't get it open. That is when the guy came from behind me and tried to slit my throat!" I told Aldo all what happened that night.

"Holy shit! Wow! I had no idea!" Aldo replied with great intensity.

"So, do you think you might be able to be free for a couple of weeks or so? I would pay you. I also think you might be better off getting a new identity and passport to match. I hope you will be able to go. Please say you will," I begged Aldo.

"Yes! How can I say no to you, especially when you ask me like that? When do you want to leave?" Aldo asked me.

"As soon as possible! Yesterday! We need to get an I.D. card for you and a new passport, just to be on the safe side. I have to actually wait about a week and a half before the private jet I want to use will be available." I informed Aldo of everything.

"What, a private jet? We are going to leave the county on a private jet with different I.D.'s and you are innocent? Ya, right," Aldo said, sarcastically!

"Oh, come on. You know me better than that. Do you really think I would be able to kill anything or anyone, let alone my own husband?" I asked in my defense. "I am paying this guy to fly us to Egypt to find out what Ralph had in this safety deposit box. There must be something really important in it because the person who attacked me mentioned he wanted the key."

"Really? Would this be the same guy that might have invaded the Gonzalez' home?" Aldo questioned after gathering evidence.

"Yes, it is very possible!" I exclaimed to Aldo.

"Well, we need to go as soon as possible then," Aldo told me.

I looked at Aldo very relieved, smiled and said, "Yes, as soon as the jet is available and you have a different identification just for precautions, we will leave." I leaned over and gave Aldo a big kiss on the cheek. He turned his head and planted a big kiss on my mouth. His tongue went into my mouth. Aldo's tongue went in and out of my mouth like a serpent's tongue. It was different than usual. It just went in and out. His hand caressed my face and cheek with his thumb underneath my chin, stroking it from side to side. I pulled away.

They think I Killed My Husband!

"We need to get to the next town and get you another identification card and passport as soon as possible. I got mine from this guy downtown. I know where this guy is now, but people like that, migrate quickly," I told him.

Aldo and I went to the next town where I knew the guy that made my I.D. card and my passport. He made one for Aldo too. Aldo wanted to be called Jesus Gamir. I had no idea why or how he came up with that name nor did I care. As long as my friend was able to make some I. D. cards with that name on them, that's all that I cared about. I just hope that in Egypt that they didn't think the name of Jesus to be sacrilegious or something. His picture turned out nice. It looks just like him. He put his new identification into his wallet and we headed back home. I told him to be ready to go next week and not say anything to anyone about today or where he is going.

The following week Aldo and I got together and I went with him to the next town. It was better that we took his car to the airport so my cars would not be anywhere but at my house. I talked to Warren earlier that morning and he said he would be at the airport all day making sure the jet was ready. I had cash ready to give to him to cover all of the expenses he would encounter. I also had enough cash to cover my expenses that I would encounter, I hoped. Aldo and I arrived at the airport to meet with Warren at the terminal 7. I was wearing my red wig that was so hot and uncomfortable. I really felt more conspicuous with it on. I had all of the money for Warren in my briefcase and the money for me in my money-belt. I could feel people looking at me as I walked through the airport. I was so nervous. I looked very different with my wig. I had pictures that matched on my I.D.'s so I should be all right. I glanced behind me and saw an airport police officer walking behind me. My stomach went into my throat and my heart fell into my belly and started to burn with nerves. I gulped my stomach back down and kept walking to keep my composure. I glanced over at Aldo, and he was unaware or oblivious to the police officer. This was a good thing. People can sense other people's nervousness. I didn't want to look back again to see if the officer was there or not, however I had to. I glanced over my shoulder and I saw the officer take a right turn down the other terminal. I felt so relieved that I blew out a sigh of relief as Aldo and I continued our journey. We stayed on track through the walkway of the airport. We were getting closer to the security where Warren would be waiting. I wanted to give Warren this money before going through the security screening. Aldo had his hands full, carrying all of the bags with clothes and I had my makeup bag in one hand and the briefcase in the other. I had my purse draped over my shoulder and my money belt was under my shirt. I saw Warren standing just on the other side of the security-check point station. Warren looked so cute standing there waiting for me to take me anywhere in the world I wanted to go. His slender body leaning against the wall with his bleached tipped hair that was spiked up. I had to walk through the Security check. I had mostly paperwork and certificates and the cash I stashed away in a pocket of the side of the briefcase. The security officers probably would not see the money in my money belt. I hid it so well under the lining. The officers are checking for weapons anyway. I hope the metal detectors don't go off when I go through the security gate. Money has those new metal strips in the bills that would set off metal sensors if the sum of money comprised was large enough. As I put the briefcase and my make-up bag and my purse on the conveyor belt to be X-rayed, I walked through the metal detectors. The officer felt he needed to go through my briefcase. I began to get very nervous as I watched him go through some of the papers and folders in the briefcase. I didn't want to let on that I was nervous in any way. As he sifted through some of the papers, I looked over at Aldo, then at Warren. Warren looked out the window and Aldo just shrugged his shoulders back at me. The officer closed the case and I gave a great sigh of relief. I gave Warren the briefcase to carry after I walked through the gate of the security of the airport. Nothing went off, thank goodness. After Aldo and I went through the gates and security, I introduced Warren and Aldo.

"Warren, this is a good friend of mine, Jesus Aldoman-

They think I Killed My Husband!

do Gamir. I just call him Aldo for short. Aldo, this is Warren. He was kind enough to lease me his family's jet." I nervously told them both as we walked towards the plane. We got right onto Warren's plane. We had no problem at all. I was very happy about that. Now, we were on our way to Egypt.

Warren led Aldo and me to his jet. It was ready to go. I felt such a rush from making it through the airport without any trouble. No one even suspects that I am leaving the country. That is what is so creepy. I better not get caught doing anything wrong anywhere. I don't know what will happen. The three of us boarded the plane. Warren said we had clearance to take off in about forty-five minutes. Warren sat up front with the pilot and he was the acting copilot. Aldo and I made ourselves comfortable in the main compartment of the plane. We sat in the white leather recliners in the center. I put my purse and carry-on bag down on the floor for a moment. Warren walked in from the cockpit to see how we were doing.

"So, make yourselves a drink if you like. May I put your bags up in this compartment so it doesn't get tossed around inside?" Warren asked me with his boyish charm look about his face. He took the bags and stretched up in front of me and leaned over my chair and placed my bags in the compartment just over my head as he placed his bags in front of my face. He looked amazing with his tight slender and muscular abdominal midriff that I could see the silhouette of his physique through the fabric of his shirt. He was so young and was so sweet for being such a great guy! Although, I was paying him a pretty penny and I just wonder if he was probably keeping it all and using Daddy's plane. Oh, who cares? I didn't. Warren smiled at me after putting the bags up in the compartment and told us both to fasten our seat belts. He leaned over to check to make sure mine was fastened. He turned and walked into the front of the jet's cockpit to join the pilot and left Aldo and me in the main area of the plane. I thought I would make myself a drink. We did have a long flight ahead of us.

The next thing I knew we were landing. The first thing I wanted to do was get to a hotel. I just wanted to get cleaned up.

The trip was too long. It was extremely comfortable, probably the most comfortable airplane ride I have ever taken. However, it was still long going over the Atlantic Ocean. I needed a shower desperately. The airplane's shower may work for now, but I wanted a real shower. The wig was really beginning to itch. The sun was up again. I could feel the heat against the window of the plane. The light was very bright outside reflecting off of the sand and concrete below.

"Welcome to Cyprus Island," Warren announced.

"Where the hell is Cyprus Island and why are we here? I wanted to know.

"We can't land a private jet in Cairo. We have to take a boat from Cyprus Island," Warren filled me in some more.

"What? Are you kidding? Why didn't you tell us that before?" Aldo yelled at him!

"I didn't know until we got over the Mediterranean Sea. I was going to land in Cairo, but when I told the air traffic controller about my aircraft, they said I had to land in Cyprus Island. That was the only way," Warren explained with force.

"So, how much longer is it going to take us? I don't have that much time, you know," I explained.

"No, I didn't know. Besides, you were sleeping," Warren defended himself. "The man in the tower said the boat ride is about an hour and a half."

"Oh, Warren, were you going to stay with the plane or did you want to come with us, or what did you want to do?" I needed to know as I stopped in my tracks and turned and looked at him.

"I can do whatever you want me to do, Anna. I can go with you and ole Charlie the pilot can watch the plane. He usually stays with it while I am out on vacation or on a business trip anyway. Did you need my help?" Warren inquired to me immediately as if he really wanted to go with us.

"Well, if you would like to come, that would be fine. Do you care, Aldo?" I inquired.

"I don't care if Warren comes. Actually, that way I know the plane will be here when we get back." Aldo said

They think I Killed My Husband!

suspiciously looking at Warren with a slight squint in his eyes. It was said slightly in jest, but I could feel the tension. I just looked at them both and ignored the comment.

We all retrieved our luggage and made our way through the airport and found the port for the commuter ship. It was convenient for the travelers. Walking through customs and getting my passport stamped worried me a bit. They were hardly checking anyone's passport that I could see. People here could care less who I was. We made it onto the boat. It was a small commuter ship from the island to Cairo. We found some chairs and sat down for a while. I started to yawn and stretch in my chair on the commuter ship. I looked up at Aldo. I had to freshen up a little while on the boat. Warren walked towards us from the walk around the boat.

"We're getting close to shore," Warren said with a slight fatigue in his voice. "Welcome to Cairo."

"I think I will go and use the bathroom," I told Warren and Aldo. "I feel a little queasy from the waves."

"Of course! We can wait for a little while," Warren ordered.

"Fine. I want to get off of this boat as badly as you do," I replied as I got up and walked into the bathroom.

"So, are you going to be hanging out with us or sit on the sidelines while we do everything" Aldo wanted to know from Warren?

"Whatever Anna wants. I'll go and help you guys if you like, but, if I am going to be in the way...," Warren answered while making himself comfortable on the chair on the ship. Aldo stood up and retrieved our belongings out of the compartments Warren had put them in. I made it out of the bathroom and walked toward the men.

"So, where should we go? I mean, where is a hotel? Does anyone have a clue? I also need to find that bank where the deposit box is. Aldo, are you ready?" I asked while I picked up my purse.

"Ready as I will ever be," Aldo stated.

I walked to the front of the port and flagged a taxi

while Aldo and Warren retrieved the luggage from the plane. I opened up the door of the taxi cab and motioned the driver to wait a minute. I saw the men coming with the bags about thirty feet away. It was so hot standing by the old car with the exhaust fumes everywhere and the heat coming from underneath the car making the heat from the sun more intensified. Warren and Aldo arrived at the cab and began to put the bags into the trunk of the car. The driver walked around the back of the car and helped. The driver had on a turban and a long dress like garment made of cotton and linen. His skin was dark, like a typical Middle Easterner. I looked down and couldn't help to notice his feet when he picked up the luggage. He wore sandals and his toes hung out over the end and his toenails were too long and were disgustingly dirty. Then, I smelled a peculiar odor. The taxi driver had an odor of curry and fishes and garlic. He had a big nose that would make Barbara Streisand's nose appear miniature with a lot of nose hair that evolved into a mustache with a beard. His beard needed a trim. It was speckled with the food crumbs he ate for lunch. When the bags were loaded in the trunk and we all proceeded to get into the car. The driver turned to me and smiled. The teeth in his smile needed cleaning too. The man was in desperate need of a dentist. We all got into the car and headed on our way into the city. The city was like stepping into the past. The buildings are old and very plain. They look like they were built in the fifties or maybe the sixties. It was very hot and dry. The taxi had no air conditioning and was very old and uncomfortable. I had to keep the windows down to have some sort of breeze in the car. It was so dry that the sand kept blowing into my eyes just a little. The streets were like the ones at home, made of concrete. The streets were almost steaming with the asphalt and concrete. They were a bit outdated though. The holes and cracks in the pavement were in desperate need of mending. The cab driver must have hit every pot-hole in the road. People wore sandals and long garments to protect themselves from the sun and the heat. The women were all covered and all I could see were their eyes peering out from the cloth. We were getting closer to the

They think I Killed My Husband!

bank I needed to investigate. I motioned the driver to stop by waving some money in his face. He promptly pulled over. We exited the vehicle and needed to find a hotel to stay in. We got our luggage out of the cab and strolled down the street the best we could without being too conspicuous. However, I don't think that was going to happen. I had on my bright red wig and I stood out like a bright ketchup stain on a Bridegroom's white tuxedo among the Middle Eastern people. The three of us walked down the street of Cairo like three glowing sparklers in the night. Warren's blonde hair wasn't helping to keep us less inconspicuous either. We found a hotel close by. The first one we came to had an available room. It didn't look in too bad of shape. I was glad that they at least had indoor plumbing. Everything was so dirty everywhere, the streets, the buildings and even the people seemed like they could use a good bath, I was glad to see the hotel had running water. Warren and Aldo and I walked upstairs to the second floor to our rooms. I had my own room and made Aldo and Warren share another one. I put my suitcase on my bed. The room was very small with only one window. The bed was an old rod iron bed that was painted many times over. The paint was faded and old, but not as old as the bed. The hotel had that old musty smell that some old buildings have. I had to use the bathroom and I looked around my room for the bathroom and all I could find was the closet.

"Hey, I can't find my bathroom," I yelled outside my door into the hall towards the boys' room.

"Well, if you were paying more attention, you would have heard the desk clerk tell us the bathrooms are at the end of the hall on each floor," Aldo came out and informed me.

"What? You have got to be kidding me. I am glad that this place has indoor plumbing, I guess it was asking too much to have a private bath. Oh well, I guess I will have to go to the end of the hall to take a shower. I have to use it right now though. Which way is it?" I asked.

"It's down to your right," Aldo pointed. The halls were dirty and needed painting and new carpet. But, it will do for a couple of days, I suppose. I reached the bathroom. It was disgusting and small. The walls were old yellow stucco with stains all over it. The floor was tile and the grout was black with filth. It looked liked it hadn't been cleaned for months and it probably hasn't. I had to use the bathroom though. I had to really pee. I didn't sit on the toilet seat. I just sort of squatted and hovered over it without touching the seat. I stood back up after wiping and pulled up my panties. I flushed the toilet and nothing happened. I sighed and tried again, but this time I held the handle down longer and it worked. The water in the toilet didn't look very clean either. I peered around the tub and wondered how I was going to take a shower because it was missing a shower head. I looked around and figured that I guess I would have to sit in the bathtub and take a bath. How revolting! The bathtub is an old freestanding bathtub with nicks in the enamel and stains that look terrible. I went to wash my hands and turned on the faucet to the sink and the water had two faucets, one for hot and the other for cold. These types are really old fashioned and inconvenient. Then I looked up and realized the bathroom doesn't even have a mirror! Oh my God! I can't stay here. This bathroom is horrid. If we hadn't already paid the man, I would suggest we get our money back. I left the bathroom and walked back to my room. The boys were settling into their room. I stopped short of my room and poked my head into the boys' room.

"Have you seen the bathroom yet? It's awful!" I told the guys as they were putting their bags on the floor. "I don't think I will be able to stay here overnight. I have to take a bath and I don't know if I can take one in that tub. It is filthy. I going to have to ask the desk man to have someone clean the facilities."

"I'll ask for you. You don't need to be making a spectacle of yourself. I will gently ask someone to have the maid or whoever it is clean it. Okay?" Aldo calmly reassured me as he began to rub my back a little bit. Then he walked away towards the stairway to go downstairs to the front desk.

"See if they know the word 'bleach' or 'chlorine'!" I yelled down to Aldo as he walked down the stairs. "And bring me some. I'll clean it myself if I have too and I bet I will!"

Aldo just kept walking down the stairs and didn't even look back at me. He just waved his hand at me to let me know he heard me and to also let me know to be quiet. I just stood there and Warren poked his head out of the room.

"What is all of the commotion? Are you going to bleach your hair Anna to match mine?" Warren wanted to know with a cute grin on his face.

"No. I don't want to bleach my hair. I want to clean this whole darn hotel or at least I wish someone else had cleaned it." I told Warren quickly. "I don't want to even touch anything in this place. Do we have to stay here?" I said as I looked up at Warren with a pitiful, puppy-dog eyed face.

"Well, we already paid and I don't think these people are the types that like giving refunds. But, we can do anything you want. We can leave or we can stay, it's up to you." Warren assured me with a pleasant sound in his voice as he placed his hand on my shoulder.

"Yea, I guess you're right. It is only money and I do have enough to spare one night in this dump. If I am going to be out a little bit of money versus having to stay here, I would rather be out a little bit of money. I am still going to try to use the water to freshen up a little. The sand has stuck to my face and I would like to get a new face on. So I will be back in a second or ten," I told Warren while Aldo was getting some maid service.

I went back to the horrid bathroom to wash some of the sweat off my face and put some fresh makeup on. I returned to my room and freshened up my wig a bit and went to the boys' room and asked them if they would like to venture out to see if we could find a better room. They both agreed there would be no harm in looking around.

Aldo looked at me and suggested, "You know, 'Anna' maybe you should buy some proper clothing"

"What do you mean?" I wanted to know.

"Well, maybe at least a scarf or something. All of the other women have their heads covered and your hair is bright red!" Aldo was trying to make a point.

I looked at Aldo and then I took him by the arm and excused us from Warren for a second. "Do you think I should buy a hat or just take off the wig here and wear a scarf too? But, what about Warren? I would take off this stupid thing, but I have to think about Warren. Right now to him, I am 'Anna'. Do you think it's safe to come clean with him?"

"I wouldn't just yet. You don't want any lawyer digging this guy up from anywhere." Aldo reassured me to hold out and endure the wig in this terrible heat. I had to get a scarf I guess. It would help protect my wig from so much sand and the sun anyway.

We walked back over to Warren. Warren just stood there waiting and wondering what was up. I told him that we were going to walk around a bit. But, I needed to get a scarf first, so I wouldn't stand out so much. We immediately bought one off of a street vendor and I wrapped it around my head. We all continued to walk down the street. I brought my purse with me, but I left the rest of my stuff up in the room for now. I wanted to look for a different place to stay and the bank with the deposit box. Warren and Aldo were walking on either side of me. It was extremely hot outside in Cairo, especially downtown. The scarf helped with the heat a little bit. I noticed a bank before finding another hotel. I wanted to check it out while we were close by. The bank was an old fashioned looking bank. However, the flooring was marble and stone and the walls were stone and stucco with very little trim. The bank was the most modern building I had seen since I arrived. The lobby had counters in the middle and old desks with typewriters at each one of them. Warren and Aldo and I walked into the bank. Warren and Aldo sat down in the lobby and I asked the bank representative about the deposit boxes.

"Do you have a deposit box here" the lady wanted to know? She had long black hair that stuck out below her forehead of her scarf wrap. Her eyes looked like two Onyx stones against two eggshells. The scarf she wore was beautiful gold silk.

They think I Killed My Husband!

"I might, or at least my husband may have. I spoke to a girl over the phone. Her name was Layla. Is there a woman that works here named Layla?" I really needed to know as I looked at her desperately.

"No, there is no one here by that name. May I help you," she asked?

"Has anyone worked here before with that name? I called few weeks ago," I told her.

"No, never had we had someone here with that name. Is there anything else I can help you with?" She wanted to know and started to become impatient with me.

"Could you tell me if Ralph Garcia had a safety deposit box here? I am his wife and I have his death certificate." I informed the woman.

"I can look up in our records and see if there is one registered in his name. How do you spell his name?" the woman needed to know.

I gave her the death certificate to show her how to spell it. I got lucky and sure enough, there was a box in his name! I was so excited! Finally, I might be able to find out what is going on around here! The woman said she had some paperwork for me to sign before she could let me in the box. She left me sitting in front of her desk as she went to get the proper documents for me to sign. Warren and Aldo walked up to me and wanted to know what was happening.

"Hey, Anna! What is happening?" Warren asked me rather loudly.

I just put my head down and thought to myself, "Oh shit. I have to get him out of here. I have documents to be signed as Pam Garcia and here is a man calling me 'Anna.'" I looked at Aldo with a cry of help on my face and he understood.

"Hey, Warren. Whatever it is that 'Anna' has to do, she can handle it without us. She is in a bank. C'mon, let's wait for her right outside the door." Aldo quickly emphasized to Warren then taking him by the arm and escorting outside with him.

I thought to myself, "Thank God. These people might

put me in jail just for being a woman in a wig with a different name or something. I don't know. I don't need to know either."

The woman arrived back to the desk and I sat up to her attention. She placed the documents before me and began to explain each of them to me. "These are stating that you are the benefactor of the estate and the deceased's wife. You do have the key to the box, correct?"

"Yes. Why do you ask? Of course, that is why I am here." I replied to the woman from across the desk showing her the key.

"These boxes are the type that you must have the key to obtain possession to its contents. Even if you were not his wife and just had the key, but the fact he is dead, anyone with the key could have access to it. Because he is no longer alive, it is like, how do you say, 'Finders-Keepers." The woman at the bank told me something very valuable.

"May I go into the box today?" I inquired as soon as I was finished signing the documents.

"You may go in whenever you wish. You have presented the proper documents to me and you have the key, so if you would like to go now, I shall permit you to your property, Mrs. Garcia. Follow me." The bank attendant instructed. I began to follow her with my key ready in my hand. I couldn't believe it. I was finally going to find out what was in the safety deposit box! My heart began to race as I walked behind the lady into the vault. She put her key into the lock and then I did the same. It was one of the biggest boxes available. I wondered what could be in such a big box. She turned her key and I turned mine. She told me that if I needed anything, the guard could assist with anything I may need. I began to pull the box out of the drawer space it was in. I can't even begin to move it. I couldn't imagine what could be inside. I did ask the guard for some assistance. It was too heavy for the guard as well. I had to help him move the box. Between the two of us, we both were able to scoot the metal lock box onto the floor. I told him that would be fine and if he could make sure that no one else came into this room, I could deal with it. He nodded and left the room. I

They think I Killed My Husband!

don't know if he understood me entirely or not, but he got the main idea. I opened the box and I couldn't believe what I saw! It was filled with gold! Gold in all shapes and sizes from coins to jewelry to even a few gold bricks!

"Holy Fort Knox, Batman! What the fuck have you been doing, Ralph?" I asked myself. I looked around the box and took out some of the coins and placed them on the ground. I banged one of the bars on the side of the box to see how it dented. Gold is a soft metal and if the bars are solid, they may dent, but they won't chip any layers off. The bars were heavy. They were about twenty pounds per piece. "I wonder how much each one is worth? I wonder how much gold is here?" I asked myself as I looked into the box. I took out another gold brick and held it up towards the light to look at the gold shimmer. It was beautiful. I started to take out a coin and some jewelry, one at a time. I had to count to see how many there were. There were twenty bars of gold in the box. There were also hundreds of coins and maybe fifty pieces of jewelry and some with diamonds. How am I going to get this to the states? Why did Ralph have this box here with all of this gold? Where did he get all of this gold? I put two bricks and jewelry into my purse and laid my purse on the floor. I retrieved the guard from his post in the need of his aid. We were able to put the box back into the drawer from whence it came.

"I will have to come back and get the rest," I thought to myself. "No one will be able to get to it. I am the only signer on it. Whoever tried to get in before failed and will again. So it will be safest here anyway," I assured myself. I made it back to the main lobby of the bank. I felt drained. I don't know if it was the adrenaline from the excitement or the weight of the gold making me feel light-headed. I asked the bank representative if there was any way anyone else other than me could get into that safety deposit box.

"The only other person is Mr. Garcia. He would have to pass the infrared fingerprint detectors if he didn't have the key and if he came back from the dead. But now, we have transferred it to you," she stated with a bit of cockiness and laughter, which was surprising considering the situation. I thought that was strange.

"Thank you." I told her routinely. I quickly walked out and immediately found Warren and Aldo. They were waiting just outside on the street. They looked incredibly hot and tired and sweaty.

"We found another hotel. It has bathrooms in each of the rooms. You can take a bath in the privacy of your own beaudois. Does that make you happy?" Aldo asked me with a smile on his dusty face and his big brown eyes looking at me with longing approval.

"Awesome! Let's go!" I shouted with excitement. I needed to bathe so badly! We all headed back to the first hotel so we could get the rest of our stuff. I was wondering if I should tell the guys what I found. I will wait and tell Aldo later, when we are alone sometime. I hope I can get it through customs and the metal detectors. Maybe, if I just put them in the baggage and since we are on our own plane, we don't need to have them checked. The way the airport looked coming in, I don't think I will have too much of a problem. The authorities looked more like they are more concerned with weapons and don't really care about gold. We all arrived to the new hotel with the private bathrooms in each room. It was a newer hotel. I don't know why we just didn't come here in the first place. I guess we just hadn't stumbled upon it yet. It looked like a newer building. It might have been built in the early seventies. A very modern building considering the city I was in. It still looked like it needed some updating. I felt like I was walking into a time warp. The décor was still like that of the seventies. The trim was done in chrome and blue and silver were the color tones. The furniture was like an art deco but old and a little worn out. It was still cleaner than the other place. I was happy. I was going to be able to take a bath in my own room without this stupid wig on.

"We already got the rooms," Aldo told me as I headed over to the desk clerk. I stopped suddenly and pivoted.

"You did? How nice! Well, let's go to our rooms then.

They think I Killed My Husband!

I can't wait to get into that tub," I exclaimed a little too loudly creating a little too much attention. We all headed straight upstairs to our rooms. I couldn't wait until I could get this wig off of my head. I went into my room and the boys went into theirs. I immediately took off my wig. I began to scratch my head. It felt so good to scratch it. It had been itching terribly in this heat and my sweat was dripping down the sides of my face and neck. I took off the rest of my clothes and became completely naked. I went into my own private bath and turned on the water to the tub. The tub began to fill up with water, when I heard a knock on the door.

"Who is it?" My voice went through the door.

"It's Aldo." The voice on the other side of the door replied. I had on a towel and that is about it.

"Just a second. I have to put something on." I yelled back through the door while I grabbed a robe that I packed out of my suitcase and put it on. I opened the door and Aldo walked in.

"You didn't have to do that." Aldo told me while delicately grabbing the ends of my robe's belt.

"Well, I just had to be sure. I didn't want to open the door naked." I insisted. "Oh, by the way, I have to show you something. It's what was inside the deposit box."

"I was going to ask you about that. What ended up being inside of it? I can't believe you found it and they let you into it, even with Ralph's death certificate. So, what is it? Tell me." Aldo wanted to know.

"Well, you are not going to believe this, but I found a bunch of gold inside the deposit box." I told him as I sat down on the bed with my robe tied around my waist and my hair was a mess. It was sweaty and straight back and just hanging off of my head like dreads.

Aldo looked right into my eyes and exclaimed, "What? Gold? You have got to be shitting me!"

"Umm, no. Here is one of the coins." I told him as I went to my suitcase and got one of the bricks out from the bottom of it. I showed the brick to Aldo. I held it up in my hands and presented it to him. His eyes became as large as silver dollars when he saw the gold brick. His mouth could catch some flies too.

"I can't believe you took a brick out of the bank with you. Then you brought it here to the hotel with you. Do you want to get us all killed?" Aldo reprimanded me.

"What do you mean?" I wanted to know. "Do you really think someone would think I would have this on my person?"

"In this place, you never know." Aldo informed me very sternly as if I were a little girl. I made my way back to have a seat on the bed.

"Besides, the gold brick could be used as a lethal weapon! I sure feel sorry for anyone that would try and attack me!" I said with a laugh.

"How much do you think one of these are worth?" Aldo was curious.

"Oh, I don't know. I guess if you started doing the math, gold is about, what nine hundred dollars per ounce give or take a few dollars on a given day? Multiply that amount times how much each of these weigh. I haven't weighed it yet, but I bet it weighs at least twenty pounds! This thing is heavy! Well, there is one step you lost, Einstein, I forgot you have to multiply that by 16 because there are sixteen ounces in a pound. So now, what do you have?" I asked him as he was punching numbers on the calculator on his phone.

"That's two hundred fifty thousand dollars a brick!" Aldo said very quietly.

"What the hell was Ralph doing with all of that gold in the box and in Egypt? Then there are the coins and the jewelry and diamonds! What kind of crap was he involved in?" I just broke down and started to cry and Aldo held me close.

"What you need to do is go to that bank tomorrow and get the gold transferred to another box. I think it would be best if you just closed that box with Ralph's name and open one up with Anna's. Somehow we can do some sort of switch, or we can get a basket with wheels like a shopping basket and just take it to another bank altogether. What ever you want, but I think that would be a smart thing to do."

"I think you may be right." I agreed while thinking that if anyone wanted the key again, I would just give it to him. They would just go to an empty box. They might get mad and get me later, but then I could get someone after them in the mean time!

Warren was in the next room and came to my door and knocked on it. Aldo and I started to shuffle about trying to figure out where to put the gold. Warren knocked again.

"Hey Anna! Are you in there? I was wondering if you were hungry. Do you want to go and get something to eat? I don't know where Aldo went. Are you in there?" Warren wouldn't give up.

"Yes, Warren, I am in here. Just a minute while I put on my robe." I had on my robe, but that was an excuse to buy some time to get the gold out of sight and Aldo too. Then Aldo pointed at my head. I grabbed my head with my hands and realized my wig was over on the table and not on my head!

"Oh, shit! Warren, I can't find my robe!" I shouted through the door.

"That's okay. Do you want me to wait or would you like for me to bring you something back?" Warren asked politely. He was such a well-mannered young man. I could tell his family was one of high ethics and education.

"Sure, that would be great!" I yelled back through the door.

"What do you want?" Warren wanted to know.

"Where are you going?" I wanted to know.

"To whatever is out there. I have never been here. I don't know." Warren replied.

"Well, just bring me back whatever. I don't care. I will eat anything. Try to keep it as close to normal as possible please." I begged him.

"I'll try. I'll be back in a few. If I am not back in thirty minutes, come looking for me please?" Warren pleaded, just before he left to find something to eat.

I turned around and looked at Aldo and sighed a sigh of relief.

"That was close," Aldo said as he came out of the bathroom.

"You think? He is going to be back in a half an hour. I hope I don't have to go out and look for him. I can't fly his jet out of here if anything happens to him, ya know?"

"Nothing is going to happen to him. Come here and let's get our minds off of this mess." Aldo said as he pulled me over towards him. He started to kiss me on my neck. He knows that is a weak spot of mine. It was so hot and humid.

"I haven't had a bath yet. I am all sticky and sweaty. I need to clean." I told Aldo.

"I can bathe you," Aldo suggested strongly still holding my hands and looking at me face to face. He smiled very willingly and raised his eyebrows a couple of times quickly to display his friskiness. "I can bathe you with my hands then I can bathe you like a cat," again with the raising of the eyebrows.

"Well, if you like, you can wash my back. I have to fill the tub. I would ask you to join me, but it is a rather small tub." I told Aldo.

"Well, let me get you all clean. That is what I am here for. I just want to take care of you." Aldo reassured me in a loving way.

The bathtub was full and I got in. The water was warm and semi-clear from the non- filtering system the city does not have. I had to get in. I would bathe in a lake right now the way I felt. Aldo followed me in with some soap and towels. The water did feel good. No, it felt wonderful. I started to feel very relaxed. Aldo got a washcloth wet and began scrubbing a bar of soap across the surface of it to work up some lather. He then took the soapy washcloth across my back. Then down into the water to bring some water up on my skin. He began rubbing my back and my neck and shoulders with the soapy cloth. It was wonderful. I was so tired. I just closed my eyes and enjoyed it. Aldo began caressing my breasts with the soap in his hands and the cloth, working both of his hands around my huge breasts like he may have been making a clay pot on a spindle. He began cleaning my underarms and around my ears. He held my hands and cleaned my fingers one by one.

"Lean back and relax." Aldo told me as he kissed my lips and eased me back in the tub. Aldo began cleaning my tummy and told me to get under completely to wash my hair. As I did, he took my foot.

"What the hell are you doing?" I yelled as I came up for air! "I almost couldn't breathe! Are you trying to kill me?"

"No! Oh, my God, Pam! I am sorry. It was an accident. Please. I got a little over zealous. Honey, please. I was just trying to clean your toes. Here, give me your foot. I'll clean your toes, your legs and anything else you want me to give a rub down," Aldo said to me again with his eyebrows going up and down.

"All right." I relaxed and let Aldo finish cleaning my toes. Aldo started to clean my feet and my legs after my toes were clean. He lifted my legs out of the tub as I remained sitting in it. He began cleaning the back of my knee and leaned over me and began rubbing my butt with the washcloth.

"We have to make sure everything is clean." After saying that, the cloth dropped and fell to the bottom of the tub. Aldo reached down into the water to retrieve the cloth. Aldo's fingers made their way to my vagina instead. He started to play with my lips. His fingers slithered up to my clitoris and caressed it back and forth with tiny circular motions.

"Is that what you had in mind by making me relax?" I asked him?

"Oh yea," Aldo said as he pushed one finger all of the way up inside of my vaginal canal.

I leaned back and moaned with ecstasy. I quickly rose out of the tub and stood up on my feet. I began to kiss Aldo on the mouth. I wrapped my arms around his neck and he put both of his hands on my buttocks and lifted me out of the tub. I stood on the bathroom floor and Aldo got down on his knees and began to lick my pussy. I put my feet further apart and he took one of his hands and held the lips of my pussy open. He began kissing and licking my clit dry that was dripping with water from the tub. His other hand was on the back of my ass holding me still so I couldn't get away. I started to tingle. I couldn't hold it in! I began to scream with pleasure! I clenched Aldo's hair until I almost pulled it out. He stopped because I started to hurt him when I was cumming and pulling on his hair. I pulled Aldo up by his hair and started kissing him.

"Oh, wow. Oh, my God." I could barely say, because I was so out of breath. I kissed Aldo and got dressed. I combed my hair and put a towel on my head. Aldo went back to his room to wait on Warren. I figured I would keep the towel on until after Warren got here so I wouldn't have to put the wig back on. Warren came back with some food. It was some fresh rice and some sort of meat. I didn't want to know. I think it might have been goat. I have heard that goat was tasty, but I really did not want to go out and try it. But, right now, I guess I didn't have much of a choice. It wasn't too bad.

"Couldn't you find anything other than goat's meat? Was there no McDonald's or something like that?" I asked, Warren.

"Not that I could find right off hand. I wanted to get back as soon as I could. I figured you would be hungry. The lady gave me a sample. I thought it tasted kind of good. Don't you like it?" Warren wanted to know with some apologetic tones in his sweet young voice. He looked at me with those big blue puppy dog eyes and I couldn't say that I didn't like it, because I really kind of did.

"Oh, it's all right. It's food. The meat is really tender and full of flavor." I told him as I took another bite. I was really hungry especially after Aldo increased my appetite. Aldo and I had to think of a way to get the gold out of the box and into another box tomorrow without creating too much attention. The gold is so heavy it will be difficult to move it. We are going to have to just keep it in the same bank and transfer it to another box. I can just put it under "Anna's" name. The trick will be 'how' will I be able to do that without leaving the bank. I will have to go in first and open up a box in Anna's name and leave it open, then go without the wig to another girl and open the box with the gold. I will have to tell Warren. He may be able to help. He has helped so far. I don't think he poses as any threat.

They think I Killed My Husband!

"You must really like it, Anna. You haven't said a word while you have eating." Warren said as he noticed I was quiet while I was thinking.

"Yes, Anna, what are you thinking about?" Aldo wanted to know.

"Oh, I have been thinking about how I am going to transfer that stuff." I said out loud and Aldo looked at me then rolled his eyes towards Warren as if to warn me that Warren was right there.

"I know he is there. I think we are going to have to let him in on it. We are going to need his help, Aldo. He has been good to us so far. He came back with food and not the authorities." I reminded Aldo.

"Yes, but that is because he is unaware that the authorities need to informed." Aldo told me angrily.

"Whoa! What are you two talking about? I brought food because your stomachs were empty. That is all." Warren stated getting up and standing in the room acting nervous. He started looking around like he may get shot any moment.

"Didn't you ever wonder why I hired you and your private jet a couple of times to take me out of the country?" I inquired of Warren.

"I just thought you had a lot of money and wanted to travel in comfort." Warren answered. "I didn't think any more of it."

"Well, there is a lot more to it." Aldo added. "Were you going to tell him everything, 'Anna'?" Aldo wanted to know.

"Well, you see Warren, I am running away. My husband used to beat me and I had to disguise myself to leave the country. My kids are with my family where he won't be able to find them or harm them. I am traveling and trying to make sense out of some things I found hidden in our bedroom. I found a key in our safe at home and found out it belonged to a safety deposit box here. Then today I found out what was in the box." I lied to Warren to get him to help us without spilling the whole truth of the matter. Aldo just smiled and looked over at Warren to see the expression on his face to see if he was buying the story. Warren bought it hook, line and sinker. Why wouldn't he?

Warren sat back down and took my hands and looked into my eyes and wanted to help me and exclaimed, "Oh my, Anna, I had no idea. What did you need me to do?"

I looked at Warren with the look of gratitude and fear and told him that I needed him to help Aldo and me at the bank tomorrow. I explained that I found approximately four million dollars in gold bricks in the box at the bank and I wanted to transfer the gold to another box.

"So, what is the problem?" Warren wanted to know.

"Well, I have to do it without creating attention. I need to stay inside the bank and put the gold in another box in another name. I can't do that being one person with two identities at the same bank and not leave the bank. But, I don't want to take the gold out of the bank, it's too dangerous out on the street. Who knows what or who may be lurking out there," I justified my actions.

"Why don't you disguise yourself, Anna?" Warren suggested.

"I thought of that. But, how do I get from the deposit vault to the lobby as a different person without anyone being suspicious? Unless, I walk in with Aldo first to open up the box, then leave Aldo there with the box open. Then come back with you as another person, like your wife or girlfriend or something and open up another box. But, we have to make this fast. I have to open up a new box first under the pseudo-name." I was thinking out loud to Warren and Aldo trying to fish for suggestions as well.

Then Aldo came up with a great idea for cutting out a shit load of time. "Why don't you rent out a box identical to the one that is filled with gold and then just switch the entire boxes. That will save time and you won't expose the gold that way."

"Okay, now we are thinking. I have been in the vault. The bank employees pretty much leave you alone. Once you are in the vault the rooms are off to the side if you want privacy. But how am I going to leave undetected?" I needed that one issue resolved.

Warren and Aldo were left a bit stumped. I was trying to think of a way to go into the vault with Aldo then be able to go in again with Warren and have both of my own deposit boxes open at the same time. The only difficult thing is I am supposed to be two different people in the eyes of the bank.

"I know, why don't I open up the safety deposit box? Then, I can just walk in and open up the box and make the switch," Warren suggested sincerely.

"Oh right! Then you would have a shit load of pure gold in your possession and out of ours!" Aldo exclaimed to Warren with a bit of distrust.

"What do you mean 'ours'? I know you are here helping, but come on. I need to have that gold where only I can get to it. I mean only me! Whether it is in some other name, as long as my picture is on that identification card for that name that is all that matters. You know I will take care of you guys. I just have to look out right now." Then an epiphany came to me, "I know how I can do this."

"Oh really? How?" Warren and Aldo both said in unison.

I looked at both of them and said, "I'll go in first as 'Anna Nelson' and open up a deposit box. I went in with a scarf on my head before so no one really saw the wig. Then I can leave and come back without the wig as Pam and Aldo you can come with me at that time."

"Hey! Hold up! Wait a minute! What are you talking about a wig? Where did you come up with the name of Pam?" Warren demanded to know.

"Warren, I will need to wear a wig when I go in as Pam or have on the scarf." I said looking at Aldo intently so he will stay quiet. "I will open up a deposit box then leave. Come back later with Aldo and my disguise. We will open up box and I can take off my disguise. Walk out of the vault and Warren, you can meet me in the lobby and act like we walked in together. Have the lady get us into the new box I opened under 'Anna's name and make the switch." I concreted the plans with the guys.

"Sweet!" Warren exclaimed. "I'm in!"

"So, what do you think, Aldo? Do you think it'll work?" I needed to validate my idea.

"Yea, it'll probably work. I can do that. I guess I can just sit there and wait while you put on your disguise or take off your disguise. Whatever it is your going to do. I can't keep up anymore. You do whatever it is you are going to do and I will do what ever you tell me to do." Aldo said to me as he leaned over and gave my shoulder a slight nudge with his shoulder.

"Cool. It's settled then. That will be our plan for tomorrow." I insisted with a nod of my head to show my approval and appreciation. "Now let's go to bed. We have a busy day tomorrow." I told the boys while looking at them like I wanted my privacy now. "You know, leave and go to your room!" I insisted again with sternness in my voice. The boys left and went to their room and went to bed as I did. I couldn't fall asleep right away. I was thinking about our plans for the switch at the bank tomorrow.

I awoke the next morning and got ready to go to the bank to open a deposit box under the name of Anna Nelson. I put on my wig and my heavy makeup and got dressed. I didn't want to take the boys with me this time. I wanted to make the initial bank visit alone. I left my room undetected by anyone and walked out through the lobby. The desk clerk was not behind the desk at the moment, so I just walked out the front door. I proceeded down to the bank where the deposit box was and went straight to another bank attendant that I hadn't met yet. I told her my name and I was interested in opening up a deposit box. I told her the size I wanted.

"Those larger sizes are quite expensive. They are two hundred fifty dollars per year," the woman informed me.

"I just want to rent one. I don't care how much it is. I can deal with the price. Is one available?" I really needed to know.

"That is the other thing. I will need to check. Those

sizes are so large and we have so few of them since they are so large, the space is limited for them. Let me check our books," she stated as she got up to retrieve a logbook of some sort to check the availability of the boxes. She combed the ledger with her finger as she looked over the pages. "Ah, yes. That's right. A couple of them were closed out a couple of months a go," she said as her memory was refreshed.

"Oh, good! So, I may have one," I pleaded excitedly with the woman.

"Yes. I just need you to fill out the proper paperwork and I need two forms of identification." She told me as she pulled out some papers from a drawer beside her desk and placed them on her desk in front of me. I pulled them towards me and grabbed a pen. I proceeded to get my wallet out of my purse to show her my identification and to help me copy exactly from my I. D. cards to the paper forms she handed me. Then she took my identification from me before I had a chance to make sure I had everything correct on the paperwork I was filling out.

"I will need to make a copy of these." She said while she grabbed my fake license and passport. I began to get really nervous.

I began to think horrible things to myself. "What if she can tell these things are fake? What if she calls the authorities? I could get into a whole lot of trouble. I could get thrown into jail just for being here. Never mind how it would look trying to set myself up to live on the run. How guilty is that? What about my kids?" I was starting to break out into a cold sweat and wondered if my thoughts were being dispelled by my facial expression.

The woman returned with my identifications and looked at me and asked, "Are you all right? You don't look so good."

"Yes, I think so. I may need some water. I do feel a bit over heated." I told her feeling a bit out of breath. She leaned over to feel my forehead. I pulled away quickly because of my wig. Her hand ended up on my arm to feel how clammy I was.

"I will get you some water. I will be right back." The

lady told me as she left to get some water for me.

"Thank you." I replied. She returned quickly and handed me some water that I drank instantly.

"Now that all of the paperwork is finished, all I need from you is the money for the box and then I can show you where it is and give you the key," the nice lady insisted.

"Wonderful," I exclaimed! I gave her everything she asked of me. She then proceeded to take me to the vault. I stood up from the chair and began to walk, but tripped on the leg of her desk.

"Do you think you can make it to the vault?" The lady asked. "You seemed a bit overheated a moment ago."

"I am fine. I just tripped. Now, where is the box?" I persisted.

Later, back at the hotel, I got undressed and took off my wig. I brushed out my long black locks and took off some of my make up. I put a scarf over my head and wrapped up my hair like I did yesterday. I also took one of my carry on bags that could double as a big purse, since I wanted to place my clothes I was just wearing and my wig and some extra make up and brush in it. I knocked on Warren and Aldo's door to see if they were in their hotel room. Aldo answered.

"Hey, now that's the girl I know. What's going on?" Aldo wanted to know. I am sure he knew I had already done something, but wanted to be up to speed on everything.

"Well, I opened up the new deposit box. Now all we have to do is switch the boxes." I told him as I walked into his room. Warren came out of the bathroom.

"Great disguise, Anna!" Warren said with his pretty blue eyes looking at me with his toothbrush still sticking out of his mouth and a plain hotel towel wrapped around his bare shoulders.

"Ummmm, yea." I said looking down, then at Aldo with a slightly shameful expression on my face I was trying to hide.

"So, what do you need me to do?" Aldo asked me.

"Well, I need for the both of you to listen. The first thing we will do is go into the bank as I am now, as 'Pam' and Aldo can come with me. He and I can go in and open the deposit box with the gold in it. We will go and take it into the room. It is going to be heavy. Maybe we can take a roller chair or something. I don't know how Ralph got it in there to begin with. He must not have done it alone, or did it in several trips. Oh, hell, knowing him he brought in his own dolly." I was saying instructions at first, then turned out to be thinking out loud.

"Anyways?" Aldo said as he looked at me with anticipation.

"Oh, um, yea, well, anyways, yea, that's it. We'll bring our own dolly and make it look like we took out something. Let's get a trunk and fill it with concrete bricks and bring it in the bank and just leave with the concrete bricks and swap the boxes as planned." I decided.

"Don't you think that might cause a lot of attention?" Aldo asked me.

"I kind of agree." Warren gave his opinion too.

"If you have people that have killed for this key to this box, it's because they know what is inside of it. They may be here right now waiting for you to come and get it. If you show up with a big box to take out the bricks for some reason they think they are entitled too…do you understand where I am coming from?" Aldo added his comments.

"Exactly. I am baiting myself. So I can get out of here as soon as this is done today, Warren. Would that be okay?" I had to clear it with Warren of course. "So, when I am back in the states, if anyone saw this take place, will try to get the gold there, in the states. Then, there will be placement of doubt upon me and I should be found not guilty. I have already had attempts on my life. He is probably the same person that killed Ralph and Mrs. Enrique Gonzalez and her son." I told them both in my defense.

"Um, Anna, what is this all about?" Warren wanted to know.

My eyes flew open and without realizing I went into great detail and just did something my father always warned me about.

My father always told me, "If you never lie, you don't have to remember anything." Boy, was he right. I totally forgot that my story was that I was a beaten woman running from her husband. What am I going to tell Warren now to alleviate him from the circumstances? I guess he is pretty much in this whether he knows or not. It just might be the polite thing to tell him. But the less he knows, the better off he may be. But, I already said everything.

"The truth, Anna. I want the truth. I am here in this Hell-hole with you and this jerk with my jet doing whatever it is you want me to do. I don't need the money. I sure could be doing something else with my time. I am not stupid either. Just because my Dad has money doesn't mean I am stupid. I am a pilot. I was trained in the Marine Corps. I am educated. Don't lie to me." Warren demanded in a way I have never seen him behave before. He started to breathe heavy and his eyes started to bug out of his head. He looked very intently into my eyes. I looked up at Warren. Our eyes couldn't have been more than three inches apart when I took a deep breath and exhaled very slowly.

"All right, Warren, you deserve the truth. I do believe you have earned my trust. I guess I can tell you." I said, with a little bit of hesitation in my voice.

"Thank you. I would never want to see anything bad happen to you. For some reason I am drawn to you. That is why I took you back from the Cayman Islands. I didn't want to see you hurt." Warren reassured me.

"Well, number one, my husband was murdered and the state is trying to pin it on me. But, I didn't do it. Everything points to me. Except that there has been an attempt on my life over what was in this box," I confessed to Warren.

"Was everything you said right now for real? You have to be found not guilty? So, you have to be like, not here? Is that it?" Warren wanted to verify his suspicions.

"Yep. That's pretty much it." I replied. "Now, if we can get to business, we should get that big box with bricks and get to the bank."

They think I Killed My Husband!

Aldo and I headed to the bank. I instructed Warren to follow approximately twenty minutes later. Aldo and I walked into the bank with the box in a wagon. The lady that waited on me earlier walked up to us.

"May I help you?" She asked us in English. She failed to see any resemblance between Pam and 'Anna' which was a great thing.

"I need to get into my deposit box. I just need to take out a few things." I replied with a smile pointing to the box. The woman smiled shyly and looked at the box. We proceeded with the paperwork and I signed my name and we all went to the vault. The lady put her key in and I put my key in. The box was open. The lady left and Aldo and I went into a room with the dolly-wagon and crate of bricks. I kept watching the deposit box. I had to help Aldo with the box of bricks. We lifted it up and off of the wagon and placed it on the floor of the little room. We then took the wagon to the deposit box where the gold was. The drawer of the box was close to the floor, so we were going to have to lift it up. But once we pulled the box out, it just fell to the ground.

"Oh shit. This is heavy." Aldo said, after it fell and he couldn't even budge it.

"Yea, I know. Do you think we can put it into the wagon?" I wanted to know his opinion.

"Well, maybe, I don't know. Here, let's try," Aldo said with enthusiasm as he grabbed the side handle of the box. I grabbed the side handle of the box as well.

"Uuummmpphhh!" I moaned with great endurance. The box hardly moved. "Oh, boy. What are we going to do?" I asked Aldo.

"Well, we could just start emptying the box out right here or take the bricks one by one into the room or try and slide this puppy over to the room." Aldo suggested after wiping the sweat off of his brow.

"If we just slide it, that would be faster and easier. We really didn't need the wagon, did we," I asked sarcastically.

"Well, you did want to let anyone watching know that

you have come for the gold." Aldo reminded me.

"I hope that wasn't a mistake." I said to myself as we slid the gold to the room on the side of the vault. I opened up the box we had brought into the bank with the plain bricks in it. I also put in my wig and a change of clothes. I put my hair up and put on the wig. I quickly changed into the other clothes I had brought. I added some more make-up to my face so I appeared slightly different in the face too. I checked my watch. I still had about five minutes before Warren's scheduled arrival. So, should I try to make it out of the bank and hope that no one notices or sees that I came out of the vault? I started to take out the bricks out of the box we brought in.

"What are you doing, Pam?" Aldo seriously wanted to know. "Have you lost your mind?"

"No. You are going to take me out of this bank in this box just in time for Warren to meet me outside. I don't know why I didn't think of it before."

"Because we wouldn't have gone along with it before," Aldo reassured me.

"It'll work. Trust me." I reassured him right back with a smile on my red haired face.

He just rolled his eyes and agreed by shaking his head and began taking out the bricks and placing them on the floor of the room. I climbed into the box and Aldo wheeled me right out of the bank. As he rolled me out, he said to the woman that escorted us into the vault, " Mrs. Garcia is still in there. I will be back in a couple of minutes. I must make a couple of trips." He continued without a lost step. I could hear him getting Warren's attention.

"Hey, Aldo. What are you doing? Aren't you supposed to be in the bank and I am supposed to meet Anna out here?" Warren wanted to know.

"Would you hush up? Don't you know the number one woman's right is the right to change her mind?" Aldo questioned Warren's knowledge of women.

"What? Where is that coming from? Where is Anna?" Warren demanded impatiently. "If you did anything to her just for a bunch of gold bricks, I'll tie you to those bricks and throw you off of my jet while we are over the Atlantic! Capische?" Warren threatened Aldo with great passion.

"Holy shit, Dude. Settle down. She is right here." Aldo told him as he pulled me to the side of some building in an alley, so I could get out of the box. I sat up and Warren helped me the rest of the way out. Warren lifted me up and out and placed me on the pavement so I was standing up on my feet next to him. I gave him a kiss for being so thoughtful. I knew now that I could really trust Warren. However, it was unfortunate that he could not really trust me. I had not been completely honest with him. He still thinks my disguise is as 'Pam' and my real name is 'Anna'. I will have to cross that bridge when I get to it.

Warren and I walked into the bank. The lady recognized me. I could tell. Oh, God. I had an awful feeling in my stomach. She smiled at me and said, "Hello, Anna. Did you need to get into your box again today?"

"Yes, please. I need to put a few things in. I shouldn't be too long." I enforced my reasoning. She proceeded with normal procedures and escorted me to the safety deposit box vault. The room I was just in was still closed and it looked like no one had been in there. The bank employee put her key in as I did mine and opened up the box. I took out the box and went into another room beside the one I was already in, so to speak. I waited a minute and peaked out of the room. The vault was still open, but no one was paying attention. I had to go into the other room and make the switch. I motioned Warren to follow me into the other room where the gold was. I grabbed onto the empty box and told Warren to do the same. We carried the empty box into the other room. I reached for the door and began to turn the knob. I wouldn't turn. I began to shake the door and tried to jimmy it open.

"Shit! I can't believe this. It's locked. Now, what are we going to do," I asked Warren?

"We," he wondered? "Unless you have a mouse in your pocket, you made it pretty clear that we were just getting our share, but it is pretty much your affair," he added coldly and sort of pissed off.

"Well, the gold is still locked up and now it will be really fishy if we need to ask for help. What do we do now? Just leave and get Aldo? We can't do anything." I rambled on to Warren.

"We can't just leave the gold sitting in there. They have to have a key to open up the door. What if someone dies or gets sick in there?" Warren was trying to justify the situation. "Besides, Aldo will be back in here in a minute anyway."

"No, he won't. That's just it. We are to make the switch and leave. Then he brings me back in inside the box. Then I leave again as Pam." I informed Warren again.

"Oh, now I get it. You come in as Pam, then he'll take you out of the bank in the box. Then you came in the bank again as Anna, and now you will leave again as Anna. You climb into the box and Aldo wheels you back into the bank like he is bringing in an empty box to take out more stuff. You walk back out again as Pam! Cool! I really didn't understand the whole scenario until now," Warren confessed reluctantly, yet proudly that he had figured it all out. We walked back into our little room. We didn't let the door shut so we were able to get back into the room.

"Me too. So, don't feel bad. I actually didn't have it all together until right now either. I sure didn't count on the self-locking rooms. I guess it would be safer. So no one could rob you and if you left your stuff, it would be locked up in the room," I sighed and sat down at the table in the little room just looking down at the box that we need to switch in a matter of minutes with the other one in that locked room. All I could do is sit with my chin in my hand and look at Warren and wonder how I could have gotten so mixed up in such a mess? How could I let this nice young man get mixed up in all of this mess? I heard a noise. I looked up. It's Aldo!

"What's up," Aldo whispered? "You were in here a little too long. I figured I could make three trips. This stuff is supposed to be heavy. Besides, who is anyone to judge me?"

"Oh, you are a life saver!" Warren answered with great

relief.

"But, we are locked out of the room! How are we going to get back in there?" I pleaded with Aldo like he could magically make the situation disappear.

"Oh, I already asked the lady to let me in. I told her you were probably listening to the headphones and couldn't hear me." Aldo replied with a smirk on his face.

"Genius! Pure, simple, unadulterated genius that's what you are! Oh my God! Do you realize what could have happened? I don't want to think about it." I said quickly and very quietly with great enthusiasm. I gave Aldo a big hug and turned to grab the box in the little room Warren and I had been waiting in. Warren quickly got the hint and grabbed the other handle on the other side of the box and carried it to the other room. Aldo held the other door open. Now all we had to do is put the box of gold in my new deposit box under 'Anna's name and leave. I will have to change clothes again and Aldo can bring me in the bank inside the box.

"Hey Aldo, is there anything around here that we can put on the door to keep it from locking, but still have it closed," I needed to know? If we were going to be successful at this, or if we need to keep messing up.

"Let me get some tape from someone out front," Aldo replied. "You two better stay here and guard this stuff until I get back."

Warren and I stayed in the deposit box vault and waited for Aldo to get back. I looked at Warren and he looked at me with a queer look on his face.

"What is he going to use tape for?" Warren asked me with the most perplexed look on his face.

"I think he is going to tape down the side of the door knob jam to keep it from being locked," I explained. "It should work."

Warren just looked at me in disbelief, "What?"

I looked back at him and smiled, "You'll see. It'll work."

He just shrugged his shoulders. Just then, Aldo returned

with a strip of tape. He put the tape over the doorknob jack on the side of the door jam so the door would not lock one it was closed.

"Let me go into the room and shut the door. That way if it still locks, I can unlock it for now," Warren stated still in disbelief.

"Okay," Aldo agreed. Warren entered the private room in the vault area and closed the door behind him. Aldo opened the door right after it closed.

Warren just looked at him and said, "Check it again. You didn't give it enough time to latch."

"Oh my God! You have got to be kidding," Aldo argued looking at him with total disbelief.

"No, I am not. You need to make sure. What if this shit doesn't work when you get back here? I won't be here. I have to leave now with her, and so do you. We have to make this really quick and discreet, right? Well," Warren confirmed to us both.

I stepped into the argument, "He's right. It won't take but 10 more seconds. If you guys weren't arguing, we could've had this done already."

"Alrighty then," Aldo said as he shut the door in Warren's face. "One, two, three, four, five. Okay, I think it had a chance to latch." Aldo opened up the door again with no problem.

Warren walked out and sheepishly stated, "I just wanted to make sure. We are all in this, right?"-

"Well, we need to switch the boxes still. The gold is heavy too. Could you two please put the box with the gold in that drawer please? I can put the plain bricks in the empty box, so I can leave." I told the men before me. Aldo and Warren put the box with the gold into the drawer slip under Anna's name and I loaded up the concrete bricks into the empty safety deposit box that I can put back into the box that had the gold. After the boxes were switched, Aldo left the bank quickly. Warren and I, as Anna waited for a few minutes before we left. The boxes were locked up so there was nothing to worry about.

They think I Killed My Husband!

Warren and I met up with Aldo outside in the alley on the side of the building.

"Are you ready to take me back in there?" I asked Aldo.

"As ready as I'll ever be. Let's do it," Aldo exclaimed! Warren opened up the crate for me and held out his hand to help me into the crate. I noticed my clothes were still in the crate, which was good.

"Oh, how sweet. Thank you, Warren," I smiled and stepped into the box with the aid of Warren's hand. The men closed the crate and Aldo carted me back into the bank. We went into the safety deposit box vault room, the one with the tape still on the door jam. Aldo opened up the crate and I got out of the box again. I took off my wig immediately and began to change my clothes. Aldo and I made sure my hair and my clothes were in order and Aldo closed the lid on the crate again.

"It'll be nice to walk out of the bank, instead you wheeling me out like you did bringing me in," I told Aldo as we began to walk through the lobby of the bank. As we were walking through the bank, the attendant called me over.

"Oh, Mrs. Garcia? Could you sign out on the logbook, please," the bank employee requested?

"Oh, of course. Sure. Here you go," I told her as I signed the book.

"Thank you. Will you be needing anything else," the bank attendant wanted to know? "No, thank you though," I answered. "Have a good day!" Aldo and I couldn't get out of there fast enough. We met Warren outside in the alley and we started to head back to our hotel. We walked with the crate on the dolly and it was hot. I am glad I didn't have to wear the wig for the time being. As we walked towards the hotel, we did look slightly odd being Americans with this huge crate on wheels.

"Now, I need to get the hell out of here and back home before anyone notices that I jumped my bail," I thought to myself. We ditched the crate in a trash bin a couple of blocks away and headed back to the hotel. We got our things packed up and figured we should get a good night's sleep. Warren said he wanted to get up early to have enough time for flight checks before take-off.

The morning arrived way too soon and Aldo and I got our things and headed for the seaport. We had to catch the commuter boat to Cyprus Island where the plane is. I had to get through customs with the gold coins and jewelry that I kept some how. The three of us were at the port and our luggage was getting ready to get randomly checked. I asked the security guard to please be gentle with my under garments and dildos. I slipped the guard some money while I was giving him my request. He didn't quite know what to do. He got embarrassed and didn't want anything more to do with me. However, he couldn't seem to keep his eyes off of me. I made myself comfortable with that as my eyes connected with his. He made no effort to make his way through my bags. I grabbed my bags and closed them back up and continued my way through the hallway and to the boat dock. We made it to the boat and settled down on a seat after our bags were boarded. We were out to sea and I could hardly see the land anymore. I couldn't help to feel paranoid, like I had eyes on me. They were all over me. I don't know where from, but they were towards me. To have a feeling of visual suffocation on a solace place as a commuter boat in the middle of the sea is beyond me how my body could sense this aura. I was anxious to be back home. I couldn't help to wonder if anyone was spying on me to know where the gold is. I was looking around. I was wearing my wig and answering to 'Anna' just in case I was being watched. We arrived at the port and retrieved our stuff and made it back to the plane. Warren was only too happy to see his plane again. We had to wait around the airport for a little while for Warren to check out the plane. Aldo and I loaded up the cargo to speed things up a bit. I fell asleep in my recliner on the plane. Before I realized, we had landed in Spain for refueling. I bought a pre-paid cell phone so I could call my kids. It started to ring. That is very strange. I registered it with my alias' name. What is even stranger is that the number on the screen is Marty's number. I couldn't answer it. What did he know? What would he do? I

They think I Killed My Husband!

just let it go into the voice message system and I will listen to it later. How did he get this number? I hope he doesn't figure out that I left the country. The plane took off again from Spain and I fell asleep once again. Aldo was pretty tired. He slept almost as much as me. We landed back in the states in a smaller municipal airport. We would be able to get through without a lot of mumbo jumbo. We would get checked, but in a more friendly manner. Besides, we didn't have anything bad. I just had a false identification. The 'customs' personnel helped unload our luggage and asked if we had anything of value.

I quickly answered, "No. I didn't have time to buy anything." The security still opened up the suitcases and just glanced at the surface. I could only think of the gold bricks I have wrapped up in a sweater. My stomach was going up and out through my throat and my heart had sunken into my stomach. I had a rush of heat engulf my upper torso and envelop my head. I tried to remain cool and calm. How does someone do this under these circumstances?

"This jet lag can really get to a person. I feel so weak and flustered." I said waving a small handkerchief at myself to divert the guard's attention. Aldo grabbed my arm to add to the effect.

"Are you all right, Honey?" Aldo asked me being concerned. "Why don't you wait over there for the taxi?" I agreed and went and sat down and Aldo went for our luggage and to get through with their questions.

The chairs were hard, plastic, typical airport chairs. I waited for a minute or so and figured I could listen to my voice message from Marty. I took out my phone and dialed the voicemail. The message was about that he was trying to locate me. He was trying to locate me to tell me that the police were trying to find me.

"Oh, fuck! What now?" I asked myself under my breath. "Are the cops going to be at my house waiting for me to get home? What am I going to do?"

I said my goodbye's to Warren and thanked him for everything. I paid him with some gold coins and told him I would send some more. He was reluctant to take it, but I insisted. I met up with Aldo and grabbed one of the bags that he had. We walked to the front of the little airport and tried to get a taxi. We had to call one on the phone. An airport employee was happy to oblige. Aldo and I still had to drive back to our town from the airport of the neighboring city. I didn't want to take any chances at a local airport where my trying to escape may seem more apparent. We were walking through the airport towards the exit when I looked up and saw Marty walking towards Aldo and me!

"What the Hell?" I asked myself as we were walking and I noticed Marty. I nudged Aldo and he looked somewhat relieved and I couldn't imagine why.

"You are a sight for sore eyes." Aldo said to Marty as he walked up to us. I stared at the both of them very puzzled. I was looking for the police to pounce out from behind the chairs and corners any minute.

"Well, I tried to call Pam, but all I got was her voice message," Marty explained as he stopped and helped me with my bag. I was still confused.

"How the hell did you know we were here?" I demanded to know of Marty. "I didn't tell anyone of my leaving. You didn't tell anybody about this did you? What about the police? You left me a message that the police were looking for me. What do they want?"

"Oh, that. Well, the police found some new evidence that doesn't look very good for you. I encourage that you talk to Jack, your lawyer, or at least make sure he is there at the station with you," Marty suggested.

"All right, but you still haven't answered me. How did you know we were here?" I demanded again.

"Pam, I need to tell you something," Aldo started to confess. "Marty is my Step-Father's cousin. I called him before I left and told him of your plans. I wanted to have a back up just in case something backfired."

"Uh-huh. When were you going to tell me this? Why did you tell him? This was supposed to be a secret! This could

They think I Killed My Husband!

have gotten us killed," I reprimanded Aldo!

"I'm sorry, I was just trying to look out for everyone's best interest. You are playing with your life! You are playing with my life and think about your kids if you ran into trouble over there," Aldo argued back!

"This could have been so disastrous! What if he came and brought the police? What if someone overheard someone say something to someone and" then I was interrupted.

"Hey! Stop it! Nothing bad happened and I am here to tell you some information and to update you on the situation. If anything would have happened to you while you two were over seas, I could have been able to help. That's it! Case closed. Now everyone, let's go so we can talk things over like civilized human beings," Marty yelled then went to a loud whisper. We left the airport, dropped off Aldo and made it back to my house in a matter of hours.

We arrived at my home and the front gate had just been repaired. We walked into the house and everything was in shambles! While I was gone, someone broke in and ransacked the place!

"Oh, my God! My house! Who could have done this?" I screamed while looking around in awe.

Marty replied, "Oh wow, Pam. I'm sorry. I should've checked on your house when I heard you were gone. What do you think they were looking for?"

"Oh, well, that. Um," I replied with hesitation.

"Pam, what do you know? You know what it is they are looking for now, don't you? What did you learn in Egypt? Tell me, then I may be better to help you," Marty demanded.

"Well, the only thing I know of is maybe this safety deposit key I found. I didn't know Ralph had it. It ends up belonging to a box in Egypt," I finally confessed.

"What was in the box?" Marty had to ask.

"Well, I guess that is where the important stuff comes in. It had just some papers that I don't know exactly what they mean. I don't know why people are getting killed for it. You have to be the owner of the box to get the contents out," I reasoned.

"Yes, but how easy was it for you to get into it? That is probably how easy it would be for anyone else," Marty added, "if someone was able to get that key. If someone knows you have the key, or about the key, then they are guilty partners with your husband that maybe didn't get their fair share of these papers?"

"Do you think that the people that killed Mrs. Gonzalez and her son may be the same people that broke into my house and may be the same guy that jumped me earlier at my gate? Do you think he could be the one and the same? Do you think it's more than one person?" I asked Marty with great optimism. I felt he was on to something.

"I am sure of it. The only thing is proving it and finding out who he is or they are, exactly," Marty answered. "You need to call the police and have this documented for your trial. If the cops and the jury and the judge sees that you are being victimized, the chances of you getting off by one reason of doubt will help."

"Oh, quite right, Marty. Let me call them right now. I will tell them I went to my brother's house for the night and came back and my house was in shambles," I agreed with optimism turning something bad into a good thing. The only bad thing was to endure another session with the cops. They were not the sharpest tools in the shed in the human world. I called Aldo at his house and he said he could come over to help. Later at my house, the police came to investigate the breaking and entering of my house. Sergeant Thomas was there with Detective Tony Perez. The Detective was looking around while the Sergeant asked me some questions.

"Where were you when this seemed to happen, Mrs. Garcia?" The sergeant asked.

"Well, my kids are staying with a relative of theirs and I went and stayed with a friend for the weekend," I responded.

"Oh, really?" he interrogated. "Who is this friend and may we call him to verify?"

"Why are you so sure it is a man?" I answered his question with a question. "How do you know it wasn't a girl I stayed with?" I looked up at him then licked my already moist lips.

"Uh, well, I don't"—the sergeant responded barely.

Then Aldo cut in, "She was with me at my house. We were talking and we had some wine over dinner and I thought she shouldn't drive. I made her a place on my couch."

"Does that convince you I wasn't here?" I asked the sergeant. "Do you really think I would do this?"

"Well, uh, no. I guess not," the sergeant replied.

"Good," I said.

Detective Tony came back from looking around and taking finger prints. He suddenly looked at everyone then at me with a really puzzled look on his face. "Mrs. Garcia, has anyone stopped to think why the alarm didn't go off? Even if the entry was a clean walk in, and that is a mystery, the alarm should have gone off, unless someone knew the alarm code."

Marty glanced over at me and then at Detective Perez, "You are right! I didn't even think about the alarm! Pam, did you remember to turn on the alarm before you left?"

"I always do. I turn it on subconsciously. Sometimes I leave and think I had forgotten to turn it on, then run back in real quick only to find out that I did turn it on," I reassured everyone.

"Well, who else knows your alarm code?" Detective Perez continued interrogating.

"Just Rita, my cleaning lady. I don't think she would do anything like this. I cut her hours way back, but she seemed good with it. The only other person was Ralph." I recalled.

"There was no forced entry and the alarm didn't go off. How do we know you didn't stage this whole thing to make yourself look more like a victim?" The sergeant asked with vengeance.

"Why are you treating me this way? I have been through Hell! My husband died, murdered, whatever! He's gone! I had to almost give my business away to have some money because the insurances aren't paying right now. My children lost their father. Someone jumped me outside of my gate at my home. I have had to put up with the press and photographers and just some random people on the streets. I have been put in jail and now you think I vandalized my own home? Are you insane?" I asked Sergeant Thomas.

"People in your situation have been known to do worse," Sergeant Thomas pointed out.

"Oh, my God," Aldo exclaimed! "I just told you she was at my house! What more do you want?"

The officers looked at Aldo and he stood his ground then they all looked at me. I was just sitting there dazed and confused about who could really be doing all of this to me?

"Did I forget to turn off the alarm? I never do. Who could have disengaged it?" I wondered to myself.

Sergeant Thomas gathered up everything they needed for the lab and Detective Perez walked over to him. "We'll be getting back in touch with you in a few days. We will let you rest for now considering the present situation."

Marty jumped up and almost pushed the officers out of the door, "Thank you, officers. We appreciate your help. I am sure Pam will want to discuss anything you may want with her attorney present. Good Day." Marty shut the door behind them.

I told Marty and Aldo I needed some time alone. I had to get some things in my head organized and I had to check on my kids. I called my kids where they were staying and told them I loved them very much and that I missed them and I would be with them as soon as I could.

Days later, at my house, Marty and Aldo and I were discussing the new found evidence the police had. Marty was informing me that the cops had investigated the murder of the Gonzalez' family and they were not convinced that it could have been linked to Ralph's death. They think it was just a random killing since Hector Gonzalez worked there so long ago. I didn't know if I should tell Marty about the gold. If I didn't, apparently, Aldo will. I wonder how much Aldo has told Marty. Has he told him everything? Did he call him from Egypt? How disastrous that could be, to have evidence of a

They think I Killed My Husband!

phone call from Egypt to the states at the time I am not to be out of the states. I pulled Aldo to the side and into the next room.

"What all have you told him?" I asked Aldo, angrily.

"Well, I," Aldo started to answer with hesitation.

"God Dammit! I knew it! What else--" I continued to encourage his answer.

Aldo continued, "I did tell Marty most of what we were going to do. But I didn't tell him about the gold or anything else! I just told him about leaving the country in case anything happened. I didn't want to be shot or be stuck or kidnapped and never be heard from again!"

"Okay, okay, I get your point. There is no telling what could have happened. The plane could've crashed or we could have been shot or kidnapped or something. Then no one would have known where we were. I guess you are right. It was better that someone knew," I finally agreed. We went back in the other room to sit down and talk to Marty. As we were walking, I was trying to think if I should tell Marty about the gold. I guess I better so, he will be better able to find out everything in regards to this whole mess. We entered the living room where Marty was sitting on the couch looking at the reports and pictures of the Gonzalez murder from the police. The pictures were spread out on the coffee table in front of where Marty was sitting.

I looked at those pictures and then looked at Aldo and couldn't help to think of Ralph. To think he may be the reason for all of this slaying. I felt so betrayed by everyone. Aldo told Marty that we were in Egypt without asking or telling me about it. Ralph had hidden some gold and jewels and cash in a box in Egypt for some reason and how he got these, I will find out. What on Earth was he into? Was he hiding the gold and money from someone? If so, who and why? All I found in Egypt was a bunch of gold and more questions. I had the fires of hell churning inside the pit of my belly. It's all I could do to sit on the couch beside Marty. I looked at the grotesque pictures of the murder of Mrs. Gonzalez and her son at her home. It was terrible. Whoever did that may be looking for the gold. I put my head in my hands and just sat quiet.

Marty saw my expression. He leaned over closer to me and softly asked me, "Do you know something? I can help you, but we need to work together." It was like he was reprimanding me. How dare him!

I lifted my head from my hands and looked at Marty as though I had to defend myself. I had to let something out. He hit a pressure point and I was about to blow! "Look, don't patronize me like I am some little girl that would never make it as a thinking man. So far I have been lied to, been set up, and have been attacked, in jail, now I can't trust anyone! Don't get me started up again!"

"Hey, don't be mad at Aldo for that. He did the right thing. The two of you leaving the country the way you did was not smart. Why did you do that? You should have taken me with you, Pam." Marty said to me in a concerned and almost fatherly way.

"I didn't want you going to the police. I couldn't risk it. Jack doesn't know either, or does he?" I had to know if these men were telling everyone.

"Pam, you hired me as a Private Investigator. My obligation is to you, strictly professional of course. You need to tell me everything you know. And no, and I didn't tell Jack. All I know is that he is your lawyer and he was disbarred and has been reinstated. I would not trust that man as far as I could throw him. I certainly wouldn't trust him with my life, Pam," Marty told me, finally with total honesty. I felt he was telling me his true belief. I felt maybe I should trust this man.

They think I Killed My Husband!

Chapter 9

The TRIAL

The time came for my trial. I was in all of the local news. "The wealthy widow, did she kill her husband?" That was the big question. I am just glad they haven't followed me around to too many places. Some of the things I have done since my husband passed hasn't been saint worthy. What was I thinking? I was looking for diversions to keep my mind occupied on something other than my real life. They may have called me "The Wild Widow" if they knew the half of it. I feel so guilty sometimes. Thank goodness, what happens out of town, stays out of town. I called Jack later that day. He said he was ready.

After gathering a lot of evidence, Jack had a significant amount of ammunition for my defense. The man trying to kill me the night at my gate of my house is still at large as well as the murderer of Mrs. Gonzalez and her son. However, the police couldn't find any hard evidence to link the cases to each other. The fact of finding the blood types at the lab didn't match Ralph's blood type may prove to be very significant. Empirically, this was valuable evidence to show reasonable doubt. The blood sucking paparazzi was outside the courthouse when I arrived. I had the children staying with my cousin on his farm, still. A place where I knew they would be safe. I met jack outside on the steps after fighting off the press and photographers.

"Jack! Over here!" I waved to Jack as I dodged the

press coming in. Jack was in the foyer of the courthouse waiting for me.

"Hey Pam. Are you ready? Do you remember everything we talked about?" Jack asked me to see if I was on my toes.

"Yes, I have nothing to worry about. I did nothing. Justice shall prevail." I replied with confidence.

"You seem cocky. That's good. But try to look distraught too," Jack insisted. "The jury would like to see some sincere distress and mourning."

We entered the courtroom together. The room was overwhelming. It seemed so big compared to me. The room was powerful with its tall wooden podium made of cherry wood and the marble tile flooring all of which went half up the walls. The small dividing gates and tables and chairs were all of the same solid sherry wood. The room simply emphasized power. I suddenly felt a little weak in the knees. I grabbed Jack for a second. I blamed my stumbling on my high heels. The trial was starting and the judge entered the room.

The prosecuting attorney handed something to the judge and wanted to submit something as evidence.

I leaned over at the table to Jack, "What is this? Go find out what is going on!"

"Permission to approach the bench, Your Honor." Jack stood up and requested the Judge.

"Granted," the Judge replied in his boisterous way.

Jack approached the benched along with the prosecuting attorney and requested a copy of what was being presented as evidence. He looked at it and asked a few questions at the bench and sat back down next to me. He looked rather upset.

"What's the matter?" I wanted to know. "You look upset. What is that paper they presented?"

"Pam, the prosecuting attorney just submitted an old invoice for the purchase of chemicals used for gold plating. One of the key ingredients in the gold solution is cyanide. This is extremely damaging," Jack said with little shock or distress. With all of the friends I have and now I don't have one, or so it seems. Jack certainly doesn't seem to give a shit.

"Another one? Well this might be not so good," I retaliated to Jack quietly at the table. "Do you think they are going to send me up for an invoice?"

"Uh, yea," Jack snapped back like a school-boy prep.

"What is with the gold plating shit?"

"Well, we did some, well, a lot of plating of metals a long time ago and when the import-export business grew, I had to just let the plating go," I told Jack the story. "I thought you knew all of this."

"I don't keep up with you, Pam," Jack blurted back then just looked down.

"All right, so they found an invoice, work with it." I insisted. "Besides, where did they get the invoice from anyway?"

"They claim to have found it later in the Gonzalez' home while investigating the murder," Jack told me. "Which I think is bullshit. I should have been informed of this before now so I would have time to prepare. This could be very devastating to your case."

"Can't you ask for an extension or a continuation to prepare for the evidence? I thought they usually do those sorts of things." I argued with Jack at the table in the courtroom just as the Judge was trying to get everything in order.

"Order! Order in the court! I will have order," The judge screamed!

The courtroom got quiet and I did too. I looked at Jack as to tell him to do something. Jack saw my face and whispered to me, "Apparently, the prosecuting attorney had this evidence since last week and it was just slipped in and made aware in the court system, but not by me."

The prosecuting attorney had the first witness to call. "I would like to call Sergeant William Thomas to the stand." Sergeant Thomas walked up to the chair and took the oath with his hand on the bible.

"You may be seated," the judge told the Police sergeant.

"Now, Sergeant Thomas, you lead the local police investigation, is that correct?" The prosecuting attorney asked initially.

"Yes, that is correct," the officer confirmed.

"Sergeant Thomas, do you have the recordings from the 9-1-1 call that night?"

"Yes, I do. I have submitted the written out documentation as evidence," Sergeant Thomas declared to the court.

The prosecuting attorney walked back to his table and retrieved some papers that must have been written forms of the emergency calls. He held them up in the air for the courtroom to see. "Now, I have on the papers everything that was said on the phone to the 9-1-1 operator that night by Mrs. Garcia. It shows that she was on the phone with the paramedics for nineteen minutes and 21 seconds. Is that correct, Sergeant Thomas?" The attorney showed the papers to the sergeant.

"That's what it says," the Sergeant stated. "So?"

"I just wanted to make that point. Now, Sergeant, the autopsy showed that Mr. Garcia died from a heart attack, which was brought on by the lack of oxygen after the administration of cyanide. Is that correct?" The attorney asked Sergeant Thomas.

"I do believe that is what the coroner reported." Sergeant Thomas once again confirmed.

"Do you have any knowledge of the kind of financial worth Mr. Garcia had, Sergeant?" The prosecutor continued asking.

"Not completely. I had my own life and finances to worry about. I didn't need to know how much more someone else had than me," Sergeant Thomas retaliated.

"You are just stating that it was none of your business, right?" the prosecutor inquired.

"Well, yes," the sergeant admitted. "I am sure Mr. Garcia would not leave his wife out in the cold after his passing. I am sure she doesn't have to cut coupons. Unless she wants too."

"Yes, quite right. I think I am finished with my interrogation of this witness, Your Honor. However, I would like to reserve the right to append the testimony and recall this witness if necessary at a later date," the prosecutor ended his questioning.

They think I Killed My Husband!

The Judge had to ask if Jack had any questions, "Mr. Schwartz, are you ready for this witness? If not, you may question him again at a later date in time as well."

"Yes, Your Honor. I have some questions for this witness. But, I may have more later," so Jack began to question Sergeant Thomas. "Sergeant, did you know my client, Pamela Garcia, before the case began?"

"No," Sergeant Thomas answered.

"So, you were not at all familiar with her or her character, in this area?" Jack continued.

"Well, I have seen her in the paper with her husband and her kids. It was either about business or something with the community," the Sergeant added.

"Oh! It wasn't anything bad? There were never reports of traffic violations or domestic violence?" Jack continued asking to clarify.

"Not that I recall. But, there was this one story going around the stations that Mrs. Garcia got pulled over for speeding one night. She was not cited," the Sergeant finished.

"That is apparently hear say. I would like those last comments stricken," Jack demanded. "Now, Sergeant, would you say that Pamela Garcia was a model citizen?"

"I don't know if I would put her into the category of 'model,' but like I said she never did anything wrong," the Sergeant confessed his thoughts.

"Just answer 'Yes' or 'No' please," Jack interrupted the police sergeant.

"Well, I would have to answer 'No,'" the Sergeant retaliated with spite.

"You just said that you used to see her in the papers with her family doing school functions, social gatherings and fund raisers. I would think that would make a 'Model' citizen. How high are your standards? Does the family dog need to be included?" Jack finished the Sergeant off.

"Move to strike! Badgering the witness," the prosecuting attorney bellowed!

"Withdrawn," Jack insisted. "Now, Sergeant Thomas, a

search warrant was issued to look for something in Mrs. Garcia's home earlier this year. Did the police find whatever it was they were looking for?"

"Nothing out of the ordinary was found," the Sergeant replied with hesitation from the stand.

"Oh, really? Then why have you been relentlessly pursuing this woman as if she is guilty?" Jack continued questioning.

"I was after justice," Sergeant Thomas blurted defending his integrity!

"I see," Jack continued with an antagonizing attitude. "So, you had an issue for a search warrant and did not find anything in her home?"

"No, but the man was poisoned. She was going to inherit the insurance money and the business all for herself," the Sergeant added.

"That is all purely speculative and circumstantial Sergeant Thomas." Jack commented to the court. "So the minute the autopsy came back with toxins in Ralph Garcia's system, you immediately jump to the conclusion that it must have been the wife that did it. Isn't that trying to rush to close a homicide case rather quickly," interrogated Jack?

"History and past cases have proven that the most likely suspect is the person closest to the victim. We were just doing our duty." The officer responded to the court and jury.

"So you immediately ordered a warrant for her arrest and came and arrested her on a Sunday morning with her children at home, purely because of past cases, not from evidence?" Jack was astounded!

"No, we found that invoice with the search warrant." Sergeant Thomas answered a little befuddled.

"Oh, yes. An invoice that is over two years old. Purely circumstantial. You had this woman spend the night in jail, exposed to prostitutes and thieves and molesters because you felt like you were doing your duty?" Jack hammered the Sergeant.

"Well, when you say it like that, it doesn't sound so good. I was making sure I went by the book," the Sergeant said.

"No further questions Your Honor," Jack excused Sergeant Thomas with disgust in his demeanor.

"You may step down Sergeant. Prosecutor, call your next witness," the judge specified.

I leaned over to Jack and was I pissed. "You mean to tell me that they found the invoice for cyanide at the Gonzalez's home where the murder of Mrs. Gonzalez happened and my husband had traces of cyanide in his system and no one can seem to link the two together?"

"It just may point more fingers at you, Pam. Did you think of that?" Jack whispered, "Would you let me handle this. That is why it is always best to never represent yourself in a case of law."

"Thank you, Your Honor. The State would like to call Hector Garcia to the stand," the prosecuting attorney, Steve Smith called out in the courtroom. Hector was sworn in and sat down. "Mr. Garcia, for the record, will you please state your name and relationship to the defendant and the deceased?"

"Certainly," Hector obliged. My name is Hector Garcia. My brother was Ralph Garcia. Pam is my sister-in-law."

"How long have you known the defendant, Pamela Garcia?" Prosecutor Smith questioned.

"I have known her for about twelve years or so," Hector answered with no emotion and with utmost honesty.

"Were there ever any harsh arguments between Pamela and Ralph Garcia that you have ever witnessed?" The prosecutor continued to pry.

"Every couple argues," Hector replied.

"So you are saying that couple argued quite a bit?" the prosecutor kept pressing Hector.

"No! I didn't say that at all! You are putting things into my mouth! Stop it!" Hector became obtuse with his words.

"How often did you see them argue in the past, Hector?" the prosecutor became relentless.

"I saw them argue only a couple of times, and it was about the kids and what…" Hector was interrupted.

"Thank you, Mr. Garcia. No further questions," the prosecutor finished.

"Your witness, Mr. Schwartz," the honorable judge stated to the court.

Jack stood up and addressed the court, "Thank you, Your Honor. Mr. Hector Garcia, would you say that your brother Rafael and his wife had a good marriage?"

"Yes," answered Hector without hesitation.

"Do you believe that in any way Pamela could have killed Rafael, Hector?" Jack continued with his interrogation.

"No, but anything is possible," Hector blatantly said.

"Hector, you said that in your opinion, your brother and Pam Garcia had a good marriage. Isn't that true?" Jack cross-examined.

"Yes, it appeared so," Hector exclaimed.

"Would you say that Pam is a good person, Mr. Garcia?" Jack continued questioning.

"Yes, I would say so, on average." Hector added.

"In your opinion, Mr. Garcia, do you think that Pamela Garcia killed her husband, Ralph Garcia?" Jack went straight to the point.

"No, I don't think she could have done such a thing. But with all of their money, she could have hired someone to do it. You know it would be like flying an airplane and dropping a bomb. You could fly right over it and not be affected." Hector spilled out his pent up frustrations about me in the worst place imaginable.

Jack immediately turned to the Judge and asked, "Move to strike, Your Honor. Purely speculation."

"Strike that from the record," the Judge said to the court reporter.

"Hector, do you think your sister-in-law is innocent of killing your brother?" Jack continued to get an answer from him.

"I don't think she directly killed him. But, I think she may have had something to do with it." Hector had to say.

"Like making love to him until his heart gave out?" Jack questioned way out of the box. "Nothing further, Your Honor."

They think I Killed My Husband!

"You may step down Mr. Garcia," the Judge said to Hector. Hector stepped down hesitantly as if he had more to say.

I leaned over to Jack, "Why is Hector acting like this? I thought he liked me."

"I was going to ask you the same thing," Jack returned the comment. "I wonder what could have set him off. Isn't it about time for lunch? I need to take a break and gather up my thoughts. Your Honor, permission to approach the bench."

"Proceed," the Judge granted his request.

"Could we take a break for lunch or have a recess?" Jack pleaded for some time to gather his notes.

"Let's see Counselor, it is eleven thirty now. Everyone take an hour and a half for lunch and be back in the courtroom at one o'clock," the Judge announced with the slamming of his gavel. The courtroom became noisy suddenly with low voices muttering all around the room amongst each other. The voices became like one low static noise like the television went off the air. It filled the room with vibrancy and was overwhelmingly loud.

"I need to get out of here, Jack. Now!" I exclaimed. We rushed through the crowd and opened up the doors of the courtroom and there they were, the vultures. The newspaper reporters were standing right outside of the courtroom door. The cameras and the microphones and the people manning the cameras and the lights and the reporters with their microphones, was the worst part. Now this was overwhelming.

"Mrs. Garcia? Did you kill your husband? Was it an accident? Is it true that it was during sex? Did you poison him to get the insurance?" Several reporters blurted out these questions at one time as I tried to get out of the courthouse lobby.

"No comment," Jack yelled in my defense. "Now, if you would all please wait until after the trial, your questions will be answered then. If you would please excuse us, we would like to get something to eat." Jack held out his arm and tried to clear a pathway so we could walk through the reporters.

We finally made it out the door of the courthouse and

got into Jack's car. We drove down the street and found a place to park and went to a small café across the street. It was light and with a friendly appeal. The tablecloths were of red and white gingham and the flooring was made with black and white tiles. Each table had a simple vase with one flower in it. There were no reporters that I could see anyway. It seemed as though we had lost them in the car on the ride to the diner.

We sat down at a corner table in the back of the restaurant so we might have some peace and privacy. "I don't know if I am going to be able to hold up through all of this. Everyone is saying those awful things about me! I can't believe my brother-in-law Hector! What a dick!" I vented to Jack.

"Well, I told you it wouldn't be easy. Unfortunately, you don't have a choice," Jack simply told me. "It's only going to get worse."

"Worse?" I sputtered loudly! "I don't know how they could be any worse, but I am sure you're right," I sighed.

"Pam, if your husband's side of the family is being this way, I don't think it will be good when anyone else on his side of the family gets on that stand," Jack forewarned.

"I didn't know they felt that way. I guess I really shouldn't have expected less. If it were my son, I wouldn't know whom to believe. Especially when I am the main suspect, but I know Ralph's mother doesn't feel that way," I hoped.

"What makes you so sure?" Jack asked concerned.

"Oh, I don't know. Just call it women's intuition. She always knew how her son was. He was always such a conniving young man." I told Jack over a sandwich and some fries and a coke.

"We'll have to see about that." Jack mumbled then at that instant a flash of light beamed at my face and blinded me for a few seconds.

I shrieked and Jack stood up and yelled at the photographer, "Jesus, don't you people let up?"

A man in plain jeans and T-shirt took the camera away from his face and said, "I didn't mean anything by it. I saw Pam sitting there and read about her in the papers. I am a tourist and was getting some lunch and just wanted a picture. Excuse me." The man left as fast as he came in to just take my picture.

"That was too weird. How did he know I was here?" I asked Jack.

"What do you mean? He said he just saw you and took your picture. You make too much out of nothing," Jack kept insisting.

"No! He was not just eating in here. He came in to just take my picture. Where did he come from? Why was he here? He wasn't just a fan. That is bullshit! You should have gotten his film Jack!" I became more demanding.

"Pam, you are over reacting. The guy was no one. Eat your lunch so we can get to the trial," Jack patronized.

I just looked at him wondering what on earth he is thinking and why is he taking everything so lightly? This is my life he is fucking with right now. This man could have been with the papers or with whomever it is that is trying to kill me to get at the deposit box that I have stashed. Maybe I do need to take a chill pill or something. I finished my sandwich and listened to Jack talk about his strategy, but was not too impressed. I was trying to figure out if he was actually serious. I may need to rethink having him for my lawyer. Maybe I am over-reacting, after all it is only the first day. Maybe I shouldn't be too over zealous. Maybe Marty was right. I should be extremely careful about what is going on with Jack. Never trust anyone with my life.

"Jack, why are you not taking this seriously? That man could have been anyone!" I began yelling at Jack and making more of a scene than necessary than what already happened.

"Let's get out of here, Pam. You are making a spectacle of yourself," Jack said as he grabbed my arm and pulled me up out of my chair and led me out the door of the café.

"Oh my God! I don't believe you! Don't you know that people could be planning to kill me and leave my children as orphans and you don't even care?" I screamed back while Jack dragged me by the arm into the street.

"What?" Jack stopped and looked at me in disbelief.

"Yes, I have been jumped and I have reason to believe that someone is trying to kill me too!" I informed Jack quickly before any more reporters found us on the street.

"Oh, you have just let your imagination run away with itself," Jack tried to convince me. Just then, someone gave me a push into the oncoming traffic of the busy intersection we were standing. I caught myself before any harm came to me. A car barely missed me.

"Shit!" I yelled. "You see? Someone is out to get me!"

"Don't be silly. That was just an accident. The sidewalk is crowded. Someone just bumped into you." Jack took my arm to console me and made sure I was all right. I just started to cry. I was so scared. I knew I was in something very serious. I had to do something to make sure I was going to get out of this alive and out of jail. If the rest of the day did not get any better I had no choice but to hire a new attorney and have Marty investigate everything more thoroughly. We were walking back to the car and I was still shaking. Jack was not too worried. There were reporters up and down the street taking some pictures and as we got closer to the courthouse there seemed to be more and more. Photographers were having a field day. I tried to hide myself, but it did not do any good.

Once back inside the courthouse, I headed straight for the bathroom. I looked in a mirror. I still had remnants of tears on my face from earlier and mascara was all down my face. I looked terrible. I just went inside a booth and sat and cried some more. Everything that I had been through was catching up to me. I felt so vulnerable. I was so scared. I did not know whom to trust. Aldo told Marty about leaving the country without asking me. Now, Jack is acting like he really doesn't give a shit whether I go to jail or not. He acts like he wants me to go to jail. I felt so alone. I have absolutely no one to turn to. No one can help me nor does anyone want to, or so it seems. The press wants to print as much dirt as possible about my whole situation and I have to try to keep my children out of harms way by hiding them out on my cousin's farm. I feel so backed into the corner of the entire universe with the world attacking me right now.

"God, please give me the strength to get through this day and the rest of the days here after," I pleaded and cried from within the walls of the bathroom stall. It felt like my barrier against the world that was my enemy at the moment, yet resembling the dark prison that soon awaited me if this is not resolved accordingly. I walked out of the stall and washed my face. I realized that the photographers and reporters must have gotten my picture with all of my mascara and tears streaming down my face. I wonder if it was a set up to get me upset or killed? Either way, it is not good. I walked out looking like a true victim or really guilty, a woman knowing her pending doom.

Jack was waiting to escort me to the courtroom. He also helped shield me from the reporters and just kept repeating the phrase, "No comment."

We entered and sat down in the front of the courtroom. The prosecuting attorney was already waiting and going over some documents. Jack walked over to him and they whispered a few words to each other.

"What was that all about?" I asked him when he came back to our table.

"I wanted to know if he wouldn't mind rescheduling some witnesses for tomorrow. I also needed to know the witness line up. I don't like surprises," Jack reverberated.

"Yea, I guess not," I agreed with Jack.

"All rise." The bailiff announced. The judge walked into the courtroom.

I leaned over towards Jack and told him quietly, "If this afternoon doesn't start to get any better, I will be looking for better legal representation." I slowly leaned back straight into my chair and looked straight ahead coldly. I could see Jack looking at me out of the corner of my eye. His face was almost comical. My life was not.

"What do you mean? I have been doing so much for you, Pam," Jack insisted. "Who else knows your case better than me?"

"Oh, I don't know. Any lawyer that might read any local newspaper," I added with sarcasm.

"Well Pam, you have a lot of nerve bringing this up now. If you want new counsel, I have a good mind to walk right out of this courtroom right now! How would you like them apples?" Jack retaliated with anger!

"Uh, well, Jack, this would be most inopportune right now," I told him.

"You're damn right it would. You're so smart Pam, why don't you just represent your own damn self? I am sure I will be seeing a lot of you in jail! I quit, you bitch! It's a shame you didn't get killed by that car back there! It sure would have benefited everyone else and saved everybody a whole lot of time and effort!" Jack spoke a bit too loudly and the courtroom was a little too quiet.

"Oh, my God! I can't believe you said that! I have two children and that would have left them orphans! You Son of a Bitch! You are fired!" I screamed at Jack. Jack closed his briefcase and started to walk out. "Excuse me, if I am going to continue with this case, I do believe anything relative to this case is my property. I paid you to obtain those items, so legally they are mine." I reminded him very coldly.

"Order! Order in the Court," the Judge demanded with the slamming of his gavel. "Mrs. Garcia, do we need to order a continuance for the case?"

"Yes, Your Honor. Apparently, my counsel would rather see me dead. I do not think my life is in the best of care with this man," I informed the Judge.

"Is this true, Counselor?" the Judge asked Jack with great despair.

"Well, she is exaggerating a bit, but I do not wish to engage in this interrogation any further, Your Honor," Jack admitted.

"Oh, that's bullshit! You sat there and said that it was too bad that I wasn't killed just now when I was pushed into the street. It was like you planned it with someone, or maybe you pushed me, then pulled me back to scare me!" I accused Jack in front of the entire courtroom. Everyone started to whisper amongst him or herself. It sounded like a static noise again.

"Order! "Order in the Court! One more outburst like that Mrs. Garcia, and I will have to alleviate you from the courtroom. Counselor Schwartz, are you not going to represent your client any further?" the Judge asked again.

"No, Your Honor, I am not. I will be leaving all of the documentation with her. As she so stated, she is the legal owner of all materials gathered and is entitled to them," Jack informed the Judge before he left the courtroom. "I am washing my hands of this." Jack emptied out his briefcase and left the paperwork on the table and walked out.

"Mrs. Garcia, I will have to ask, are you going to obtain new counsel or will you be attempting to represent yourself?" the Judge had to inquire.

"I will be obtaining new counsel Your Honor," I replied with respect of the Bench.

"With no further adieu, I will make a judgment for a continuance for two weeks from today. Will that be enough time, Mrs. Garcia?" the Judge asked me very nicely.

"I hope so Your Honor. I need to get this trial over with so I may go on with my life." I told him.

The Judge looked at me with a bit of a surprised look, "Very well, so be it. The trial will convene in exactly two weeks at nine o'clock in the morning. Court adjourned until then. Mrs. Garcia, Good luck." He slammed his gavel.

I smiled at the judge and gathered the papers that Jack left in a mess on the table in the front of the courtroom and hoped I could get through the flock of vultures that were made up of the press.

The prosecuting attorney just looked at me like I was dead meat. I just held my head up with dignity and finished gathering the papers and put them into my briefcase. I wanted to try to get out of the courthouse the best way I could. I approached the bailiff and asked him if he was doing anything right now. He said that he would not be able to escort me out of the building, but he could see if another security guard might be able to help me out. It was obvious that it was not going to be easy. I was about to get ambushed by the reporters. I thought I might just wait a bit. Maybe the reporters will get tired and leave. They may think I left via the back route out of the courthouse.

I waited for about fifteen minutes and started to leave out of the courthouse with the security guard. He knew of a way to get out through the basement and then to the parking garage. That was awesome. We were able to by-pass all of the reporters. After the chaos in the courtroom, I really didn't need any more headaches. Now, I need to find another lawyer, quick. I wonder if Marty knew of any. I had to think for a minute. I also need to find my car. I looked around in the parking garage for my car while walking and trying to think of lawyers I know. "What about Tom, my other accountant attorney? He may know someone," I thought to my self.

I immediately called him on my cell phone. The receptionist answered. "DeBeauois and Associates. How may I assist you?"

"I need to speak to Tom, now please," I demanded forgetting how busy he is.

"I am sorry, Ma'am. Mr. Cooper is out of the office at the moment. May I take a message?" She politely and eagerly asked of me while I could almost see her perfect huge smile over the phone.

"No, that won't be necessary. I will try him later. Oh, wait. Yes, tell him to call Pam. He has my number. ASAP. Thanks," I hung up as soon as I got that out. I put my cell phone away in my purse. I found my car. I put my document bag in my car and walked around and got in. I began to drive out of the garage and at the opening of the parking garage is a huge mob! I guess it isn't going to be that easy after all. I stopped the car and looked behind me and put it into reverse and gunned it. When I saw the turning area, I slammed on the brakes, turned the wheel to the right and made it spin to a 180. I then took my feet off the brakes halfway through the turn and swerved the steering back straight and floored it forward after putting it in gear while it was in the middle of the spin. I had to try to find a way out of there. If I had to hide in the courthouse or the garage all day, I will. I went to the roof. I parked the car and got out. I walked to the elevator and went back to the building. I had to just get out through the walkway or someway. The doors opened and I saw a security guard standing by the door. I walked over to him and explained the situation.

"Do you think you could escort me out, or tell me of a way to get out? Is there an employee or delivery entrance or something?" I begged the guard to divulge some information to me.

"Well, the back exit where the deliveries are made is right through that hallway and go through the double doors at the end. I may have to walk you down. But, I have to get someone to relieve me from my post here," the guard reassured me.

"Maybe I could just go by myself?" I suggested.

"Oh, no. You can't go back there without someone with you," the guard told me earnestly.

"Okay. Can you escort me out then?" I asked the guard sweetly with a smile trying to talk him into it.

"I said after I find someone to relieve me from my post, then I would," he assured me.

"Oh," I replied humbly. He picked up the phone and called someone and he agreed to relieve him. I didn't know what else to do. I couldn't leave my car at the top of the garage. The reporters were blocking my way out. He walked me back to the parking garage. There they were, just like I figured they would be. The newspaper reporters and the photographers were all in the parking garage waiting for me to come back and get into my car. What whores they are.

I just ignored who I could and had to tell the others "No comment."

"Get back! Let the lady through! Don't you people have any manners?" the guard yelled at the reporters while pushing them back so I could get to my car. If I didn't have the guard with me, I would have never had made it to my car. He literally had to push these people away from me. I can't believe they made up to the top floor so fast! They are vultures. I asked the guard to help make sure the reporters weren't blocking the exit downstairs so I could drive out of the garage. He radioed his staff and he had them clear the exit for me.

I made it home and had to start looking for an attorney right away. I called Marty to see if he knew of anyone reputable. Private Investigators often work closely with several attorneys on cases for many reasons.

"What do you mean you need a lawyer? What about Jack? Isn't he a personal friend of yours and your late husband?" Marty asked me over the telephone.

"Well, we got into a little argument today during the trial," I informed Marty.

"Really? What kind of argument?" Marty wanted to know.

"Well, the usual kind where two people want each other dead. Only I accused him of it in front of the judge." I told Marty over the phone.

"You have got to be shitting me! You have one huge set of balls on you Pam! I can't believe you did that! What on earth made you do such a thing?" Marty kept pumping me for information while trying to keep his composure and not laugh.

"Can you come over? I don't want to keep talking on the phone." I requested.

"Yea, sure. I have to stop by the store first. Do you want anything?" Marty said.

"Pick up some wine and some good cheddar. That's all I feel like eating tonight." I replied.

"You got it. I'll be right there." Marty said just before hanging up the phone.

Marty arrived later with some wine and cheese that I requested. I opened the door to my house and let him in. We made ourselves comfortable in the kitchen while I opened the cheese and Marty found the corkscrew for the wine.

While opening the wine in the kitchen, Marty asked me, "Now, tell me why you fired Jack again?"

After getting a couple of wine glasses down from the

cupboard, I told Marty, "No, you need to fill this wine glass first. Then I need to drink it and you need to fill it again. Then after that, I will tell you."

"Oh. Well then, here you go," Marty said as he turned and poured the wine into my glass. I began eating some cheese and Marty poured himself some wine and sat down at the table with me. We both ate some cheese and just sat there in silence. I had to just sit and take everything in for a second. Somehow, Marty knew this and was giving me the space and time I needed. I ate some cheese and drank it down with some red wine that Marty had picked out.

"This is pretty good wine, Marty. What kind is it?" I wanted to know.

"It came recommended by an old man that ran a vineyard in Napa Valley." Marty told me.

"What? Napa Valley? That is in California, isn't it?" I confirmed.

"Well, yes," Marty answered back across the table modestly. "I was in California last year. I bought a few bottles of some red wines while I was there. There was this old man that I met while I was touring the Napa Valley and he personally selected this particular bottle of wine for me."

"Really? And you saved it all of this time?" I continued to be inquisitive.

"Well," Marty replied shyly, "I have been busy. Besides, I haven't had anyone to share it with at least anyone I would like to share it with."

"Ah, aren't you sweet." I told Marty from across the table and smiling at the same time. "It couldn't be that I pay you?"

"Oh, come on, Pam," Marty whined as he slumped back into his chair. "I have been here when you needed me and when you didn't even know you needed me. I don't want to see you go to prison for something I feel I know you didn't do," Marty told me to reassure me that he was out for my best interest.

"Oh, sounds like something I have heard before." I

told Marty with cynicism.

"No, really. I like you Pam. I wouldn't want to see anyone that is truly innocent go to jail. That's why I want to help you, for what it's worth. When Aldo told me you guys had left the country, I almost lost my mind!" Marty exclaimed.

"Really?" That was the only thing I could think of to say. I held out my glass for Marty to refill.

"Well, yes!" Marty exclaimed as he stood up and leaned over to refill my wine glass and then sat down and topped off his own glass. "I couldn't imagine what on earth you could be thinking. I know when someone is desperate he or she will do things a little out of character, but Pam, what are you thinking?"

"Well, I have to find out what my husband was doing before he died. I think that whatever he was into may be what got him murdered!" I began explaining to Marty.

"You mean the gold and the safety deposit box in Egypt, right?" Marty confirmed.

"Exactly. I have to get to the bottom of all of this. I have to find whom Ralph was dealing with and who was helping him here. I believe that if I can figure that shit out, I can probably prove or show a reasonable doubt. What do you think?" I asked Marty.

"Sounds logical, but I think your best bet is just trying to make a case of reasonable doubt. If you try to find out who did do the actual killing or what exactly Ralph was doing, you might end up killed yourself. Like that night you were jumped outside your gate?" Marty reminded me from across the table then grabbed the last piece of cheese.

"So, do you know of a good lawyer that may take my case? I would love it if he or she could wait for payment. I can pay a fee, but the final pay off will have to wait until the insurance benefits pay. Right now, I am living conservatively," I reminded him.

"Oh, yea, with all of that gold you found. I can imagine," Marty said with a bit of sarcasm in his voice and a role of his eyes.

They think I Killed My Husband!

"I can't just cash the gold in just like that! I don't think most people can make change for me when I use some of those coins. I have to wait and just live like I don't even have them until I can find a way to exchange them somewhere and still remain safe," I reminded Marty.

Marty looked at me like I was crazy, and suggested, "You know Pam, you could take the gold and have it melted down and made into jewelry or something else that can be exchanged or sold for some money."

"Well, do you know where or who does that, Mr. Smarty Pants," I asked?

"I have heard of a jeweler in the area that may be able to or know someone that could do it for you. Then maybe you won't be so strapped for cash," Marty continued with his insight.

"Okay, so I am not so broke after all, for the moment. But what if whoever killed Ralph wants me dead too? Or what is it that is the center of all this?"

"What do you mean, the center of all this? Apparently you are the center of all of this mess." Marty replied.

"No, no, no. You don't know what I mean. I am talking about the gold, the secret box of gold in Egypt and the killings. It is all so strange and something else is going on bigger than we realize," I snapped back.

"Well, I will need everything you can give me. I will need records of cell phones bills, and what about those airline tickets that you found? I could use those to inquire from the airlines if he had flown before and get the records from them when and where. That should help and will be a start from what you are telling me." Marty said and got up to get some more cheese.

"You know, what have you been doing anyway? I have been doing almost everything!" I exclaimed with a little hostility to Marty from the table.

"Whoa, I have gathered more intelligence than I have revealed. Besides, you did not tell me anything about the gold, or going to Egypt or any of that stuff. You need to tell me about that stuff. You need to tell me everything, Pam." Marty demanded while sitting back down with more cheese.

"Well, I didn't know whom I should trust. I guess I can tell you the things I find out now." I told Marty as I leaned back in my chair and he refilled my wine glass and put some more cheese on my plate.

"Well, you better. You still haven't told me what the hell happened that you had to fire Jack today. Now, I want to know every detail about that. I thought he was your friend too. So what happened Pam?" Marty wanted to know.

I leaned over the kitchen table and picked up my wine glass and took a drink and proceeded to tell him exactly what happened earlier today. "Well, we went to lunch and on the way back, someone pushed me into the street and he pulled me back just before I was hit or run over by a car."

Marty looked at me rather confused, "You fired him for saving your life?"

"No, it's more complicated than that. He just disregarded the urgency of my situation. I was almost killed and he thought I was over reacting!" I began to explain to Marty.

"Over reacting? When you were almost ran over? So, you fired him for that? That sounds a little drastic, Pam." Marty told me.

"I know, but you weren't there and I was. He just took everything a little too lightly. I think he may be a part of this whole thing," I started to think out loud and tell Marty at the same time.

"What makes you think he may be part of this whole thing? Do you mean a part of the gold? Do you think he knows about the gold?" Marty continued interrogating me.

"I haven't even thought about that. He just acts like he would like to see me ending up in jail. He didn't do as much work as I thought he should have," I told Marty.

"Okay, so maybe he hadn't had the time to get into the rough stuff yet," Marty tried to defend him.

"Oh my God! I just remembered something! How long does a Power of attorney last?" I asked Marty.

"Why? Did you sign one?" he replied.

"Yes, I did. When I was incarcerated. I had to get bail money, so Jack had to get the money out of my accounts. It nearly drained what I had in hand, but he did it." I informed Marty of my memories.

"Was it just for the duration of your incarceration?" Marty continued asking.

"Oh, let me dig the thing up and see. He can't get my money if I am out of jail now, can he?" I pleaded with Marty.

"I wouldn't think so. Usually a Power of Attorney acts for someone if they are unable to do things for themselves. You better check for any clauses in the paper work, though. If there is anything that says it goes back into effect if you are back in jail, well, then he may want you back in jail," warned Marty.

After hearing that, I had to make sure I found the Power of Attorney that night. It was getting late and I was getting tired. The wine was making me very tired and if I was going to get the Power of Attorney out by morning, I had better let Marty say his good nights.

"Marty, I will get that out of the file and call you in the morning," I told him as I was getting up from my chair.

"Oh, would you? That would be awesome," Marty said as I gave him a hug and walked him out to the front door. I went to my home office in the back and opened the file cabinet and found the Power of Attorney that Jack had me sign while I was in jail. I started to read the fine print. It was a continuous Power of Attorney. It was in Jack's favor. It said that at anytime I was incarcerated or out of the country or hospitalized or mentally incapable, he would have Power of Attorney.

"What a schmuck! I can't believe it! He probably does want me in jail so he could rob me and my kids blind! He will get his." I folded up the papers and put them into my purse and went upstairs to bed.

The next morning, I phoned Marty and told him I had found the Power of Attorney that Jack had me sign.

"Marty, would it still be valid if he is no longer my attorney?" I asked.

"Unless you make it invalid in the court system. You need to go to the courthouse and have someone in the courts put a stop to it, quickly." Marty strongly suggested over the phone.

"Do you know of any good lawyers?" I needed to know. "Maybe my new lawyer can do whatever it is to have Jack stopped."

"What do you mean?" Marty had to know.

"I mean, to have Jack stopped from being able to get anything of mine, especially my money." Do you know of any good lawyers? Or do I need to get one myself?" I kept interrogating Marty over the phone a little impatiently.

"Well, I do know of a few. I know of a real good one. His name is Adam McCann. Why don't you give him a call and tell him I told you to call him. He might give you a good deal. He might work with you if you explain what you have," Marty continued.

"What do you mean, Marty? Explain what I have? Do you mean about the gold and stuff like that?" I had to ask.

"Well, yea. I imagine he would take some collateral like that as payment," Marty told me.

"I don't know. Do you think that is wise?" I kept looking for reassurance from Marty.

"Well, don't mention it right out of the gate, but it might be all right. I don't know of anyone refusing gold as payment when the dollar fluctuates so much." Marty reassured me over the phone. "Well, I have to go, bye."

"Bye." I hung up the phone and started to look in the phone book for Adam McCann in the attorney section of the yellow pages. I started to think to myself of how much more can I take? I just wanted to have my life back to normal. I wanted to be able to have my kids at home with me. I didn't want to be in danger and worry about anyone trying to harm my children or me. I wanted my happy home the way it used to be. Ralph playing with the kids. They would run around in the

They think I Killed My Husband!

yard or just roll around on the floor while watching television. It was almost better than the Cleaver's. Our normal, healthy, happy home I had at one time, I want it back so bad. Just then, the doorbell rang.

"Why would someone come all the way up to my door this early without calling first?" I thought to myself. I got up and went to the door and looked through the peep-hole. I couldn't believe my eyes! Why on earth would he be here, of all of the people in the world? He must have some ulterior motive. I better keep my guard up. Maybe I should just act like I am not home, or not out of bed yet. I just stood behind the door like an imbecile.

"Pam?" I heard from the other side of the door. "Pam, are you there? I know you are there. Will you open up, please?" The man shouted from the other side of the door.

"What do you want? I fired you yesterday remember? Why are you here, Jack?" I yelled through the door.

"So, you are home. Please open the door. It's me, Jack. As you already know. I need to talk to you," Jack screamed from the other side of the door.

"What do you want?" I yelled! "I don't want to talk to you."

"Oh, c'mon Pam, open the door. I have some papers for you!" Jack kept yelling through the door.

"Oh, I bet you do. Why don't you go out and play in the traffic?" I asked him angrily.

"Pam, are you still on that? Would you let me in?" Jack would not stop begging to be let into my house.

"Why should I let you in my house? Give me one good reason, Jack." I challenged through the door.

"Did you know your Private Dick, Mr. Marty is working for the C.I.A.?" Jack yelled back through the door trying to keep my attention.

I got so angry that he would actually use such a ploy to get my attention that I opened up my door and looked him straight in the eyes and asked him, "So, what? That's even better for me. Of course, I know." I only got those words out of my mouth when a blaze of rushing argyle and tweed plaid suit wearing metal frame glasses plowed through the living room clutching my neck. I tried to fight him off. He pushed me up against the wall and put his left hand around my neck and his shoulder was pressed onto my body. His right hand was in his pocket or holding something. It was pressed against my stomach. I couldn't tell exactly, but he had something in his pocket. My back was flat on the wall with Jack's stomach against my stomach. I was literally pinned up against the wall! I couldn't move and was beginning to be unable to breathe.

"You can't fire me, Pam! I won't let you," Jack threatened!

"Let me go," I muttered gasping for air. "Then we'll talk about it."

Jack released my throat so I may speak, but he grabbed my ear and hair and remained pressed against my body so he could remain in control of me. I felt something else sticking into my back. I believe it's the alarm keypad.

"Now, what on earth do you want?" I had to ask.

"I want my job back," Jack demanded.

I had to laugh at him. He looked like such a geek that had gone mad. The receding hairline with his metal-framed glasses just made him a classic geek. I couldn't help myself. Plus, with my irresistible advantage of having the police alarm button to push within seconds kept me smiling. I do believe my laughing made him more desperate and mad.

"Now, why should I give you your job back? You haven't done a thing for me that I haven't done for myself."

"You need me on this case, Pam. I know the history and every detail of this whole case so far. You won't be able to find anyone to manage this case like I can manage this case for you," Jack pleaded his case into my ear while still brushed up against my body pinned to the wall. He slowly eased up after he made his point and let me down off of the wall. I had to try to be smart with this man. I do believe he may be sick in the head a little. He seems to be desperate and willing to do anything to try to represent my case again. He may be the one that is out to retrieve the key for the deposit box. I had better be careful for my own life. He was just choking me a minute ago. I remained in front of the alarm panel, leaning against the wall to appear intimidated. I stood erect and strong.

"Jack, you want me to hire you back, but you came charging through my door and started choking me and making threats! Do you think I am stupid or something? I think you had better go before I call the police right now and have you arrested for breaking and entering," I told him sternly, but nicely.

"You wouldn't dare call the police on me. I know you are hiding something. Besides, I am a lawyer. I'll be out in a few hours or less. I can come back," Jack came back saying to me not less than an inch from my face with his body still pressing against mine. "I can come back."

"Jack, you are really scaring me now. Come back and do what? I think you need to leave. Have you been taking your medication?" I questioned Jack about drugs just in case he had taken any or not enough.

"How do you know I take medication?" Jack asked me and took his face back a few inches with surprise.

I began to ease my arm up to the alarm keypad and said, "Oh, don't you remember? You told me when you first came back to work for me. You told me all about your rehabilitation and the two years you were disbarred from practicing law and it was because of your manic/depression disorder."

"Oh." Jack said as he backed up and put his guard down. He looked down at the floor and started to remember the times he came to work for me. He was in a little better shape then. Jack began to walk around the room a bit, pacing and remembering. Meanwhile, I pressed the police button unknown to Jack. Now, I knew the police would arrive shortly. I had to try to keep Jack calm until the police came, however.

"But, you didn't have to fire me like that yesterday!" Jack yelled to me and started to get aggressive again. Jack quickly walked back over to me still standing against the wall and then back away again like he did not know what to do exactly.

"Jack, you don't seem sincere about protecting my best interest in this case. If I am going to pay someone, I want 110% out of him. I don't believe you are doing that. At least not for me," I told him calmly, trying not to make him mad.

"But I didn't do anything!" Jack retaliated.

"Exactly! You weren't doing anything! Besides, you quit and walked out, remember?" I reminded Jack of the sorted details of yesterday.

"That's because I had to save my dignity! I couldn't let you fire me! Especially over something as ridiculous as blaming me for pushing you into traffic! Like I would do something like that. C'mon, Pam." Jack kept insisting he was innocent.

"I am still not going to hire you back. So, you can just forget it." I answered him. Just then I heard the sounds of sirens and two police cars were pulling into my driveway. Jack looked out of the window and saw the police cars.

"You Bitch! How did you get the police here? You didn't use the phone! What do you have, one of those medic alerts or something? You'll be screaming, 'Help, I've fallen and I can't get up!'" Jack mocked totally surprised looking at me with his hands up from the window. He was desperate indeed. In a split second, Jack pulled out a gun and ran to me by the wall and grabbed my arm and twisted it behind me. Jack pulled me in front of him. He cocked his gun and placed the barrel to my temple. "Now, I need to get some things straight with you, I need to be your attorney. I need to remain as your Power of Attorney. God knows if anything should happen to you Pam. What would happen? What would happen if this gun should go off right now? Who would take care of all your paperwork, your banking needs, your contracts?"

I was silent. I just didn't want to die right now. I didn't want to show how scared I was either. Then I remembered the police and got the nerve to say, "The police are right outside, Jack. What are you going to do? Shoot me now? The police will come running in here so fast and just kill you for killing me!"

"Fuck you! I can do whatever I want to do." Jack

started to scream. "You think you're so smart, don't you?" Jack asked as he pulled on my hair with the same hand he was holding the gun.

"NO! Really, Jack. Please, let go of my hair. You're hurting me," I pleaded with Jack to let me go. Just then, the cops raced through the door. Jack turned and pointed his gun at the cops then back at me.

"Don't shoot! I'll kill her!" Jack shouted at the policemen.

"Now, Jack. Why would you want to go and do a stupid thing like that? All that is going to do is land your sad ass in jail for a really long time," the first cop tried reasoning with him.

"Yea, and be roomies with Bubba! You know what Bubba likes!" I reminded Jack.

"Come on, sir. Put the gun down and let go of the lady," the other cop demanded.

Jack looked up at the cops, then at his gun in his hand. Realizing, he felt my wrist in his other hand and let my arm go and looked at his now empty hand. "What am I doing?" Jack asked himself as if he were coming out of some manic rampage. I ran away from him as fast as I could towards the cops. The cops immediately jumped on him and forced him to the floor and put his hands around his back and slapped some handcuffs on him. They stood him up on his feet with his arms still behind him, and began to march him to the patrol car. The policemen came back into the house to confirm the status of my health.

"I am fine. A few less hairs, and this bump on the head, but other than that, fine," I told them.

"Would you like to press charges, Ma'am?" the policeman asked.

"You bet I would! That Son of a bitch had me pinned up against the wall with a gun! I am not letting this slide. If I did, I would be really stupid!" I exclaimed.

"Yes, Ma'am. We will take him to the station now. There will be another squad car arriving any moment to have some paperwork for you to fill out," the officer stated.

"Can't I just come down later?" I asked.

"Well, the other officers are on their way, and you might as well get it over with here in your house. They need to gather some vital clues here to establish exactly what happened." The officer continued explaining.

"Very well. It couldn't hurt, I guess," I answered back to the officer as he made his way out the front door to his squad car. Just then the other car pulled into my driveway as the first car drove away. The other officers got out and came to my door where I was standing.

"Are you Pamela Garcia?" the officer asked.

"Yes, I am her." I answered back.

"We have to do an investigation here. May we come in?" Officer Donovan, a blonde pudgy man in uniform asked before entering.

I opened the door wide and let the officers in the front door. I showed them into the living room and offered them some coffee and a place to sit. We all sat down on the couch. The policeman pulled out their paperwork for me to fill out. I began doing the filling out of the papers and the officers started to get a little bit nosy around the living room.

"Hey, What is it exactly you two are looking for?" I had to ask and stop them from getting into something that wasn't of any of their concern.

"Oh well, why don't you tell us where you were attacked?" Officer Donovan looked over and asked me.

"Well, it started at the door. The minute he heard I unlatched it. He pushed it open and rushed me and I didn't stop until that wall stopped me." I pointed at the wall next to where the broken lamp was lying on the floor. The men made their way over to the wall and the area around the broken lamp. They both started to work together and gather evidence around the wall and the surrounding area. I just sat back and tried to put myself back together.

"Well, if you gentlemen don't mind, I am going to change. I would like to get out of these clothes and freshen up a little," I told them as I got up to leave the room.

"Well, yes, Ma'am. I do." Officer Donovan stopped dusting the wall, looked up towards me and continued saying, "You need to stay in those clothes until we gather the evidence from you. You will need to be taken to the lab at the hospital or the police station. Did he hurt you in any way, Ma'am?"

"Yes, a little. He just slammed me up against the wall and I hit my head in two places. Would you call that hurting someone, Officer?" I looked at him like he was stupid.

"I guess I should call an ambulance and have you taken to the hospital for X-rays, just to make sure," concentrating solely on my well being, Officer Donovan justified his negligence.

While he was calling the ambulance I sat back down and waited for them to finish gathering intelligence and to be taken to the hospital. I did not need this today. I should call that lawyer Marty mentioned to me. Adam McCann was his name. I looked in the phone book for the name of McCann under 'Attorney's and found his number. I picked up the receiver and then looked over at the officers investigating the situation within ear's reach of my telephone conversation. I quickly put the telephone back down and went into my bedroom. I knew that these creeps did not need to know everything.

"Hello. May I speak to Mr. McCann please?" I asked the receptionist over the phone while sitting on my bed in my room.

"Mr. McCann is out of the office at the moment. May I take a message?" She very politely informed me and professionally offered to take a message from me.

"My name is Pamela Garcia. Do you expect him in today?" I quickly asked her.

"Oh, Mrs. Garcia, the widow," she had to remind me of infamous the local media has made me.

"Well, yes. I fired my attorney yesterday and I would like for Mr. McCann to call as soon as he can, please?" I quickly and coldly stated to the woman on the other end of the phone.

"Yes, of course. He should be in later this morning. He has a court appearance this morning. That should not take all morning. I expect him in around 10:30 or so. I can have him call you as soon as he gets in. May I have the number you can be reached?" The receptionist continued while getting out a pencil and paper to write down my number and information.

"Sure, it's 388-555-0876. Please have him call me as soon as he gets in. I want to be the first one he calls when he returns," I demanded.

"All right. I will see what I can do. He has several messages here before yours," the receptionist said.

I noticed that she might be developing an attitude, like some young women do when dealing with my demanding attitude, so I asked, "What did you say your name was?"

"I'm Natalie," she answered back into the phone with a chipper and cynical attitude.

"Thank you, Natalie. That will be all." I said then hung up the phone before she could get the entire word 'Good' out of her mouth to finish her 'Good byes.'

"Women!" I uttered while getting up off of the bed and walked back into the living room. The ambulance had just arrived to take me to the hospital. "Oh, God!" I said after seeing the ambulance from the living room window. I saw the two policemen still working on gathering intelligence and information. "Aren't you two finished yet?"

"Yes, Ma'am. We were just finishing up now," Officer Donovan said while getting up off of the floor and looked over towards me and pulled up the back of his pants.

"Good. Because it looks like the ambulance is here to take me to the hospital. I don't know why you guys couldn't have taken me to the hospital." I told the officers.

"Well, we didn't know what time we would be finished. You need to get yourself checked out as soon as possible," the other officer added.

"I don't know you two characters. I don't want to leave you alone in my house without me here. You are not searching

They think I Killed My Husband!

my house, but what is to stop you if I am not here? Who are you? Are you with the police? I am not leaving unless you are out of here. I don't care if the ambulance is outside. How about if I just drive myself to the hospital? That would be cheaper. I am going to have to pay the ambulance bill anyway, right?" I retaliated and became a little too loud and defensive with the officers.

"What do you care? Look at you. You live in this beautiful house on the lake. You have nice things. You must have plenty of money. Why are you worried about anything being cheaper?" The officer interrogated as if he had a right.

"Look, I don't like your attitude," I told him coldly. "Who are you? I wouldn't think a well trained police officer would speak with such ill mannerism."

"Sorry. We'll be going now. Are you going to drive yourself to the station?" Officer Donovan asked me.

"Some gentleman you are," I told him. "Yes, I suppose so."

"Well, I can drive you down, if you don't feel up to it." Officer Donovan stated with complete insincerity.

"Don't put yourself out. How do they train you guys down at the force anyway? Do they beat you guys so you will think everyone is out to get you?" I asked with great sarcasm. "I have a friend that is on his way that can take me down. I would rather go with him anyway. If I went with you guys, it would just look like I was some creepy prisoner," I told him sternly so they would definitely get on their way.

"Well then, good day Mrs. Garcia." The officers said then turned around and left my home and drove away. I called Marty on the phone to see if he could come over and pick me up to take me to the hospital to get checked out. I had to have the attack on record.

"Hello," Marty answered his phone.

"Marty, you need to get over here, please," I told him before anything else came out.

"Who is this? Pam, is that you?" Marty questioned over the phone.

"Yes, it's me. I need you to take me to the hospital so I

can get checked out," I pleaded with him.

"Checked out for what?" he kept asking questions.

"I was attacked this morning," I informed him.

"What? You have got to be kidding me! By whom?" Marty demanded over the phone and nearly broke my eardrum.

"It was Jack! He lost his mind. I think he stopped taking his medication," I informed him.

"His medication? What? You mean to tell me that your lawyer was crazy? It's a good thing you did fire his ass! You would have ended up in jail and he, in the looney bin!" Marty stated with a small snicker.

"Ha ha very funny. Not! Can you get your ass over here and pick me up to take me to the hospital or not?" I needed to know.

"Yea, sure. I am on my way. I'll see you in a few." Marty said still laughing a little.

"Okay, bye." I answered back in to the phone.

"Bye." Marty hung up and was probably on his way.

I tried to get my self together while I waited on Marty to arrive. Since the officers were gone I felt more at ease. I walked around the house and smoked a joint to calm my nerves. I took a Tylenol to ease my soreness and headache while I was waiting. I sat alone and couldn't believe that little fucker tried to kill me. Does Jack know about the safety deposit box? Does he know about the gold inside of it if he does know about the box? I am going to find out. I guess I have to go the hospital first to make sure I am okay physically. Marty arrived at my house to take me to the hospital.

"Are you ready to go?" Marty said as he opened up the door. I got up and walked over towards the door.

"Yes, let's go," I answered in route whisking my jacket around my shoulder and grabbing my purse off of the end table. Marty stood by the door and held it open as I walked out and shut and locked the door.

"You have quite a big bump on your head, Pam. Does it hurt?" Marty asked me. We got into Marty's car. He had a different car everyday. One day he would have his nice car, a black SUV, or one of a half dozen, cheapo cars he would use on his detective cases. He had these modest cars to be less conspicuous. Today, he had the nice, new SUV. I think that is his personal car.

I sat down in the passenger seat and answered, "Only when I touch the bump. Does it look that bad?"

"It's the size of a golf ball. You poor thing. Pam, what do you think Jack wants?" Marty asked me.

"What do you mean?" I wanted clarification, but still looking out the window out into the street and the sidewalks with a few people walking in front of the old brick homes along the road.

Marty glanced over at me while driving and said, "I mean, what do you think Jack is really after? Jack is like in on something. Don't you get that? Or is it me? Or is it he is crazy and didn't take his medication?"

"I think it's the latter," I replied laughing nervously. I looked over at him and thought a minute about what he just said. Maybe Jack is mad. But there is some truth in madness.

"Well, he did seem pretty demanding to be my lawyer again. Why would that be so important?"

"Don't know," Marty replied. "Maybe it's something on that Power of Attorney document. Maybe it only applies if he is your appointed attorney."

"Oh, of course. But, wait a minute. That means he wants to make sure I get put somewhere that would make him in control of my estate! That son of a bitch," I exclaimed accusingly.

"Yea, sounds like it. Pam, did Jack do dealings for your husband a lot?" Marty began to ask some questions I haven't heard before.

"They would play the stock market a lot. You know, talk about business and economics. I suppose they would do a lot of business trading and shipping with the business we owned. Jack was always drawing up contracts. He knew how. Even if he wasn't licensed at the time, a person can still represent himself, and Jack knows what to do. So, Ralph saved money in lawyer's fees."

"You mean at the time some contracts were made, Jack wasn't a licensed lawyer?" Marty repeated what I said with a question.

"Yes. What is so bad about that? I thought it was a good idea at the time. It saved us a lot of money." I retaliated.

"Yes, but Pam, there could have been a lot of monkey business going on. Illegal things done that any real lawyer wouldn't have even wanted to know about." Marty told me.

"Why are you being so cynical?" I asked.

"Pam, do you think your husband was such a saint?" Marty kept asking me.

"Well, I know he wasn't perfect. What are you getting at, Marty?" I looked over at him and questioned intently.

"Do you care if I pull in here and grab a cup of coffee? I really need some caffeine," Marty muttered and turned the steering wheel into the parking lot.

"Sure, do I have a choice? Quit trying to change the subject. We are not finished with this yet." I told Marty as he quickly got out of the SUV and went inside and got a cup of coffee in the local coffee shop. I sat in the truck and waited for him to return. After about five minutes he returned back. He opened the door and placed his coffee in the cup holder and hopped in. He did not say anything more.

"I said we weren't finished yet. Why are you being so down on my late husband? Everyone is accusing me of being the bad one. I am glad you are not one of them. But why are you making it seem that my late husband was a bad person?" I questioned Marty inside the SUV. Marty continued driving down the street and had to stop at the light.

He turned to me and said, "I just think it is weird that Jack is so determined to be your counsel. I think he knows about the gold and maybe there is something more," Marty told me as if he was thinking out loud.

"Do you think Ralph and Jack were both involved in the gold stuff? Then Jack must know what the whole situation is! He would've known all about the gold all along. Do you

They think I Killed My Husband!

think?" I asked Marty looking over at him, yet thinking in my head why hadn't I seen any signs of any of his possible knowledge?

"I bet he does. I bet he wants to see you put in jail and he gets to go through whatever you have and take control. That means bank accounts and safety deposit boxes and anything that takes your signature. There is no telling what is in that sick head of his," Marty reminded me.

"Well, after we leave the hospital, I want to go to where ever they took Jack and ask him point blank. Do you think he will be at the station or do you think they took him to a hospital?" I continued to interrogate Marty as he interrogated me.

"He is probably still at the station. We'll go when you are finished at the hospital. You have to have the attack on record with medical records on file with the police report, just in case," Marty said.

I finished my business at the hospital and we continued our daily venture to the police station. Marty walked right in. I followed behind him.

"May I help you?" The receptionist with short brunette hair and in her uniform asked.

"We need to speak to Jack Schwartz, please," Marty demanded from the receptionist once we entered the station.

"And who the hell are you," the receptionist replied with a great attitude.

"I am the man that will have your job if you don't cooperate, that's who I am. Now, get someone with some authority so my client and myself can speak with Jack Schwartz," Marty demanded as he held out his identification that was rather impressive. I don't think I had seen it. It looked very official from what little I could see it.

"Yes sir," she said with great cooperation and excitement. She was almost too happy to oblige. She went and got another officer that could help us to see Jack and we could get some questions answered.

"What was that you showed her?" I had to ask.

"Oh, my identification? I haven't showed it to you? Oh

well, here look. It's a terrible picture. Now, I am going to have to kill you," Marty said in jest.

"Please don't tease me about anything like that," I begged. "I know you think it's funny, but remember who you are talking to."

"Sorry," Marty said and he put his wallet back in his pocket. Officer Thomas came to the front with the receptionist to see exactly what we wanted.

"Madge here, says you want to speak to Jack Schwartz. May I ask why?" Officer Thomas questioned us like he was protecting his prisoner.

"We would just like to ask him a few questions, sir," Marty told him very nicely. He wanted to try to persuade him to permit us to interrogate Jack in our own words.

"Well, if you make it quick. I know the nature of your case. He will remain in custody, because that is your request. But this is highly irregular," Officer Thomas added. Officer Thomas took us down to see Jack in his cell. I thought he might bring him to a room or something. We walked down the corridor and I saw Jack sitting there behind the bars and he looked absolutely pathetic. His hair was tousled and sticky. He was sitting on the cot in his cell looking down.

"Jack, you have a visitor. Make it quick," Officer Thomas told Marty and me.

"Thanks, we will," Marty replied.

"Jack, what in the hell do you think you were trying to do back there at my house?" I asked him point blank.

"You stupid bitch. You aren't supposed to be here. You should be in here and me out there. This is all wrong," Jack said to me with great resentment.

"What do you mean 'this is all wrong?" I had to ask. "What is it you are not telling me?"

"What I am telling you is that you are a stupid bitch and you are the one that is supposed to be in jail. I am supposed to get what is coming to me," Jack replied.

"Hold It!" Marty yelled out in the jailhouse. "Spit it out Jack. You know something, something that I have always suspected of you. What is it?"

"Fuck you, and the horse you rode in on!" Jack yelled back to Marty. "I have an attorney coming and I don't have to tell you anything! LALALALALALALA!" Jack said with sarcasm and then plugged his ears and just began acting crazy.

"Oh, my God! Hasn't anyone gotten this man his medicine?" I wondered out loud.

"Medicine? Who needs medicine? I have mine right here!" Jack exclaimed as he held out his hand and opened a napkin that contained some pills.

"You mean you haven't taken them yet?" Marty asked him with suspicion. "Pam, we can't deal with him now. He needs to get proper treatment before we can continue any more questions."

"Yes, I think you are right. Let's go," I agreed to leave with Marty and wait for another day. As we were leaving, I couldn't help to wonder what he meant by 'he suspected of Jack,' and I didn't know how to bring it up other than to just ask. We got into the SUV and started towards my house.

"Hey Marty, what did you mean that you had suspected something of Jack all along? What is it you suspect of him?"

"Well, Pam, I have been doing some investigating of my own with the C.I.A. and there may be a link to the gold you found and national affairs," Marty told me.

"What? Get the fuck out of here. You have got to be kidding me. How could the gold be linked up with something of national importance? I found it in Egypt," I reminded him.

"I can't tell you anymore yet. It is a matter of national security. The investigation may lead to something bigger than you know or could imagine! Jack may be at the heart of it all. He knows something, I can feel it," Marty told me. All of the sudden we were almost hit by a garbage truck!

"Look out," I screamed! Marty swerved and we just missed the truck by inches and my heart was racing and my stomach felt like it was doing flip flops in my chest! Marty pulled over for a second.

"Oh, my God! That was close! Maybe too close," Marty

said with a voice of suspicion again. We sat for another minute to catch our breaths and recollect ourselves. Marty started up the SUV and we continued on our way to my house.

I had to know what Marty was talking about. It could get me off for the murder of my husband, since I didn't do it. The cops are so lazy that they just want the case solved, but don't care if the person is actually guilty or not. But I will trust Marty for now. I will have to wait until further evidence reveals itself.

A few days later, Mr. McCann, the attorney I called, returned my phone call. I really needed to speak to him sooner.

"Mrs. Garcia?" Mr. McCann said through the telephone lines.

"Yes," I replied.

"This is attorney Adam McCann returning your phone call. I apologize for not calling sooner, but I was out of town. What can I do for you?" He went straight to the point.

"Yes. Well, I had to fire my legal representation. I would very much like it if you would be retained as my counsel?" I asked him intelligently as I knew.

"Well, what happened to your last attorney?" Mr. McCann kept interrogating.

"I guess you were really out of town or just want to hear my version. Okay, I had to let him go because of lack of drugs. Yes, you heard me, the lack of taking his medication. The man went bonkers. He needs to be on medication and he apparently went manic or off somewhere. He tried to kill me. I don't think that made the papers." I told him abruptly and coldly into the phone.

"Wow. That's a new one. I never had heard of someone getting fired for not taking drugs before. I guess for your sake, maybe it is for the best you found out before it got totally out of hand," he replied more sympathetically. "When would you like to come in for consultation, Mrs. Garcia?"

"Well, of course as soon as possible. Are you free today?" I was really desperate to have someone to handle my case. I went down and met with Mr. McCann later that day. I

They think I Killed My Husband!

am exhausted. I hope I can endure this torture. I have to put up with all of this ridicule and the people closest to me seem to be the people I have to watch out for the most. They are the ones that know the most about me. I have to sit down and evaluate everything, the people the situation, everything. Marty is working also with the C.I.A. and now tells me that this whole situation that Ralph was involved with, the gold and the foreign affairs may be of federal significance. Jack, my lawyer, who I thought was a friend, is simply crazy. I think, or maybe he is just desperate about something he knows and just seems crazy. He won't do hard time if declared insane. How long has Marty been an onlooker? Has he been spying on Ralph for years, months? It all just seemed to weird. I didn't know whom to trust anymore. What does everyone want? The gold, of course. I have to keep that gold for me. I need to go and see my kids. I need my sanity back.

  I made some reservations at a nearby hotel and met my children in a middle place just outside of town, in the country. I had my cousin bring them to me. We stayed in a hotel that I paid cash for and leased under an assumed name. I hugged my kids, Rafael and Serena as soon as I saw them. I was so happy I started to cry. We just stayed in the room and I ordered room service for lunch. Earlier, we went down to the pool area and went swimming. The pool area was very elaborate. The hotel must have been in its off-season. It wasn't very crowded. We all had a wonderful time in the pool. There were a couple of other people in the pool, but they were on the other side. Rafael and Serena were having a great time with me in the water. We were splashing each other and having a wonderful time. I hate to leave them when the time comes. We went back up to the room to have our dinner in our room. We had a delicious prime rib with mashed potatoes and gravy with green vegetables. It was a perfect day. The only bad part about it was leaving them. My cousin came later to take them back to her house. I was so glad they were able to stay with my cousin on her farm. No one suspected they were there. I was able to feel secure about that. I went down to get my car, and left before my kids did. I left at night in the dark, so I wouldn't be seen or noticed. The kids stayed in the room overnight with my cousin and left the next day. The hotel had a continental breakfast in the lobby by 10:00AM. So Serena and Rafael and my cousin could eat breakfast before they left in the morning. I told my cousin to call me when they made it home. It is so wonderful to see my kids again. I didn't think about anything. I didn't think about the gold, or the fact that Marty was linked with the C.I.A. and may have been spying on Ralph for years. So, what was Ralph exchanging for the gold, if anything? But there must have been something else involved. I don't want to think about it right now. I had to keep myself alive and out of jail. That is the number one priority for now so I can get my kids back home and keep us all safe. But, I couldn't do that until I could prove myself innocent. Funny, we are supposed to be innocent until proven guilty.

    I had a meeting with the attorney Mr. McCann later that week. I couldn't believe Jack was in the mental hospital. I hope my new lawyer can think and act accordingly. It seems that everyone in this world is out for himself. I know one should be, but sometimes it is not that difficult to help others too. It may turn out that one day you may need the help of that other person. It seems that the people that I have helped or thought I helped are not there now. I cannot trust anyone. I really need to be careful whom I tell things to.

    I had a couple of other meetings with my new attorney, Adam McCann. I brought him up to date on the case. I didn't tell him of the gold quite yet. I told him of the safety deposit box in Egypt and there may be some valuables in it. I don't know, or led him to think I didn't know. I didn't until after the fact anyway. Marty recommended him to me. I don't know if I should use this guy. I made a few more phone calls from a new cell phone I bought to some lawyers out of the phone book. I set up a couple of more interviews with some attorneys that I did a little bit of investigating myself. I cannot afford to do this in a trusting way. People are shit. A met about three other attorneys that week and I really liked one that seemed to have

They think I Killed My Husband!

a great reputation. His name was Harry Fluxenberg. He was very smart and was very factual. He just wanted to get the case solved and did not like the facts about the middle Easterners involvement and the Cubans. It seemed extremely far-fetched, but somehow relevant. Mr. Fluxenberg took some gold jewelry as payment and presumed not to ask questions. He was extremely intelligent and I presumed he knew as well as I did where it came from after hearing just part of my story. He told me he was going to do some research for me with the information I had given him and we will get together in a couple of days.

"Wow, that's fast," I exclaimed in his office just before our initial meeting came to an end.

"Well, I need to work fast. You paid me adequately, and your trial picks back up in less than 10 days. Let's Rock and roll," he told me in his most exciting way he knew how, which wasn't that exciting.

"OK, I'll see you in a couple of days. Any particular time?" I questioned.

"Oh, say about noonish. Is that good for you?" he wanted to confirm.

"I'll be here at noon," I replied with a grin. He was so serious, yet so gallantly cute. I left the attorney, Mr. Fluxenberg to do his work so I could go about my business. I telephoned the other attorneys to tell them I would not need their services. When Marty recommended that other guy right away, my first instinct was to use him. But, what does Marty really want? Why the special wine? Or was it special? He may have just bought it at the store and said that some old man hand-picked it at a Napa Vineyard. Men are such liars. He probably didn't even bring it over from California on the plane or car or train or nothing. He said that he was talking to the C.I.A.? He probably is the C.I.A.! Jack may be crazy, but he isn't stupid! Marty is probably lying to me too! I have to talk to him. I don't know whom to trust. I hope Marty doesn't try to kill me either.

Marty called me and wanted to come over to talk to me about the situation with Jack and my lawyer and the gold and what the trading may be for. I agreed and he came later that evening to talk about the situation in more detail. He arrived with another bottle of wine and some cheese and grapes and crackers.

"What's all this?" I asked him at the door. He was also dressed nice and I could smell his cologne a second after I opened the door.

"What do you mean?" He answered with a question like he was a pure and innocent person.

"I mean you! You are dressed nice with a bottle of wine and cheese, to talk shop?" I questioned again as he went into the kitchen to put the cheese and grapes on a plate and to open the bottle of wine. I just looked at him still holding the door open. I realized I was in shock and closed the door and walked into the kitchen.

"Can't someone put on a pair of slacks and a colored shirt and bring someone that is stressed out after losing her husband and then being accused of killing him too, some wine?" Marty asked me like I should be ashamed that I am thinking that people are not nice to others that are suffering.

"I am sorry. Thank you. That is very kind," I told him putting my guard down.

"Sheesh, you are stressed, aren't you? Here, sit down. You do need this, and here are some fruit and cheese. Relax for a few minutes and tell me about your day," Marty said handing me the wine then we sat on the couch in the living room to talk. I started to tell him I found a new lawyer.

"So, you hired that guy I told you, Adam McCann?" Marty asked me all bright eyed and excited.

"No, if you would let me finish, I will tell you more. I did not hire that guy you told me," I told Marty, while his face went from a happy one to a concerned puckered looking one.

"Well, whom did you hire?" he asked me in a very serious tone.

"Well, gee, you have such a look on your face, I don't know if I should tell you." I answered him.

"I will find out sooner or later, Pam. You might as well

tell me now. I have my ways of finding things out," Marty told me sharply.

"So, you do work for the C.I.A.! Jack told me you did, but I didn't know if I should believe him or not. I didn't know if he was just crazy or what!" I exclaimed to Marty.

"NO! I don't work for the C.I.A.! I was just insinuating that the newspapers publish news all of the time and I can find out very easily who he is. That's all. You really come up with them, don't you?" Marty reassured me.

"Well, you even said you were talking with the C.I.A. and the situation that Ralph was in may have concerned the C.I.A., did you not? So, don't go acting like this just came out of nowhere." I told Marty sternly then taking a sip of wine and biting on a grape.

"Why are we arguing, Pam? I came over to talk to you about your case and I am trying to help you," Marty said trying to redeem the situation between us.

"Don't go and try to switch this around. How do I know you haven't been following this for a long time? That is why you are here now. I only know what you have told me about yourself," I told him with skepticism in my voice.

"Oh, my God! I can't believe this! Pam, you know that I don't work for the C.I.A.," Marty kept trying to convince me.

"Well, whatever. I just want to drop this right now. We could go on forever like this. So let's just drop it," I demanded.

"Fine, I agree. We do need to drop it. Now, why can't you tell me what the name of your lawyer is?" Marty still wanted to know.

"Well, I don't think his name is that relevant do you? If you must know, it's Fluxenberg, Harry Fluxenberg," I finally told Marty with an attitude.

"Oh, I heard of that guy. He's supposed to be very good. Why didn't you use the guy I told you?" Marty kept asking me to the point it is really aggravating.

"Because you told me," I snapped back. "Why do you want me to use this specific lawyer so badly?"

"I heard he was the best. He may help you the most I

thought," Marty responded with a kind voice. I didn't know whether to believe it or not. I didn't know if I should believe anything anyone has advised me of. I need to sit and evaluate everything and meet with my new attorney in a couple of days.

"So what is with the wine? Why are you bringing me the wine always? Do you really expect me to believe that you had it from when you went to California?" I looked at him and wondered if he would answer me honestly and if I could trust any answer he gave me.

"I had it forever and I thought I'd bring it. I didn't have to stop and buy anything, and so I just grabbed it and brought it over. I didn't realize you would become so suspicious of me over it," Marty informed me.

"Oh," I responded humbly. I sat quietly and took another sip of the wine. I put the glass back down on the table. The silence was engulfing our surroundings. I spoke up, "It is good wine." I took another sip and grabbed a chunk of cheese. Marty just looked at me like he didn't know what to do. He seemed glad that I was not arguing any more and he seemed frustrated that I was thinking the things that I was. I looked at him with my big brown eyes innocently and sweetly. He laughed and shook his head.

We finished the bottle of wine and the hor's deorves he brought. The talking didn't amount to much other than gossip about Jack and a little shop talk. I didn't have much to tell him since I hadn't met with my new attorney to find out what his strategy will be. Marty continued talking about some of his old cases and stakeouts he had been on. The wine was getting to my head a little. I was wishing he wasn't such a prude about professionalism and client-contractor relationships. He sure is cute with his gorgeous green eyes and the way he would talk about his stories. I realized the time and it was really late. So, I told Marty I was tired and I had a busy day tomorrow and it would be best to call it a night.

A few days later, I met with Harry Fluxenberg about the situation I was in. He had done some investigating of his own. Which was nice to see that I was getting my money's worth for a change. Harry had found out that the man that worked for Ralph in the warehouse had gone to high school with Ralph. He disappears, then his wife and son are murdered is very strange to the case. He told me this should raise some reasonable doubt in my defense. He said he was waiting for some confirmation of other things he was investigating, but it would be a couple of more days.

"Wow! That is great!" I exclaimed. "You really get down to business and don't waste any time!"

"Well, like I said, we don't have any time to waste, Mrs. Garcia. I need everything, now!" Mr. Fluxenberg told me.

"Keep up the good work. I guess I will be off now. Should I meet you back here Thursday? That will give you two days," I told him.

"That should be fine," Harry replied barely looking up. I had my meeting with Mr. Fluxenberg on Thursday. It was quite interesting. He had found out that Jack had been involved with Ralph's business accounting for exporting some goods out of the country to Egypt on a regular basis for many years. No one knew what it could have been, except Jack apparently.

"How did you find out all of this?" I asked Harry sitting in front of his desk.

"Well, I dug deep and I have some good friends," Harry told me.

"I am glad you are on my side," I told him. We finished up going over everything else he had and together with I had, we should be ready to back into court.

We arrived back in the courtroom the following week. It was raining this morning. The reporters were not so obtrusive because of the rain, which was a good thing. Harry and I sat down in the courtroom. I looked around to see who is here. I saw some reporters that were in the room with some good seats to get some good pictures and notes. The Judge walked in from his chambers. The bailiff stood up called everyone to rise. Everyone stood up and the judge walked up to his podium. The trial was beginning to commence.

Harry explained briefly how he intends to approach the

situation and to enlighten the jury to the fact that everything is circumstantial evidence against me. I am sure he can do it. I don't want to count my chickens before they are hatched though. The prosecuting attorney was at the other table just sitting there waiting to fry me at the stake. The things the papers have been writing lately. Most of the things are just made up and pictures are old or fabricated.

The Judge asked the prosecuting attorney to call his first witness to the stand. He called an old employee of mine, Elizabeth Watts. She never liked me that much. I think she envied me a little. She was young and a pretty girl, but she was still struggling financially. She sat up on the witness stand and was sworn in.

"For the record, would you state your name and occupation Ma'am?" The prosecuting attorney asked politely.

"Elizabeth Watts. I am an Executive Assistant for a Purchasing manager at a Warehouse Supply club," the witness routinely stated.

"How long have you been there?" he continued questioning.

"I have been there for over a year," Elizabeth replied.

"Elizabeth, did you ever work for the defendant, Mrs. Garcia?" the prosecutor asked Ms. Watts.

"Why, yes I did. I worked for her prior to my present job," Elizabeth answered back almost too cheerfully.

"How long did you work for the Garcia's, Ms. Watts?" He continued with his interrogation.

"I probably worked for her about three years or so. Mostly for her, but if Mr. Garcia asked me to do something, I would do it too," she added.

"Do you think Mr. and Mrs. Garcia got along?" the prosecutor asked.

Harry quickly stood up, "Objection! Purely speculation, Your Honor! What does the opinion of Ms. Watt has to do with anything?"

"Sustained. Move on Counselor. Can you rephrase the question?" the judge insisted.

"Tell the court what you observed while working for

the Garcia's," he rephrased the question.

"Well, they would argue a lot. Sometimes it would really get loud and they would have to go outside. I just thought how sad it must be to be that bitchy," Elizabeth said with a Valley girl attitude.

"Objection," Harry said with disgust and frustration sitting with his arms folded while shaking his head at the table. "Motion to strike, Your Honor."

"Sustained," the Judge concluded and looked at the Prosecutor then to the court reporter. "Strike that last comment."

"Elizabeth, did you ever hear the defendant say anything relevant to putting the victims life in danger during one of their arguments?" the prosecutor continued his questioning.

"Oh, yes! On several occasions," Ms. Watts replied with enthusiasm. I just wanted to jump the next flight right then and there. I knew where she was going with this. People fight and say things they would never do. It's like you would like to kill someone, but would you really?

"Well, Ms. Watts, that is interesting. What did Mrs. Garcia say and to whom did she say it to?" The prosecuting attorney asked with a note of sarcasm to his voice while looking over at Harry and me.

"Oh, she would say things like, 'Just you wait, when you least expect it. You won't know what hit you!' Or she might say, 'Don't sleep with your eyes shut,' and 'I could just kill you sometimes!' In that tone." Ms. Watts explained with emotional detail exactly how I said those things in a fit of rage during heated arguments that Ralph and I were having. I leaned over and explained this to Harry. He had already figured it out and probably half of the jury did too.

"Nothing further, Your Honor," the prosecutor put it to rest. "Your witness." He held out his hand as to present Ms. Watts to Harry so he could ask her some questions. Mr. Fluxenberg stood up to begin asking some questions.

"Ms. Watts, you say you worked for the Garcia's for over two years, correct?" Harry wanted confirmation.

"Yes," Elizabeth said.

"Now aren't these accusations you are claiming resulting from the fact Mrs. Garcia fired you and you want vengeance on Mrs. Garcia?" Harry interrogated Ms. Watts further.

"No! She threatened his life. Now, he is dead. What are people supposed to think?" Elizabeth continued.

"In the two years you worked for Mr. Garcia, you had to attend business functions and you hated Mrs. Garcia, isn't that right, Elizabeth?" Harry slammed the question to Ms. Watts.

"I didn't like her much, no. I always had to do the things she didn't want to do. She was a bitch," Elizabeth added.

"Move to strike the last comment," Harry said.

"Stricken," the judge ordered it so and waved to the court reporter.

"Why did you stay as long as you did, if you were miserable, Ms. Watts?" Harry kept asking.

"Because I was hoping to get a promotion," Ms. Watts said.

"Oh, were you up for a promotion soon?" Harry continued.

"Well, Mr. Garcia was promising me a promotion if I kept doing some favors for him," Ms. Watts added to her testimony.

Harry looked puzzled at the vagueness of her response and had to know more details so he inquired, "Favors, Ms. Watts, what kind of favors were you doing for a promotion?"

"Well, I needed the money and Ralph said that he would make sure that I would advance in the company if I made sure some clients were satisfied in more ways than one," Elizabeth stated putting her forehead in her hand seemingly ashamed.

"Were you compensated for these actions?" Harry continued asking.

"Yes, at the time. But, I was supposed to be promoted to a salary position where I didn't have to do those things. Ralph said that he would take me on a business trip with him to Egypt one day as a special bonus," Ms. Watts added to her testimony to add to my disbelief. What on earth could she be saying? Ralph planning to take her on a trip? Ralph making her perform 'favors' for customers? I could hardly believe my ears! Was she doing things for Ralph?

"Why would you think this was a way of advancement for a woman in a legitimate business Ms. Watts? It doesn't sound like you are very smart," Harry asked and commented at the same time.

"Objection! Move to strike the last comment, Your Honor," the Prosecutor exclaimed from his chair.

"Strike the last comment," the judge said to the court reporter.

"I thought Ralph cared about me. He gave me bonuses and advances in my pay to help me pay my bills. I needed extra money for my little girl and myself. I was getting so far behind in my bills. I didn't know what to do," Elizabeth sobbed. I couldn't believe all of this was coming out.

"Did you and Mr. Garcia have sexual relations, Ms. Watts?" Harry went straight to the point.

"Not according to Bill Clinton," Ms. Watts told the court and the jury. There was some laughter heard but I was about to faint and be infuriated at the same time.

"Are you saying you had oral sexual relations with Mr. Garcia?" Harry got more specific.

"If you put it that way, yes," Elizabeth said with a note of more confidence and pride in her voice than before. She seemed rather proud of having an affair with Ralph. I just wanted to kill Ralph. But, he was already dead.

"You didn't get that promotion you were looking for, did you, Ms. Watts?" Harry interrogated Elizabeth with more persistence.

"No, Mrs. Garcia let me go for coming in late from lunch," Elizabeth coldly stated.

"So you will say anything to get back at her won't you Ms. Watts? She cut your future short, so you will cut her future short too?" Harry began to get on a roll of excitement.

"No! I am not lying!" Elizabeth yelled in her defense.

"But, you are stretching the facts a bit. Taking emotional discussions that a married couple were having and twisting their words into literal meanings. I think everyone in this courtroom can agree that we all have said that we would like to kill someone. But to actually act on the statement are two different things," Harry stated to the court.

"Ask her! Stop yelling at me! She fired me! Her husband promised me more money and he would take care of me! I should have sued the crap out of him! Now, he's dead and they don't even have a job at the company any more. I am the victim here, not her! She got everything, the bitch!" Ms. Watts kept yelling and crying. The Judge started to pound his gavel on the podium.

"Order! Order in the court!" The Judge began to shout. Then he leaned over very nicely and asked Elizabeth if she would like a glass of water.

"Nothing further, Your Honor," Mr. Fluxenberg stated.

"The witness is excused."

"You may step down, Ms. Watts," the Judge told Elizabeth. "Call your next witness."

"The prosecution calls Frank Richardson to the stand," the other attorney summoned the man that helped me sell the business so I could at least have some money to live on. I wondered why the prosecuting attorney would call him to the stand. I thought he helped me when I needed it.

"State your name and occupation for the court," the prosecuting attorney asked Frank.

"Frank Richardson. I own several businesses and I am a business broker," he said from the stand. Frank had this important demeanor about him. He seemed very confident.

"Frank, what was your connection with Raphael Garcia and the defendant?" the questioning continued almost non-stop.

"I helped Ralph find some good investments and he helped me with some over sea trading," Frank confessed.

"Did you ever witness the defendant and the murder victim engaged in any arguments?" the prosecutor continued.

They think I Killed My Husband!

"They argued constantly. Pam Garcia is an impossible woman to deal with. I had to deal with her once exclusively and I would not wish that on my worst enemy. She is a cold hearted bitch." Frank told the court these things about me just to throw me under the bus, so to speak.

"Objection! Your Honor, please," Harry pleaded to the Judge and jury.

"Sustained. You will strike the last comments from the record." The Judge told the reporter.

"What was the exclusive deal you did with Mrs. Garcia?" The prosecution interrogated while pacing the floor of the courtroom.

"I helped her find a buyer for her company after her husband died," Frank replied.

"Can you describe your experience to the court?" the prosecutor requested.

"Yes. She was very demanding. She wanted an astronomical amount for the business and I got her what I could get in the urgency she needed it by. It still wasn't good enough. She literally took the initial offer and threw it in the trash." Frank told everyone. I couldn't help to think that a woman acts like a professional bad ass, and gets condemned for life. A man acts the same way and he gets bonuses and promotions.

"So, you aided her in the sale of the business?" the prosecutor kept questioning.

"Yes." Frank confirmed.

"Did Mrs. Garcia get the amount she wanted?" the prosecution went on.

"Oh, heavens no. She got like ten percent of what she wanted. She was worried about how she was going to survive on only a couple of million or so. I forgot the exact amount." Frank told the prosecution and the court.

The prosecuting attorney was stunned! "A couple of million of dollars! And she was worried how she was going to live? I think I could live just fine! But that is just me. How long did you know Mr. Garcia?"

"I knew Ralph for about fifteen years. I met him when

I was finishing my Master's Degree in Business," Frank admitted from the witness stand.

"How long were Pam and Ralph together?" the attorney questioned Frank.

"They were together for about 10 years I think," Frank answered to the best of his knowledge.

"Nothing further, your witness Mr. Fluxenberg," the prosecutor waved his hand and sat down. Harry sprung out of his chair and fixed his tie and straightened his belt. He picked up a pen and rocked it between his fingers and thumb. Harry slowly walked with his Florsheim wing-tipped shoes and his silk suit up to the witness stand. He leaned close to Frank.

"Frank, you and Ralph were close before he even knew the defendant, huh?" Harry quietly asked Frank.

"I said I met him about fifteen years ago. I didn't say I was close," Frank corrected Harry.

Frank stood up and began to pace the courtroom, "Oh, my mistake. You said you met while you were finishing your Master's Degree. Isn't it true that the two of you shared an apartment while you attended college?" Harry questioned Frank with a little bit of aggression and closing in on Frank again.

"How? Well, yes," Frank confirmed.

"I would think that two people that shared an apartment together would know each other very well, wouldn't you agree, Frank?" Harry asked Frank.

"I suppose so," Frank confirmed with a whipped tone to his voice.

"You two were like brothers, best friends weren't you?" Harry continued to almost badger the witness.

"I don't know if I would say that. We were friends." Frank rephrased the verbiage.

"I see. Frank, how long have you been doing business with Mr. Garcia?" Harry asked from a few feet away from the witness chair after turning around from his short pace.

"For as long as I have known him," Frank returned the answer from the witness stand with confidence.

They think I Killed My Husband!

"And how long is that exactly?" Harry quickly needed to know.

"Like I said, since we graduated, or for about thirteen years or so," Frank filled in the blanks.

"You were the one that initiated the sale of Mrs. Garcia's business after the death of her husband, is that correct," Harry asked?

"Yes," Frank confirmed.

"To whom did you sell the company to, Frank," Harry continued?

"Well, I had sold it to an anonymous owner in Delaware. A person can remain anonymous in the state of Delaware to be able to no declare it on his income and can file bankruptcy without declaring the ownership of that said business and keep the income from it. It is one of the loop holes that attorneys have made in that state that very few people know about," Frank stated.

Harry looked surprised, "Well, isn't that interesting? You have no idea who you sold the company to?"

"That is correct," Frank agreed with Harry.

"Now, why would someone sell a company to someone that they have no clue to whom they are selling it to?" Harry continued asking Frank.

"She needed the money," Frank told Harry and court.

"Do you think she got a fair price for the company Mr. Richardson?" Harry wanted to know. "Tell the truth, you are under oath."

"Well, she could have gotten more, but she needed the money fast. So, I found a buyer but the only stipulation was that he wanted to remain anonymous," Frank informed the court.

"Now, why do you think that is?" Harry asked Frank.

"I don't know, I am not that man," Frank said.

"Well, how did you draw up the paperwork? How could the business be purchased? Did Mr. President by it?" Harry kept interrogating.

"His business and another attorney was in charge of the

deal. The actual man was absentee. Business deals are done like that everyday," Frank stated.

"In your opinion, Mr. Richardson, did Mrs. Garcia murder her husband in cold blood? Did she premeditate this whole scenario and put poison into something her husband would ingest to kill him so she would have to go through all of this turmoil and havoc?" Harry asked loudly.

"Well, nothing is ever as easy as it looks. Anyone can slip some liquid into a drink and try to survive the turmoil to end up a very wealthy person in the end," Frank stated.

"But, she was already a wealthy person. Why would she destroy her family? Destroy the love she had and her children's lives?" Harry continued to make the case stronger.

"I don't know. Ralph was an ass at times. They fought a lot. Maybe she just wanted to stop working and live an easier life. She is young and attractive and to be single and rich too. I am not her, but it doesn't sound like a bad idea if you can get away with it," Frank was stating such damaging things to the case. Harry needed to get him off of the stand.

"No further questions, Your Honor. The witness is excused," Harry said to the court and turned to walk back to our table to sit down. The Judge looked at the Prosecution and told him to call his next witness.

"The Prosecution would like to call attorney Thomas Cooper to the stand," the lawyer yelled as he stood up and turned to find the witness in the courtroom. Thomas stood up in the courtroom and approached the bench. Mr. Cooper was sworn in. "For the record, Mr. Cooper state your name and occupation to the court."

"My name is Thomas Cooper. I am an Attorney at Law," He stated the facts to the courtroom.

"What is the nature of your business with Mrs. Garcia," the prosecution kept pushing.

"I am Mrs. Garcia's corporate attorney. I manage her company affairs and her money and investment advisor," Mr. Cooper so stated the facts again.

"I see. So did you advise her on the sale of her company

to the unknown purchaser," he asked?

"Yes, I did," he kept his answers short as possible.

"Do you believe Mrs. Garcia will receive the insurance money from the death of her husband," the prosecutor quickly asked?

"Yes, I do." Thomas, the witness quickly answered back.

"Nothing further, Your Honor. Your witness," the prosecutor sat back down at his table. Harry got up from our table. I felt a little sick. That made it sound like I was for sure going to get the insurance money and that is motive for me to kill my husband. It didn't sound that great to me. Tom got tricked a little bit. I could be just a little paranoid. Harry started to begin his line of questioning.

"Now, Mr. Cooper how long have you known the defendant?"

Mr. Cooper replied, "As long as they have had their business. I think it has been 9 years."

Harry responded, "You have been taking care of their accounting and investment advising for that long. What happened to their money?"

"Ralph put most of the money in insurance and back into the company for growth. He also spent a lot of it too. I can lead a horse to water, but I can't make him drink," Tom made a point.

"Point taken, Mr. Cooper. So most of the Garcia's assets were tied up within their corporation?" Harry continued asking.

"Yes," Tom confirmed.

"I would say that is very accurate," Tom agreed.

"After losing her husband and the father of her children, she sold the company that she sweat long hours over and help to build from nothing with her now dead husband, to an unknown party for an amount she knew was too little? Why would someone do such a thing, Mr. Cooper?" Harry continued with an escalating voice.

"She really needed the money. The funds were frozen and the insurance wasn't paying until the autopsy was final and the police report was finished. Then when the autopsy turned up showing cyanide was in his system, well the wife is always the first choice of suspects. The police just figured she would be the easiest target," Tom added to his testimony.

"Objection! Purely speculative! I would like to have the last comments stricken from the record," the prosecutor yelled from his chair!

"Sustained. Just answer the question Mr. Cooper. You should know better." The judge leaned over towards the court reporter and told her to strike the last comments from the record.

Harry began to question Tom some more. "Tom, would you think that a woman that premeditated murdering her husband would have been so negligent to have become such a desperate person after the fact?"

"Mrs. Garcia is not capable of planning such a devious act." Tom stated to the court.

"Why would you say that, Mr. Cooper?" Harry continued.

"She has children to raise and she needed her husband to help with the business and to help raise her children. I don't think she would do it," Tom confirmed Harry's questioning.

"The police seem to think Mrs. Garcia is the only one with motive, would anyone else have motive," Harry tried to find out some other alternatives?

"Well, whoever may have purchased their business dirt cheap for one," Tom stated.

"I don't have anything more for this witness at this time, Your Honor," Harry told the Judge.

"Mr. Cooper, you may step down for now," the judge said to him. "Does the prosecution have any more witnesses?"

"Yes, Your Honor the prosecution would like to call Pamela Garcia to the stand," the prosecuting attorney stood up and coldly stared at our table and said.

I was very nervous about getting up on the stand. I looked at Harry. He gave me a tight squeeze of my hand to ensure that I would be just fine. Harry pulled me down towards his face and whispered to me, "Don't let them see you sweat.

They think I Killed My Husband!

You didn't do anything wrong." He gave me a reassuring nod and I slowly walked up to the stand. I stepped up to the witness stand and turned around and the bailiff held up the bible and swore me in. I sat down slowly in my burgundy cashmere suit with matching pumps. My long black hair was up in a bun because the weather was warm and windy outside. I was scared, but I didn't want to let it show.

The prosecutor walked up towards me very slowly and asked me, "Now, could you state your name to the court please?"

"Pamela Garcia, I used to own Garp Import/Export Business and the mother of two," I stated to the court in a cool and calm way.

"Could you tell the court what you also did before the importing and exporting became the major money maker," the prosecutor asked right off of the bat.

"I did metal plating," I had to tell them because it may come out later and prove more damaging if the jury thought I was trying to hide it for some reason.

"So, you did metal plating. I remember studying that in chemistry class in college. There are several chemicals that are used when plating metals. Is that correct?" the prosecution kept asking.

"Yes," I answered briskly.

"Someone uses acids and electricity and in the final metal solution there is a hardening agent so the metal will harden. Can you tell us what that chemical agent is?" the prosecuting attorney snidely asked me like he knew the answer anyway.

"I don't believe I ever read up on that," I answered like I didn't know.

"Really? Well, I don't believe you, but my opinion is irrelevant. I will enlighten you, Mrs. Garcia. It is cyanide. Cyanide is the chemical in the metal solution that when combined with the electrodes in a positive Alternating Current hardens the metal to the base metal in which it is applied," he stated to me and the jury and to the whole courtroom like he had just done a grand finale! There was a loud gasp from the jury box and the audience in the court. The judge started to pound his gavel on the podium.

"Order! Order in the court, or I will have the courtroom cleared," the judge yelled out as he slammed the gavel several times.

"Objection!" Harry stood up and yelled in my defense. "Circumstantial evidence which has no evidence relevant to the case."

"Over-ruled," the Judge apprehensively stated. "Proceed, Mr. Bailey. May I remind you that you are on a very fine line."

"Yes sir, Your Honor," the prosecuting attorney, Mr. Bailey told the judge very gratefully. "Knowing that cyanide is mixed with the metal solution that you plate with, how easy would it be to put cyanide into your husband's food or whatever you serve to him?"

"I haven't done any plating in years. The importing and exporting took up all of my time. I haven't had any metal solution lately. We were out when he was poisoned, it could have been any sick fuck," I told the prosecutor.

"I would like to admit as evidence these invoices, Your Honor. These are invoices for pure cyanide purchased by Garp Import/Export in the last year," Mr. Bailey went back to his table and picked up the invoices and approached the bench with them and handed them to the judge.

"I object Your Honor! I wasn't informed of this evidence." Harry stood up and was very angry. "The product could have been purchased by anyone in the company. There are several employees and this is speculative. I would also like to see the search warrant in which made it authorized to obtain these invoices."

"Sustained. Yes, Mr. Bailey, Mr. Fluxenberg does make a point. Do you have a search warrant? I would also like to see who signed the authorization for the purchase of the cyanide," the judge stated to the prosecutor as he was examining the invoices.

"And isn't that the chemical that was found in your

husband's system causing him to asphyxiate and have cardiac arrest, Mrs. Garcia," Mr. Bailey kept badgering.

"I really don't know! You probably know and understand more about it than I do."

"Objection, Your Honor. The prosecution is badgering the witness," Harry stated with frustration. I looked at Harry with desperation and wanted Mr. Bailey to stop his questions. Just sitting up in front of everyone and remembering all that I have gone through is torturous. Harry saw the look on my face and knew that I should just sit down, "Your Honor, may the witness be excused?"

I cradled my face sobbing into the palms of my hands. The prosecutor and the Judge looked over at me.

The Judge replied, "Yes, considering the demeanor of the defendant, the witness is excused at this time. Mrs. Garcia, do we need to call a short recess?"

I looked up and wiped my face off. "Thank you, that would be nice," I tried smiling a little and got up to walk to the table. Harry was there waiting. We waited until the courtroom cleared out a little. I needed to use the restroom. He said that is what the recess is usually used for. I gathered my purse and Harry began to walk me out of the courtroom. We made it through the double doors and I went to one end of the hall and Harry went to the other. I did my business and exited the ladies' room and started to walk down the hallway. I couldn't believe my eyes. I saw Jack! Jack Schwartz was in front of me about 20 feet! Why and how was he out of jail?

"Jack! Jack Schwartz! What are you doing here?" I yelled through the crowd to get his attention. I had to know. He began to walk over.

"Oh hey, Pam," he spoke rather calmly.

"Jack, what are you doing here," I had to ask again?

"Mr. Bailey called me in. Didn't you know?"

"No, no one tells me anything," I told Jack.

Harry walked up, "Jack, you were able to come."

"So you knew about this?" I asked Harry.

"Yes, I just found out. I hadn't had time to tell you,"

Harry said in his defense.

"Fine. Like I said, no one tells me anything."

Jack laughed and was extremely calm. So calm it was creepy. "I guess I will see you two inside," Jack finished and walked into the courtroom.

I looked at Harry very concerned and wide-eyed, "I don't like this."

"Don't worry, it's like the calm before the storm." Harry and I re-entered the courtroom. We both sat down, up front at our table. The Judge started to come back in and the bailiff told everyone to rise. We sat back down. The Judge asked the prosecutor to call his next witness. The prosecutor called Jack Schwartz to the stand! I couldn't believe it, already!

Harry leaned over and told me, "He probably only has a limited amount of time from where ever he is."

"Really," I asked?

"I don't know."

Jack sat down on the witness stand chair and the bailiff swore him in. The prosecutor walked towards Jack slowly collecting his thoughts it seemed. Mr. Bailey had a scrunched look on his face, "Jack, what is your occupation?"

"I am an Attorney at Law."

"Who was the last person you worked for," Mr. Bailey continued asking Jack?

"I was working for Mrs. Garcia last until she fired me for no reason."

"Objection, Your Honor! Strike the last opinionated comment from the record. Purely speculative," Harry stood up and demanded!

"Sustained. Just the facts, Mr. Schwartz, you should know that," the Judge stated in the courtroom.

"Yes, sir."

"Jack, didn't you work for Mrs. Garcia in their Import and Export business?" Mr. Bailey questioned.

"Yes, as their legal advisor."

"So, you would know about any contracts drawn up?"

"Yes, I would draw them up myself or read most of

them and advise them on most things."

"How long did you work for the Garcia's" the prosecutor inquired Jack?

"For about six years."

"Wouldn't you say that you knew the two of them pretty well?"

"I would say so, yes."

"In your opinion, do you think the Garcia's got along?"

"I don't think anyone could get along with that bitch!" Jack said with a vengeance. There was a gasp heard in the courtroom.

Harry stood up, "Objection, Your Honor!" Harry had much frustration welding up inside of him.

The Judge looked back at Jack, "I won't tell you again, Mr. Schwartz, one more outburst like that, and I will hold you in contempt of this court. Strike that last comment from the record."

"Yes, sir." Jack just sat there looking like he was sorry but he really was not.

Mr. Bailey continued with his questioning, "Mr. Schwartz, did the Garcia's act like they were in love?"

"I never witnessed any such muse."

I whispered over to Harry's ear, "Jack only saw us at work, we never hardly talked or would act unprofessional at work!"

"Mr. Schwartz, do you think Mrs. Garcia, to receive the money from the business and the money from the insurances and the house, could have slipped her husband some cyanide to kill him?" Mr. Bailey questioned while pacing the front of the courtroom and waving his finger in the air.

"Yes, I do," Jack so very coldly stated.

The prosecutor walked back to his table and sat back down and said, "I have nothing further Your Honor.

Harry just kept sitting and I was stunned. I looked at Harry and he said to me in a deep whisper as he got up, "I am going to get him." Harry walked up towards the witness stand and leaned in very close to Jack. Jack began to feel very uncomfortable. "Jack, for those six years you worked for the Garcia's, didn't you work mostly on proofreading the contracts before they signed them?"

"Of course, that was my main job."

"Why didn't you handle the legal matters first hand?" Harry questioned Jack with cynicism.

"Because I didn't have my bar at that time." Jack defended himself in a way. He was getting a little nervous. Harry continued pacing a bit, but stopped and turned abruptly.

"You mean you just recently passed the Bar?"

"No. I had it suspended for a couple of years." Jack told the courtroom in a slightly shameful way.

"Suspended? What did you do to have your legal bar suspended?"

"I was caught trying to find some evidence in my former partner's office. I guess it was frowned upon when they found me on tape after the silent alarm went off," Jack confessed to Harry.

"Exactly how long was your Bar suspended for?" Harry continued to Jack.

"Exactly five years. After the suspension was lifted, I had to retake the exam before I could practice law again."

"Didn't you have to get some recommendations from people to submit before the Bar as well?" Harry looked at Jack to make sure he would answer honestly because he already knew the answer.

"Yes, I had asked Pam to help me out after I had left the company. I needed some time to try and study before I took the test. I needed some reference letters as well," Jack pleaded his case now.

"Oh, did you go in to your partner's office after hours?"
"Yes."

"The Garcia's are good enough people that they hired you knowing this?"
"Yes."

"The Garcia's paid you a salary, Mr. Schwartz?" Harry continued questioning Jack. I was wondering where he was trying to go with this. He was making Jack look bad. I just didn't know the relevance.

Just then the prosecuting attorney, Mr. Bailey stood up, "Objection! I fail to see the relevance of Mr. Schwartz's salary to the murder case of Mr. Garcia."

"Over-ruled. However, please get to the point, Mr. Fluxenberg," the Judge commanded. "Answer the question, Mr. Schwartz."

"Yes, sir. I was paid a salary. Not what I was used to getting paid as an attorney, but the Garcia's were paying me for legal advice and I was doing some marketing for them too."

"Mr. Schwartz, one weekend you disappeared and your wife couldn't find you. You didn't show up for work until Wednesday morning, on the dates of April 5-9, two - three years ago. Where were you?" Mr. Fluxenberg asked Jack, out of left field. Jack was hesitant to answer and for good reason. That was the weekend he had spent smoking crack after I gave him a big commission check.

" I don't remember."

"Do I have to refresh your memory, Jack? I know for a fact that you personally told Mr. Garcia you had spent the weekend at a crack house smoking crack the entire weekend."

"Objection, Your Honor! Speculation!" Mr. Bailey stood up and yelled from his table.

"Withdrawn. Mr. Schwartz, didn't you go out of town quite often for the Garcia's to do some of their Public Relations for them too?" Harry continued questioning.

"Yes, I did."

"Mr. Schwartz, didn't you specialize in their middle Eastern affairs?"

"I went wherever Ralph told me to go." Jack pointed out.

"Ahh, I see. So when you were told to go to Egypt to negotiate whatever it was to negotiate over, you did."

"Yes, that's right," Jack answered.

"What was it you were negotiating over, Jack?" Harry questioned more.

"Different things. What ever we were trading that day," Jack replied.

"Can you be more specific?" Jack demanded. "Can you give us an example of something you were trading with the Middle Easterners?"

"Oh, I don't know, like metals and sometimes silks," Jack insisted as he started perspiring from the witness chair.

"Really? Metals and silks? What kind of metals, Jack?"

"I can't tell you, the company was the mediator for two other companies. The Garcia's were the Import /Exporters and they were the "go-between" for the other companies. What ever merchandise was traded is completely confidential and between the companies," Jack explained.

"Well, to please the court, you don't think you can give some examples of the merchandise? You are not divulging the names of the companies. The merchandise is not illegal merchandise is it?" Harry asked Jack and turned to the court. "After all you did give the Garcia's legal advice, and if you advised them to help negotiate to trade illegal goods, well, that would be aiding in criminal activity. Is that what you are afraid of Mr. Schwartz?"

"No. All right, I'll tell you. Sometimes we traded gold."

"Gold, well, Jack, that is not illegal and what did you trade the gold for?" Harry kept pushing.

"Look, you are making it look like I did something wrong up here. I am not the one on trial here." Jack protested on the stand while pointing at me.

"Well Jack, maybe you should be." Harry insisted. "I can get some other people in here to testify if you like."

Jack was about to let go. The calm before the storm was about to erupt! Jack twitched in his chair uncomfortably and began to get out of breath, "I am sitting in rehab because she had to fire me! It wasn't supposed to be like this!"

"What do you mean, 'it wasn't supposed to be like this,' Jack," Harry look puzzled and wanted Jack to continue with his thoughts.

"Pam was supposed to be in jail accused of Ralph's

murder! I was to be in control of all the assets! Then, I could get what is coming to me!" Jack blurted out in the courtroom with the gold on his mind!

"What is it that you have coming to you, Jack?" Harry questioned Jack, "Because there is definitely something you are not saying."

"I forgot," Jack conveniently stated. "I plea the Fifth Amendment."

"Why is it that you said, Mrs. Garcia should be in jail and you should be the one in control of her funds?"

"Because she signed the Power of Attorney over to me if she is incarcerated," Jack replied angrily.

"Right now, Mrs. Garcia doesn't have much in liquid assets. Why would you want to control little or nothing, Mr. Schwartz?"

"NO, no, no! You don't understand! There is a lot more than even she knows." Jack slipped.

"Really, why don't you enlighten the court?" Harry requested.

"No, I can't."

The Judge turned to Jack, "Mr. Schwartz, if you don't tell what you know, I will have to hold you in contempt of court and give you a fine as well."

"Fine! Everybody is for the pretty girl. If people just knew what a bitch you really are!" Jack yelled at me from the stand. "I don't know where, but there is some money or gold or something hidden somewhere. I was supposed to get it, somehow. Ralph told me to figure it out. But, it didn't turn out that way. I figured it out, sort of. I just got fucked. Why don't you ask her? I bet she knows all about it!" Jack screamed pointing at me! There was a loud commotion in the courtroom. People were whispering back and forth that it was sounding like thunder inside the huge room. The Judge pounded his gavel several times on the podium.

"Order! Order in the court!" the Judge yelled at the top of his lungs!

Harry was gathering his thoughts and thinking of what

to ask Jack next. Jack was losing it and Harry had to take advantage of it. "Jack, if there is gold or some money that Ralph hid, do you think that there is more than just you may have known about?"

Jack sat there stunned for a moment. He never had thought of that. "I don't know."

Harry looked at Jack, "Could someone else have been looking for the 'goods' like you and maybe that person or persons killed Ralph or the other related victims?"

"All I know is I didn't get it. I was supposed to get what was coming to me."

"Aren't you in jail right now Mr. Schwartz for attempting to kill Mrs. Garcia in her own home?" Harry wanted to point out Jack's flaw at the end.

"Well, I missed my medicine. I wasn't well. I am in a hospital treatment center."

"Oh, so you are getting what is coming to you, Mr. Schwartz. No further questions, Your Honor. This witness is excused." Harry said to the courtroom and walked back to the table where I was sitting.

"This isn't supposed to happen this way! She is supposed to be in jail! She did it! She is supposed to get the blame! I am innocent of everything! You have to believe me! I won't be disbarred again! I won't!" Jack was yelling as the bailiff pulled him up out of the witness chair. I was about to pass out from the excitement. I do believe that he really made Jack look crazy. Jack was escorted out of the courtroom by the bailiff. I assume he was still staying at the jail or at the mental hospital for trying to kill me that day after breaking and entering my home.

The Judge looked up and asked the prosecutor to call another witness. He said he had no other witnesses at this time. The Judge looked at Harry and asked him if he had any more witnesses to call. Harry said he had one more witness.

"I would like to call Martin Powers to the stand," Harry shouted after standing up in front of the courtroom. I looked all around the room and did not see Marty anywhere. But all

They think I Killed My Husband!

of the sudden, he came walking in through the double doors. He walked up to the front and stepped up to the witness stand and held up his right hand and the bailiff held the bible out and swore him in.

"Marty, would you state your occupation and relationship with Mrs. Garcia?" Harry asked.

"I am a Private Investigator, I was hired by Mrs. Garcia to help her with this case."

"Oh, so Pamela hired you? Why did she hire you, Mr. Powers?" Harry continued with his questioning.

"My cousin recommended me to her. She needed some help with this matter."

"Did you find out anything?"

"I had been working on a case that dealt with a lot of conspiracy with the government. Internal Affairs of the C.I.A. had hired me quite some time ago. But that case had been put on hold and I needed some work so my cousin told me about Mrs. Garcia and I told him I could help."

"Could you tell the court who your cousin is?"

"Yes, It's Aldo Gomez."

"Gomez? You two are cousins with two very different last names." Harry acknowledged. I don't know why he is being so picky, Marty is supposed to be on my side.

"Our Fathers are not of the same nationality. They are different."

"Have you found anything that could of any help to Mrs. Garcia since you started working on the case, Mr. Powers?"

"Oh, yes. I have found that there have been other murders committed that could be tied in with the murder of her husband. Mrs. Garcia has in fact been threatened." Marty pointed out to the jury.

"Really? In what way?"

"While coming home one evening, she was jumped just outside of her gate of her home. The murders that occurred were past employees of the Garcia's that may have known something and to this day it still remains unsolved," Marty stated the cold hard facts to the courtroom. There was a gasping and some confusion of whispering that quickly died down as soon as Harry began asking his next question.

"You mean to tell me that there is still a murderer out and about, and Mrs. Garcia's life has been threatened as well?" Harry wanted confirmation as he turned to the people of the jury with a look of surprise.

"Yes, that is what I just said. I don't want to repeat it." Marty confirmed.

"Why do you think Mrs. Garcia is being threatened?" Harry wanted Marty to make a point for the jury.

"Probably over whatever it is Jack was talking about. As crazy as he is, he must be talking about something. Mr. Garcia must have left something behind. Maybe Jack is the one arranging it. After all, he was disbarred for some similar actions." Marty said in the courtroom and the people of the courtroom got in a tizzy once again. The whispers turned into talking and mutters and it sounded like one big loud buzz. The Judge banged his gavel down on his podium again and again.

"Order! Order in the court!" The Judge was yelling over the loud buzzing.

"No more questions, Your Honor. Your witness, Mr. Bailey," Harry said as he sat back down next to me at the table in the front. I was sitting there hoping that everything would turn out okay. So far, it looked like it might.

Mr. Bailey stood up and approached the stand. He looked at Marty with a cold stare. He leaned over the pit of the stand where Marty was sitting and he remained calm.

"Mr. Powers, if Mrs. Garcia is innocent, why would she have to hire you to prove it? Wouldn't the truth come out in the end?" Mr. Bailey inquired from the front of the witnesses' podium.

"Of course. But it seems that these days, people believe the dirt before the truth. The police also seem to want to close the case as well," Marty stated.

"Why would you say that the police wanted to close the case? They will work on a case until it is closed, wouldn't they?"

They think I Killed My Husband!

"Not necessarily. Mr. Bailey, you should know there are many, many unsolved cases in the police files. That is something they do not like to admit to either."

"Didn't Mrs. Garcia have a huge insurance benefit coming to her from her husband's death?"

"I don't know. I think you already covered that by asking her, didn't you?" Marty made his point.

"Well, Mr. Powers, what exactly have you found out since Mrs. Garcia hired you?" The prosecutor asked with a snide attitude.

"I have found that a lot of things that have happened could have been done by anyone. The evidence is purely circumstantial," Marty pointed out to the prosecutor.

"Really? I believe that Mrs. Garcia had the knowledge and the power to get the cyanide to poison her husband and she had all of the profit to gain from it, therefore she was the one with the motive. Now what makes you think it is purely circumstantial, Mr. Powers?"

"They were out in a nightclub. A number of people could have slipped him a Mickey with the cyanide. Just like sick men do to girls all of the time." Marty made a valid point, a sick but true point to help in my defense. The two went on arguing back and forth for a while, Marty still making his points and the prosecutor trying to make his. Marty actually confessed that because he worked for the government, he was able to find out some classified information about Raphael Garcia and the dealings he was doing overseas. Mr. Garcia had been trading a lot with the Saudi Arabian Government but the company books were showing a different story. The courtroom became very unruly and the media was ordered to leave afterwards. My mouth fell to the floor. Marty hadn't said a word to Harry or me. Marty was excused after more questions were answered and some were not. The jury finally left for the deliberation of whether I was guilty or not. After all of the deliberation, the jury re-entered the courtroom.

"Will the defendant please rise?" The bailiff said after receiving the verdict from the jury. I stood up at the table in front of the courtroom to hear the verdict. I grabbed the edge of the table. Harry stood up with me. I grabbed his hand to hold on to while I waited for the response of the jury.

"We, the jury find the defendant not guilty," the jury foreman stated to the court. I leaned my head back with relief and hugged Harry! I was so happy! Harry whispered that justice was served and the reasonable doubt because of circumstantial evidence probably is what convinced the jury. I was free to go and Harry and I walked out of the courtroom together. I had to get with my tax/accounting attorney, Tom to find out about the insurance benefits now that I have been found not guilty, they should pay.

Tom began working on it even before the court proceedings were over. As soon as the verdict was in, he called them and told them. He also faxed them the necessary documentation then sent it overnight so I could have it that much sooner. Even though I paid Harry with some gold initially, later I paid him a percentage of the insurance money proceedings I received.

Now, I had to figure out what I could do with all of that gold I had found. I separated the funds from the insurance benefits and I felt better with actual money in the bank and my home paid off and the cars too. I had to do some errands downtown transferring some funds from one account to another. I need to make arrangements to go to Egypt too. I had to get a hold of Warren to see if he would be willing to take me back to Cairo.

First, I had to get some of these cashier checks I had made into the banks in the Cayman Islands. I walked back to my car in the parking garage. I had just gotten off the phone with Warren. He said he would be happy to take me back to Cairo. I rounded up Aldo and I needed Marty to come this time too. I was still on the phone with Marty while I was looking for my keys in my purse when someone jumps me from behind. He grabbed my hand that I was holding my cell phone with and it fell to the ground. He twisted my arm behind my back and covered my mouth with his other hand. He was embracing me and I couldn't move. I couldn't see him either. I was very scared. He tripped up my feet and knocked me down face first to the ground. The next thing I knew, I was lying face down kissing the concrete. I

They think I Killed My Husband!

scraped my knees and almost broke a tooth! I was really frightened. I could hear Marty on the other end of my cell phone. I tried to fight, but he was sitting on top of me by now still holding my hands together behind my back. The man leaned down very close to me. I could feel his breath on the back of my neck. His hands held my wrists very tightly, so tight that it was really hurting. I was trying to wriggle my hands free, but it was useless. He just grabbed that much tighter. His breath was awful. It smelled like the crap out of a dog's ass.

"I want that key," he demanded with his ass breath. I was still lying face down with my cheek scraping the concrete.

"I don't know what you mean," I explained through the side of my mouth.

"The key to the gold we bought. You imported it for us, but all we received was some gold plated lead bars. We gave your husband the artillery, and he gave us fuck!" The man yelled in a loud and stern whisper right to my face while tightening his grip.

"I still don't know what you are talking about," I continued with my retaliation. "What kind of artillery did you give my husband? I don't know anything about what you are talking about. I think you are fucking nuts! That's what I think!" I spoke a little out of turn as he twisted my wrists harder. "Oowww!" I said under my breath as I breathed in. He pulled up off of the ground and pushed me against the wall. I was in the same position as on the ground, but now I was upright against the concrete wall. Now was my chance. I head bashed him with the back of my head and hit the front of his head. All I did was stun him and piss him off.

"If you think you are going to get out of this like the last time, I don't think so." The attacker told me. Suddenly there was a group of people coming off the elevator and onto to the floor of the parking garage.

"Auuuuuuugggghhhhhhhhhh!" I screamed at the top of my lungs! "Help me! I'm being raped!" A couple of the larger men from the crowd of people came running over. He looked up and wanted to kill me right then and there.

"I'll have to kill you later," he said then he let me go and ran away before the other perpetrators caught up to him. I rubbed my face to see if I was bleeding and the nice men stopped to see if I was okay. Then they continued to chase the guy that attacked me. I left.

I didn't just leave the garage. I left the country. I sent the kids to stay with their grandmother while I was gone. Warren flew his dad's jet and Marty and Aldo came with me. Warren stopped at the Cayman Islands for me first. I put the little bit of gold that I had at home, in a safety box in the islands. I also deposited the checks I had made, down in the islands to divide up some of the money until I figure out what I am going to do with it. Warren was an absolute doll doing everything he is doing. Aldo and Marty are great for coming so I feel better. I am so scared. People are trying to kill me to get the gold that is in Cairo in the lock box. I switched the box, so if anyone else might have the key, the box is empty. My life is apparently in danger after the incident in the garage. But, what the hell is the artillery is about? I kept thinking about that on the flight over the Atlantic. The men were quiet as me during our flight. On the plane, Marty made a valid point that it would be very dangerous for me to go anywhere by myself. He wanted to be by my side any place I decided to go for my own protection. We arrived on Cypress Island and caught the ferry to Cairo. We arrived at the port and immediately went back to the place we stayed before that we found was nicer and checked in. I later went with Marty and bought a pistol for protection. Warren and Aldo checked into the hotel and settled in their room and unpacked. They carried my stuff up and put my suitcase into to my room. Marty didn't like the idea of my having a gun.

"Did you know most people get shot with their own gun? I can stay with you. I have clearance for carrying a weapon. I should have the gun, not you," Marty reprimanding me like a male arrogant pig.

"What in the world are you saying? I want a gun! I know how to shoot and how dare you talk to me like that!" I yelled at him while leaving the place we bought the gun.

They think I Killed My Husband!

We made it back to the hotel. I couldn't wait to take a shower. I went to my room where I was staying by myself and the men had their room next door. It was getting late and I felt better having a gun next to me while I slept and the men were right in the next room. The next morning the four of us went to the bank where the deposit box is. The men waited in the lobby while I went to the bank desk to sign in to go into the vault. I took out the box to take a good look at the gold and take some of it out. I put some of it out onto the table. I hadn't really looked at any of it. All I know it is really heavy. I couldn't even lift it out of the slot in which it was placed. I peeked out of the vault and asked if one of the men that accompanied me could come in. Marty scurried into the vault as quickly as he could without creating much attention to himself. Marty helped me set the box on the floor so we could at least open it and look inside.

"Wow! I have never seen so much gold since I was in Fort Knox!" Marty exclaimed with his eyes beaming and his facial expression in awe. We began taking some of the gold coins out of the box and there were some jewelry and the gold bars. But, after clearing some of the stuff out, I uncovered between the gold bars and under all of the treasure, was a wonder of all wonders. Marty lifted it out of the box. It was too heavy for me to lift. It looked like an ancient Egyptian Sphinx. It stood upright and was gold with blue stripes. It looked like the huge God statue from the old "Ten Commandments" movie. The one Ramses put his son on to bring back to life. It had the head of a coyote and the body of a man holding the rods crossed in front of its' chest. Its head was crowned with a blue and gold headpiece. It was absolutely beautiful.

"Marty, I have never seen anything like that. Do you think it is authentic?"

"The way people have been getting killed, I am sure it is. This is some major dealing, Pam. This is high dollar black market shit. This should be in a museum in New York or Washington D.C. somewhere. How did your husband get a hold of something like this?" Marty questioned me like I knew anything about it.

"You probably know more about it than I do," I told him.

"You are going to have to keep it here until you can get it and sell it to a museum. That is the proper place for it. It needs to be where everyone can enjoy it," suggested Marty.

We put it back along with everything else and put the box back into the vault. We walked out into the lobby of the bank. Aldo and Warren were still waiting for us in the lobby.

I signed out and the four of us went to find something to eat. We sat and discussed what Marty and I found in the box. Marty seems to think it may be worth over on hundred million dollars. I was hoping no one around us could understand English. We finished eating and decided to go back to the room. We went back to the hotel. The boys went to their room and Aldo and Marty and Warren decided to go to the local police to check out the laws on the lost Egyptian artifacts found. I told them not to worry, I was going to take a shower and I had my gun.

"Besides, who even knows I am here? Go on, I will be fine," I told them. Marty thought about it again, and asked if Aldo could stay here while he and Warren went and check out the finder's fees on artifacts. Aldo said he would and he stayed in his room while I showered and the other two left.

"I might take a shower too. That sounds like a good idea. I might as well while these two are gone," Aldo made a point. Marty and Warren left and I went in to my room and Aldo went into his room. I started to get ready to take a shower when I heard a knock at the door. The man at the door said he was room service and had fresh towels for me. Since I only had taken off my shirt already, I put on my robe. I was still a little apprehensive, so I grabbed my little handgun that I just bought and put in the back of my jeans.

"Warren must have told room service to bring me towels," thinking to myself. I got up to answer the door. I looked through the peep-hole and saw that he in fact had a stack of nice white towels. He looked unshaven, but so did most of the men in Egypt. I opened the door and the man stepped closer to me and put the towels up to my face. That's the last thing I remember. I awoke inside of what seemed to be a trunk of a car. My mouth was taped shut and I was tied up. My ankles were tied together and my wrists were tied. The man hog-tied me too. I don't know how long I have been in here or where I was in the world. It was still dark in what I am assuming is the trunk. I tried to lift my hand to feel my aching head. It hurt so much. I couldn't touch my head because the ropes weren't long enough. The roads were bumpy and the man was swerving all over the road or so it seemed.

    The car stopped suddenly and this crazy looking man whom I have never seen before pulled me out of the trunk. It was a different person than the towel by at the hotel. This man had a full beard and wore a long white dress like gown and sandals and turbine on his head. His skin was dark and his nose was big. He looked similar to the taxi driver that drove me the first time I was here. He didn't say a word. I landed on the ground again. I screamed in pain because I landed on my gun, which was still in the back of my pants. It hurt like hell. The man leaned over and ripped the tape off my mouth so I could at least breathe easier. Then he reached to his side and pulled out a knife.

    "Don't kill me, please!" I pleaded with the man. He untied my feet so I could walk and escorted me to the train. We were in the parking lot of the train station apparently. There were more men with beards and turbines and suits. These men were bigger and looked like they were in shape. One man draped a cloth over my hands that were tied so no one would see. I walked between all of them and they would not let go of me anyway while we got on the train. I was so confused. We got onto the train. I sat down inside and no one would tell me anything except to be quiet or they would put the tape back on my mouth. I was so exhausted. I could barely walk. I saw from the signs I was still in Cairo. The men were holding me up by my arms. I guess the man at the hotel used chloroform to put me out.

    The train took me to a place I was not familiar with. We went through in a rural place, through the desert at first, then it turned to the rainforest. I just sat and looked out the window. I wish that Warren and Marty and Aldo were here. I hope they can figure out where I am going. I doubt it though. I don't know how, unless they are really quick to figure out that I am even missing. The train had a straight shot to our destination where ever that may be. The train-ride seemed like it went on forever. We had our own private compartment with beds and the bathroom adjoined the compartment. One man would not take his hand off of my arm. I could barely go to the bathroom by myself. The first time I went, the gun fell to the floor. I picked it up and put it in the cup of my bra. It barely fit under my breast. I didn't want it to fall again and I didn't want them to find it. I figured that would be the best place to keep it for now. I wish I had that shower before this happened. The way these men smelled, I wished they had a shower within the last week of this happening. I just tried to sleep while sitting there. I didn't know what else to do. I was glad to be alive for the moment. No one was talking to me and if the men spoke, they spoke in Arabic. I felt like my legs weighed a thousand pounds and my body like a brick tower. I fell asleep for what seemed a little while again. I couldn't help it. One of the men woke me up almost instantly and told me to sleep in one of the bunks in the compartment. He actually helped me up into one of the top beds and I went to sleep. The next thing I knew it was morning. One of the men started to wake me up. I felt a lot better than I did the day before. I reached to see if the gun was still in its place. It was. The big goon with the long beard and long hair with his grotesque teeth pulled me down from the bed by my arm.

"Ow, that hurt!" I yelled like he gave a shit.

He just said something back to me in Arabic and I could only just imagine what it could be. I closed my mouth and kept quiet. The train was still moving along. I couldn't believe it. I wished I could get off the train.

After a few days, the train began to slow down. The train finally stopped at the depot. I did not know where I was. The signs were all in a different language. People were speaking in a different language I didn't understand either. The three men tied my hands back together again and draped a jacket over my wrists to hide the rope. They led me by the arm and walked me out of the train. A taxi drove up and the men shoved me into the back seat of a taxi cab that was an old four door Chevy. It didn't smell good. The car had dirt and mud in it like the rainforest that may be out in the rural areas of the vicinity. The taxi driver was a colored man with short curly hair and bright clothes. The Arabic men got into the car with me. The car didn't have air conditioning and it was hot outside and humid. The smell of the car mixed with the smell of the men was really beginning to get to me.

"Could you roll down the window?" I tried to ask one of the men. He looked at me like I was really stupid. He apparently couldn't understand me anyway. I had to sit there and try not to get sick. One man reached and turned on the radio. It still didn't do me any good. The disc jockey spoke the language of whatever country we were in. We pulled into a hotel. The big Arabic Goonies quickly got out before I could think about anything. The man next to me grabbed my arm and pulled me out of the car. His fingers dug into my skin, squeezing my forearm until I screamed. He loosened up only a little. They led me into the hotel and through the lobby. I still had my hands tied with a jacket draped over my wrists. The Arabic chaps and I entered the elevator and went to the Penthouse Suite. The big one that seemed to be in charge opened the door. He sat me down on a chair in the room and turned around and left the suite. I heard the lock on the door latch. I knew I had to try to get out. I walked over to the door. My hands were still tied up. I struggled to get my hands free. I didn't make a sound. I put my ear to the door to try to find out if the men were still on the other side. I could hear them breathing and talking and their feet shuffle a little. Even if I could open the door, or if I did, the men would be there to block me from leaving or escaping. I went back through the apartment to look for something to cut my wrists free of this bondage. I ransacked the penthouse for something to cut these ropes. I looked almost everywhere in the little time before I heard someone come out of the back bedroom. I looked around for only about five minutes when I saw a silhouette of a man coming down the hall. I tried to make out the face, but the brightness from the room behind him made the front of him too dark. He slowly kept walking towards me. The shadow he cast was the shadow of a man that looked very familiar to me. Then he stepped into the light where I could see his face. The man looked amazingly like my dead husband! I looked again at this man. He looked exactly liked Ralph. I looked into his eyes. Oh my God, it is Ralph!

"Ralph, is it really you?" I asked him trying not to faint since I felt weak at the knees. I stumbled a bit. Ralph helped me back upright then unbound my wrists.

"Hey, babe. Are you all right?" he asked in a soft, familiar voice that I thought I would never hear again as he helped me to the couch.

I was so confused. I saw him dead. I looked at him, he looked so real, so alive. I couldn't help but to grab him and just hug him for a good minute. All the while I was hugging him, so many questions entered my mind.

"Ya, it's me. Did ya miss me? I bet you have a lot of questions, don't you?" Ralph asked me in a soft, sweet and sincere voice.

I sat on the couch with him next to me and I grabbed my head in confusion and asked, "What the hell just happened here? Are you for real?"

"You almost fainted. I had to help you to the couch before you fell. Are you okay?" he asked, almost laughing.

"Ya, but how can you be here? You are dead! I saw you die and everything. They did a thorough autopsy and I had a funeral and do you know what hell you put me through?" I told him climaxing into madness.

"Well, I am glad to see you made it over here. I knew I didn't marry some stupid bimbo. I knew you would figure it out."

"Figure what out?" I demanded to know. "That you are an asshole?"

They think I Killed My Husband!

"No, well, maybe. Now that we are on that subject, why did you fire Jack?" Ralph asked right out of nowhere. How could he have known about any of this? Jack must have been involved! That is why he had me sign that Power of Attorney. He wanted to get access to everything I had, including the things in my house!

"What is the story about the gold?" I demanded to know.

"Oh, the gold. Well, I need the gold, Pammy. You took the gold from me. I have been working very hard for years and now I don't know what happened to it. Some people are pretty mad about it and especially me. I want it back." Ralph told me with an attitude.

"I was almost killed by some thug back in the states!" I told him indignantly, "He wanted the gold! Frankly, I was disappointed that I couldn't give him his gold. If it meant that he would have left me and my kids alone, I would have given him whatever. He didn't ask for money, just the gold. So tell me Ralph, what is your story?" I inquired of him very anxiously.

We went to the bar by the window to fix a drink. "Would you like a drink?"

"Uh, no, I don't think so. Not right now. I have had enough toxins from the thugs that brought me here," I reminded him with a glare.

Ralph walked back to the couch where I remained seated. He went on to explain what happened and what he has been doing. "Well Pam, it went down like this. I started doing business importing and exporting some weapons for this company in Saudi Arabia. The owner of the company lives in Saudi anyway. In exchange, he paid me in solid gold from Africa."

"Okay, that explains where you got the gold, but why the secrecy? Why did you fake your death? Why did you leave me and the kids? Why Ralph? Why?" I just kept asking him trying not to cry.

"Well, it gets more complicated than that. I was getting the weapons from a man that worked for the government. He had access to old military weapons that weren't used anymore. These weapons were in 'retirement' so to speak. They were just in an old storage facility. I didn't question where he got them. At first, I sold some of the gold and gave him some of the money and kept the rest of the money. Then later, I found out that the weapons were actually old military weapons," Ralph explained calmly.

"Oh, gee, do you think? Where do you think a massive amount of weapons would come from? And why on earth would you supply weapons to the Middle East? Are you really that retarded?" I asked him.

"Don't be such a smart ass. You lived a great life for a while, you ungrateful bitch." Ralph cynically stated.

"Oh, my God! I don't believe what I am hearing! So, why are people trying to kill me even if they think you are dead?" I had to know the answer to that question. "And what the hell! How did you fake your death? I saw you die!"

"They took me to the hospital in the ambulance. When I arrived there, I had some friends ready to take me to the airport. There was already another body there to be sent to the funeral home as my body." Ralph continued to inform me. I couldn't believe what I was hearing! Does he even realize what he put his children through? Does he realize what he put his parents and his siblings through?

"But, I saw you dead! I don't understand! I had your body cremated! You are dead!" I told him. " I identified you! You were blue and stiff! How can you explain that?"

"Well, when you have money, you have a lot of friends. I told some people that I was making a haunted house and I needed a body made up to look exactly like me, but dead on a slab. You know, like they do in the movies. So, they made one up. The same friends at the hospital that sent the John Doe to the Funeral Home had you identify the fake me. I had to make sure you of all people were truly convinced," Ralph confessed to me. Why he had this sudden urge to clear his soul with God, I hadn't a clue. But thoughts of my death were entering my mind if I confessed where I put the gold.

"This can't be happening. I must be dreaming. That bump on the head must have been a doozy. I must be still asleep somewhere." Yelling to Ralph at first, then looking down talking to myself trying to make heads or tails of all of this.

"That was me on the gurney at first, but later I got out of there. I left the country as soon as I could," Ralph continued.

"Who bought the gold from you? If the guy that supplied the weapons didn't, who else is involved in this?" I wanted to know.

"I was doing business with some Asian guys. They bought the gold from me for a great price, top dollar then some. The gold was African and Egyptian so they paid even more than the going rate per ounce. I profited all of the way around," he kept explaining.

"Lucky you. So, why is everyone trying to kill you?"

"You know how you used to gold plate?" he asked me.

"Yes?" I gasped! "Oh no! You didn't!" I started to figure it out!

"Ya, I did. I got the idea once I saw the gold bars, I figured it would be easy to recreate those and gold plate them."

"Oh shit, Ralph! Do you know what kind of trouble you are in?" I kept interrogating.

"Yes. Why do you think I had to kill myself? But, who wants to do that?" Ralph asked me.

"But, why did you have to get so greedy? Why sell weapons for gold anyway? Weren't we doing all right without all of that bullshit?" I tried to make a valid point.

"Yes, but I made a great connection to make a whole lot more, and I did!" Ralph finished informing me.

"You greedy Bastard! Don't you hear the news? The killing going on in the Middle East? Our own American soldiers over there? Are you such an imbecile?" I continued to get really angry. "Now you have nothing. No more company, the company is gone. I had to sell it for practically nothing. I used the money from it to live off of until the death benefits paid me for your dying after the trial. Do you realize I was blamed for killing you? Do you know what you put me through?"

"Oh, you were accused of killing me?" he asked. Ralph

had this look on his face like he knew all along.

"You are a terrible actor," I told him. "I was put through hell, not to mention your kids. Your kids had to see their mother get arrested for murdering their father, not to mention they think their Daddy is dead!" I yelled angrily to him. I stood up and looked out of the window at his wonderful view of whatever city we were in. I could only guess somewhere in South Africa.

"But, I sold some of the gold so I could buy back the business since you sold it. I have an agency through Delaware that a person can remain anonymous and I now own my business again. I was the one that bought it from you! Since my death, the business rate went down and you wanted to sell the majority stock so bad, I bought the business real cheap and rebuilt the business again so it is thriving better than ever! I still have some cash from the gold I sold to the Asians. I am making more money with the business than ever. With all of the profits I bought into the major oil refinery businesses. I am now importing and exporting crude oil after making the connections with the Saudi Arabians that I made the deals with the weapons with," Ralph informed me of his past premeditated thoughts.

"You mean to tell me that all of this mess the world is in, you are profiting from it? You ripped off some Asians for some gold trinkets to add to this pile of shit you just told me!" I confirmed his confessions. "Not to mention me and kids and the crap you put us through!" I stated calmly and sullenly and heartbroken again.

"Where is all of this money, Ralph?" I asked him still in disbelief. All I could think about was all of the crap I have gone through in the last year. The pain of a broken heart and having to tell my children their father was dead. Going to his funeral with the kids and dealing with the lawyers and the press. I had to hire a private investigator, was almost killed by these people he stole the gold from and just dealing with losing my husband on a daily basis. I still can't believe he put me through all of this for money. We had money. My head was spinning. I had to keep myself from almost fainting. I felt weak in the knees again.

They think I Killed My Husband!

"Where is the gold?" Ralph asked me.

I regained my strength, realizing I had better. This man is not the man I thought I had married. He was all about himself. He was 'All Show' and what he could do or get for himself. He didn't give a rat's ass about me or the kids.

"I don't know what you are talking about," I quickly told him. I looked at him straight into his eyes and stared at him without looking away.

"Oh, come now, Pam. You know exactly what I am talking about. Why do you think I brought you here?" Ralph argued with me in a calm manner that was uneasy to me. I know that tone. When he was quiet, yet demanding, I know he means business.

"You tell me where all of this money is you are talking about. Where do you conduct your business from? What name do you use now? Who the hell are you?" I asked.

"The money is in a bank account here in town," he openly told me.

"Well, where is here?" I demanded to know.

"South Africa. Where else?" he rhetorically stated.

"Are the accounts in your name? Did you put everything in your real name or did you have a fake name or is everything in someone else's name?" I questioned him thoroughly.

"Oh, no. Everything is in my name. This is South Africa. Do I have to remind you why I am here? No extradition! I don't have to hide." Ralph continued explaining. He kept explaining and I just kept looking off into space in disbelief. Was I going crazy? How could a man I loved so much and whom I thought loved me as much in return do this to me? How could he do this to his family? Just for money? Didn't seem to fit. I didn't get it.

"What is the name of your bank, honey?" I wanted to know. I felt like I was losing my mind. If I hadn't had a nervous breakdown yet, I think I was getting ready to have one right at that instant. I wanted him to think I was still his loving wife that would do anything for him.

"Cape Town National is my bank. I can give you all of the routing numbers and you can transfer our money from the states over here and then you and the kids can move over here permanently," Ralph told me like nothing has even happened.

I couldn't believe what I just heard. Was he the idiot? What is he thinking? Like I am going to just start doing what he says after all of this time. I don't think so. I have a lot going on back home. I need to take care of these jewelers though. But, oh, my god! What an egomaniac! I have my own money. I am in control of myself. I don't have to take orders from anyone, anymore! I looked straight at Ralph with just a blank look on my face.

"Ralph, how did you know I was in Cairo? Why did you have your thugs kidnap me like that and bring me here?" I had to know the real answer to the billion-dollar question.

"Well, Pammy, I left behind the key to the box in my haste in the safe at home. You found it. Before I could get to it, I discovered my widow had closed out the box. That wasn't hard to figure out who has all the gold. I had to get you here so I can get my gold back, maybe you and my children too. What do you say?

"I need to use the bathroom. I'll be right back out." I told him as I walked into his bathroom. I was numb. I couldn't think. I just went with instinct. My instinctive reaction of a mother seeking revenge on someone that is evil and I thought about all of our soldiers that had died. I thought about the many women that lost husbands and have gone through similar things with their kids losing their fathers. I went inside and pulled out my little gun I purchased in Egypt when I arrived. I wasn't going through this again. I walked out of the bathroom and before I could think about it anymore, I looked right at Ralph and pointed the gun at Ralph and said, "There is only one glitch in your carefully thought out plan Ralph, you are already dead." So, I shot him.

They think I Killed My Husband!

The Wild Widow Part II
"Running For Justice" coming soon

Read and find out how Pam escapes and reunites with Aldo and Warren and Marty. Will she make it back to the States? Is Ralph really dead, again? What will happen to the gold? What about the second key and the lady Layla she talked to at another bank? All will be continued.........

Marty Penate

ISBN#: 978-0-9842497-2-5
The Library of Congress Number: TXu001267535
Written by Marty Penate
Edited by Martha Nelson
Photographer, Michael Murphy
Cover design by Martha Nelson

Printed in the United States of America

A fictional novel by Marty Penate
To order, send a check or money order to:

MAP Productions
P.O. Box 1305
Mt. Dora, FL 32756

Or visit online: www.theythinkikilledmyhusband.webs.com
www.facebook.com/thewildwidow
www/myspace.com/wildwidow   (click on the wildwidow poster to reach the link)
www.twitter.com/wildwidow
www.youtube.com/wildwidow

They think I Killed My Husband!

This book is dedicated to my two wonderful children that have grown up with me through the years. They have been patient and loving as I have been with them I could not have accomplished this feat without them! They are my best friends and always will be. I love you!

www.ingramcontent.com/pod-product-compliance
Lightning Source LLC
Chambersburg PA
CBHW070552100426
42744CB00006B/261